Before You See a Lawyer

Before You See a Lawyer

AN EVERYDAY GUIDE TO LAW

Robert Weber

NEW CENTURY PUBLISHERS, INC.

Printing Code
11 12 13 14 15 16

Library of Congress Cataloging in Publication Data

Weber, Robert, 1928 Jan. 28-
Before you see a lawyer.

Includes index.
1. Law—United States—Popular works. I. Title.
KF387.W38 349.73 81-11258
ISBN 0-8329-0101-6 347.3 AACR2

CONTENTS

PREFACE

The law like a person is always growing and changing. It is changed when the various legislative bodies pass new laws. It is changed when courts interpret and apply these laws. Sometimes these laws are the same from jurisdiction to jurisdiction, as when "Uniform" laws are used. Sometimes they are different from jurisdiction to jurisdiction, as in the case of marriage or divorce laws from state to state. Sometimes they are different even within the same state when different courts interpret the same law differently.

In addition to its chameleon quality, law and lawyers have and use a technical vocabulary which may not be comprehensible to one not a lawyer.

Therefore, my purpose in writing this book is not to make practicing lawyers out of laymen. It is, however, to help the nonlawyer understand what is involved in various legal matters and to understand the procedures being followed as these matters progress.

It is also my hope that by reading this book my readers will become so informed before they see their lawyers that they can ask the right questions of their lawyers and even help to gather evidence or volunteer pertinent information where required.

With these goals in mind, this book was written to cover comprehensively the legal subjects of most interest to the public. It is written to be informative and applicable no matter in what area of the country one lives, and the use of legal terminology was held to a minimum. Where the use of legal vocabulary was unavoidable, I explained the meaning in the context of its use.

Instead of using the usual question-and-answer format books of this nature usually take, I felt that the material could be presented in a more interesting way if it was written in a narrative style with anecdotes and examples. I hope, as a result, that you, the reader, get as much enjoyment from reading this book as I did in writing it.

Robert Weber

1

THE LAW

DEVELOPMENT OF THE LAW

During every step of our travel through life we are bound and controlled by the Law. From the recording of our birth, as prescribed by law, to the recording of our death, as prescribed by law, each step of our existence is circumscribed by the Law.

We are told how we must care for our children, the age at which they must enter school, the age to which they must continue going to school, and the subject matter taught in their school. The Law decides the age at which one can be employed, places restrictions on the hiring or firing of employees, determines what food or cosmetics can be sold and what drugs can be sold, who can sell these drugs—as well as who can prescribe them or prescribe our glasses or check our teeth or hearing or represent us in legal matters or comb and style our hair. The Law dictates how fast we can drive (or even if we can drive) where we can drive (or walk), when we can work and where, whom we can marry, and how we get divorced. The Law also tells us our rights and obligations when we buy or rent anything, how much of our incomes we can keep, what we can say or write about anyone, and what our standard of conduct should be.

How did this great body of rules that so completely regulate our lives develop?

At first there were unwritten agreements between and within ancient tribes to provide some order in their relationships and to eliminate private vengeance. These rules were later formalized in writing as the Ten Commandments and still later expanded by the Bible and its commentaries by setting a retribution for harms done by one individual against another.

Over the centuries, such objective punishments developed into Criminal Law. Individual compensation to the individual victim became public punishment for sins committed. The community administered punishment according to legal forms that continue to this date. The State, not the individual, brings an action on behalf of the injured party; and the State, not the individual, collects for its coffers the fines imposed. Criminal Law is written in either *statutes* or *ordinances,* which are described later under "Source of Law." There are also Federal Criminal Laws. These are defined in the Constitution of the United States and in the laws passed by the Congress, called *acts.*

Civil Law, which also deals with relations between people, grew from the same roots as Criminal Law. In a civil action, however, the individual rather than the State brings the action, and any compensation for the injuries goes to the person injured rather than to the government.

Civil Law is not only written in acts, statutes, and ordinances but also embodied in the law developed by the courts. This body of law is called *case law* or *common law.*

American common law was brought over and developed from English common law. Some states, notably Louisiana, Texas, and California, use Roman civil law as the basis of their legal systems.

Civil Law and Criminal Law are independent of each other, and the fact that the State may bring a criminal cause of action for a wrong does not mean that an individual cannot bring his own cause of action for the same act if the wrong is also a civil wrong. Trespass, assault, and battery are some examples of this.

THE COURT SYSTEM

Each of the political bodies under which we live is subject to its own set of laws.

Matters involving federal laws are heard in the federal courts, which have been established under Article III, Section I of the United States Constitution, which provides that "the judicial power of the United States, shall be vested in one Supreme Court, and in such inferior Courts as the Congress may from time to time ordain and establish."

Under this permission, the Congress has established district trial courts. Because these are the courts in which most federal cases are originally tried, they are called *courts of original jurisdiction*. Cases may be tried before a judge alone (a *bench trial*) or before a judge and jury (a *jury trial*).

Appeals from decisions of a district court are taken to the federal appellate courts. There is an appellate court for each of the judicial circuits in the United States. In turn, appeals from a federal appellate court's decisions are taken to the Supreme Court of the United States. The Supreme Court need not hear all cases brought before it on appeal. The justices usually elect to hear only cases involving substantial constitutional questions. When the Justices of the Supreme Court elect to hear a case, they are said to *grant certiorari*. When they elect not to hear a case, they refuse to grant or deny, certiorari.

It is said that the United States Supreme Court is the most powerful body in the government. The president can veto any act of Congress and the Congress can override any veto of the president; but when the Supreme Court of the United States rules some law or action unconstitutional, its decision can be reversed only by the Court itself if at some later time it reverses or modifies its previous opinion in a case involving a similar issue.

In certain circumstances, the Supreme Court acts as a court of original jurisdiction. This occurs only in cases involving foreign diplomats or a state of the union. In all other cases, the Supreme Court hears cases only on appeal from the lower federal courts.

In addition to the district, appellate, and supreme courts, special courts have been established by the Congress to hear matters involving special areas of the law. These courts are

The customs court, which reviews the appraisals of imported merchandise and all decisions of collectors of customs, including orders on rate of duty, exclusion of merchandise, and liquidation of entries.

The tax court, which reviews deficiencies the commissioner of internal revenue claims are due for additional income, estate and gift taxes, or taxes imposed on private foundations.

The court of claims, which allows individuals an opportunity to sue the federal government for certain claims. Appeals from decisions of this court are heard directly by the Supreme Court.

Besides the courts, various federal boards and commissions arbitrate claims between individuals. Their decisions, like those of the Courts, have the force of law. Some examples of these are the National Labor Relations Board, the Board of Patent Appeals, the Fair Trade Commission, and the Federal Aviation Administration. And there are many others, touching and controlling almost every phase of our lives.

The organization of the state courts broadly parallels that of the federal courts; but there are many more state courts and certain significant organizational differences.

Although each state has a supreme court established by its constitution, the decisions of these courts, unlike those of the United States Supreme Court, can be appealed further. If the matter before a state supreme court involves a question arising under the Constitution of the United States, the states court's decision can be appealed to the Supreme Court, which may or may not grant certiorari.

In the federal district court system, the trial court, called the circuit court, may hear both civil and criminal cases. In state courts in many areas (particularly in large cities) there are separate systems of courts for hearing criminal and civil cases.

Probate courts (also called orphan's courts or surrogate courts) and courts of equity are found only in the state court system. Probate courts hear matters concerning the disposal of estates and matters concerning those considered incompetent because of age or mental infirmity.

In a court of equity, cases are heard that have "no adequate remedy at law." This means money damages alone cannot fully compensate the injured parties.

Divorce courts are likewise found only in state court systems.

Finally, another court unique to the state courts is small claims court. This court is set up to handle matters involving small dollar amounts, usually less than a thousand dollars. The parties usually represent themselves—in fact, lawyers are barred from some courts, and the pleadings and the trial itself are informal. The purpose of the court is to give individuals a fairly inexpensive way to have their differences heard and judged.

There are also, of course, state administrative boards and commissions that hold hearings and issue rulings the same way as their federal counterparts. Appeals from decisions of these bodies are made to state circuit courts, where the only matters decided are

1. Whether the hearings were conducted fairly;
2. Whether the administrative body had the authority to hear the matter and rule as it did; and
3. Whether or not the ruling was arbitrary and capricious.

Circuit courts will not review any issues litigated before boards or commissions.

In some localities there are local courts presided over by justices of the peace, police magistrates, or municipal court judges. For the most part, these courts hear traffic cases and other cases of ordinance violation, but they may also function as small claims courts.

APPEALS

The appellate courts, both federal and state, are courts of review. Before an appellate court, a case is argued only on the written record of the trial court. No witnesses are heard, nor is additional evidence presented. Only briefs containing a summary of the facts involved, a transcript of the original testimony, and arguments of counsel supported by citations to legal authorities are presented. The appellate courts sit as panels of judges. After reading the briefs and listening to the oral arguments of the attorneys for both sides, the judges issue their written opinion. If the appeal is denied, the matter usually ends there. As stated earlier, however, if the state supreme court or the United States Supreme Court grants certiorari, the decision of the appellate court is reviewed by the higher court sitting as a panel. The entire written record, including the briefs and oral arguments, which may again be presented, is reviewed again and a written opinion is again issued.

The decision of an appellate or supreme court to sustain an appeal may reverse the decision of the lower court or remand it back to the lower court for further action in accordance with the new decision. The decisions of appellate or supreme courts, unlike jury decisions, need not be unanimous. The ruling decision need only be concurred in by a majority of the judges hearing the matter.

SOURCES OF LAW

How do the judges in our courts know what law applies to the cases they hear?

There are several sources of law. Federal law originates in the United States Constitution and its amendments and takes the form of legislation passed by the Congress. Of course, whatever legislation Congress passes can be invalidated by the United States Supreme Court, which potentially wields the highest power in the federal government because it can rule that any act of the legislative or executive branch of government is unconstitutional.

Judges in the state courts preside under laws contained in the state constitutions and in legislation passed by the state legislatures, whose laws are called *statutes*.

In addition, municipalities may pass laws to control the conduct of people within their confines. These are called *ordinances.*

Besides the above, which is sometimes referred to as the *written law,* a great body of law has grown up through the *common law,* based on centuries of English and American usage and custom; and an even greater body of law has developed, consisting of judicial decisions that interpret the Constitution or the legislative acts.

2

HOW DO WE GET TO COURT?

JURISDICTION AND VENUE

Before bringing an action to court, we must first determine which court can hear the matter with which we are concerned. To do this, we must know whether the matter involves the United States Constitution or any congressional acts, a state constitution or its statutes, or a municipal ordinance.

Of course, we may decide that our matter involves none of these and must be brought before a federal or state board or commission for resolution; but if we find that a court has original jurisdiction, we must then determine before which particular court to bring it. *Jurisdiction* and *venue* make this determination.

Jurisdiction means the right of the court to hear the case. For example, probate matters are heard only in probate court, bankruptcy cases only in bankruptcy courts, constitutional questions only in federal courts, and so on. Sometimes the dollar amount of a claim determines jurisdiction. For example, a small claims court whose jurisdiction is limited to claims of a thousand dollars or less cannot hear matters in excess of that amount.

For the federal courts to have jurisdiction in a civil case that does not involve a constitutional question, the suit must involve citizens of different states and the amount involved must be $10,000 or more. If Mr. Jones of Illinois makes a claim against Mr. Smith of Illinois for $12,000, the case must be brought in the state courts of Illinois. However, if either Mr. Jones or Mr.

Smith lives in Wisconsin, the case can be brought in a federal district court; but even if Mr. Jones and Mr. Smith reside in different states, if the claim is $9,000, the case must be brought in the state court where the cause of action or transaction took place—it cannot be brought in federal court. Even if the parties agree that they want the matter heard in a certain court, if that court does not have jurisdiction, any judgment by that court is void and unenforceable.

Venue, on the other hand, generally refers to the location of the court, and venue can be waived by the parties to the suit. Venue is waived in one of two ways: The parties can actively waive it by agreeing that the matter shall be heard in a certain location, or unknowingly by failing to object to the venue at their first opportunity (failure to object amounts to a waiver of venue). A judgment by a court where venue has not been waived is voidable. Venue is usually determined by the place where the incident complained of occurred, where the parties reside, or (if the matter involves real estate) where the real estate is located.

CIVIL ACTIONS

After we have determined the proper jurisdiction and venue, how do we proceed?

In a civil case, the person who feels aggrieved may himself, or more frequently through his lawyer, prepare and file with the clerk of the court having jurisdiction a list of his complaints. This document is called a *complaint,* and the party bringing the action is the *plaintiff.* The person (or persons, if there are more than one) who will be called upon to defend against this complaint is the *defendant.* The complaint, which comprises not only the complaints against the defendant but also any damages the plaintiff demands for these alleged aggrievements, is served on the defendant by the sheriff (in some jurisdictions small claim complaints may be served by certified mail) along with a summons. The summons notifies the defendant where and when he should appear in court.

The defendant then takes the complaint and summons to his lawyer, who will have one or more conferences with his client before filing an *appearance* on behalf of the defendant on or before the date indicated in the summons. At the same time, he may file an *answer,* in which the defendant denies some of the allegations of the complaint while admitting others or denies all of them.

If the defendant's lawyer feels he cannot answer the complaint, he may file several *motions,* written and oral arguments by attorneys for both parties heard by a judge to get certain parts or all of a complaint stricken because they are too vague or irrelevant or immaterial or are merely recitals of conclusions rather than facts. The defendant's attorney may also request the plaintiff to state certain facts with more particularity and specificity or admit certain facts or produce certain documents or other tangible evidence for inspection by the defendant's counsel and any experts he may hire, or he may file a *special and limited appearance* to object to the venue.

The plaintiff's attorney may of course file similar motions against the defendant after the defendant has filed his answer.

Because these involve question of law and are argued solely by the lawyers, notice that a motion is going to be heard on a day and time certain and in a certain courtroom is only to the lawyer representing the party who must respond to the motion.

In addition to filing motions or an answer to the complaint, the defendant can also file a *counter-claim* for any grievances he feels he has against the plaintiff that will reduce, eliminate, or even exceed the damages claimed by the plaintiff. If the defendant feels that a necessary person has not been made a party to the action, he may join this other person or persons as *third party defendants.*

In a civil case, lawyers for each side are permitted to find out as much as they can, subject to certain limitations in regard to privileged information, about the other side's case. This is done by submitting questions in writing called *interogatories* to the other side, who must answer them in writing. Attorneys may also require witnesses to answer questions orally under oath before a judicial officer by giving depositions. Discovery takes place well ahead of trial.

Many people feel that the use of motions or the use of techniques of interogatories and depositions for the purpose of discovery are abuses by one side or the other to delay the administration of justice or to obtain some other, baser objective. However, a trial is a complex situation, with its own rules governing procedure and the allowance of testimony. In addition, two capable attorneys representing opposite sides as adversaries can and do create questions and indecision in the minds of a jury. Therefore, the purpose of the discovery and the effects of the judges' decisions on the motions are only to narrow the issues so as to shorten the actual trial and keep areas involved as concise as possible during trial.

At the time the plaintiff files his complaint with the court, he may demand a jury trial. Should he not do so, at the time the defendant files his appearance, he may then demand a jury trial. Should neither side demand a jury trial, the matter is heard only by a judge, in what is called a *bench trial.*

In a bench trial, the judge decides all questions of law and fact. In a jury trial, the judge decides questions of law and the jury questions of fact.

If the trial is by jury, each party's attorney is given a list of the prospective jurors. Through a series of questions asked of the jurors, individually by the judge or the lawyers or sometimes by both, the requested number of jurors is selected.

When the trial starts, counsel for the plaintiff speaks first and presents his theory of the case and the basis of his client's claim. When he is finished, counsel for the defendant gives his reasons why the plaintiff's claim should be denied.

After the respective lawers have given their opening statements, the plaintiff's attorney calls all of his witnesses, who testify under oath. After each witness has testified, the defendant's lawyer has the right to cross-examine him to impeach his credibility or obtain admissions the defendant hopes will be beneficial.

After the plaintiff has presented all his witnesses and they have been cross-examined, the plaintiff rests his case. Ordinarily at this point, the defendant's attorney claims that the plaintiff has not carried his burden of proving the case and asks the court to direct a vertict in favor of the defendant. If the court so directs, the trial is ended. If the court does not, the defendant's attorney presents his witnesses, who also testify under oath. The plaintiff's counsel of course has the right to cross-examine each witness at the conclusion of his testimony.

After all witnesses for both sides have testified and all evidence has been presented, the attorneys for each of the parties make their closing arguments. Because the plaintiff has the burden of proving his case and his burden remains with him all through the trial and never shifts to the defendant, the plaintiff's lawyer presents his argument first. When he is finished, the defendant's lawyer then presents his argument. When he has finished, the plaintiff's lawyer has the privilege of again speaking to rebut the defendant's argument. This privilege is extended only to the plaintiff's lawyer; the defendant's lawyer does not get an opportunity for rebuttal argument.

In a bench trial, at some time after the plaintiff's lawyer has concluded his rebuttal argument, the judge renders a verdict. However, in a jury trial, after the plaintiff's lawyer has concluded his rebuttal argument, the judge instructs the jury as to the law so the jury can apply it to the facts as it heard them and then render its verdict.

If either side is unhappy with the trial verdict, it may first move for a new trial. If that is denied, it may then exercise its right of appeal.

CRIMINAL ACTIONS

In a criminal matter, the procedure is much different. In the first place, the plaintiff is a government body—United States of America, State of Illinois, City of Los Angeles. The accused is charged with the crime by either an *indictment*, a *presentment*, an *information*, or a *complaint*. The method used is usually governed by the seriousness of the offense.

A *complaint* is generally used when the offense is a petty state charge, called a *misdemeanor*, or a municipal ordinance violation. The complaint originates with either a private citizen or a police officer, who appears before a magistrate and describes, under oath, what he represents the accused did. The complainant's testimony is then reduced to a written document, that he signs. The written complaint is put in the words of the criminal statute that characterizes it as an offense. If the magistrate is satisfied that an offense has been stated, he issues a warrant for the arrest of the accused.

When a police officer sees a crime being committed or has reasonable grounds for believing a crime has been committed and that a particular suspect has committed it, he may arrest that suspect without a warrant. A citizen may also make an arrest if he has reasonable grounds to believe that a crime other than an ordinance violation is being committed. It is not required that a police officer actually see a crime being committed. He may make an arrest without a warrant upon reasonable belief that a crime has been committed and that the person arrested committed the crime. For this reason, a lawful arrest, with or without a warrant, should never be resisted—even if you believe it is illegal. A police officer has the right to use as much force as necessary, even to use his gun when circumstances apply, to affect an arrest. The best procedure is to permit the arrest and then employ legal counsel to protect your rights.

More serious crimes are called *felonies*. Most felony arrests are made without warrant, the complaint being filed after the arrest. In addition, station-house bail is seldom authorized for a felony. Therefore, most defendants arrested for felonies get at least a short taste of jail, sometimes a day or two, sometimes longer.

Shortly after his arrest, whether for a misdemeanor or for a felony, the defendant is brought before a judge for a preliminary hearing. At the preliminary hearing, the attorney for the government, called the *prosecutor*, presents evidence to determine if there is sufficient evidence (or *probable cause*) to hold the defendant or set bail for his release until charges have been brought against him in a court of record. Should the judge decide that a *prima facia* case has not been made by the prosecutor, he discharges the defendant from custody. This finding is not a trial on the merits, and the defendant can be rearrested on a fresh record for the same crime. Should the Judge find that there is probable cause that the defendant committed the crime with which he is charged, the defendant is *bound over* to the grand jury for a felony charge; and the judge sets bail, so that the defendant can be released from custody upon the payment of the bail until his trial.

If the crime charged is a misdemeanor or ordinance violation, there is usually an immediate trial without the intervention of a grand jury. A more detailed description of the grand jury is given in Chapter 18.

Should the grand jury issue a *presentment* (a written accusation initiated by a grand jury for the purpose of having an indictment submitted) or return a *true bill of indictment* (a written accusation, under oath, drawn by the prosecutor). The accusation is presented to a court for the issuance of the accusatory pleading on which the defendant is tried.

An *information* is a sworn statement by the prosecuting attorney describing what the defendant did and characterizing it as criminal presented directly to the court without the intervention of a grand jury.

After a defendant has been served with the complaint, information, or indictment, he appears in court on the date set by the court (of which he has advance notice) and pleads guilty or not guilty to the charges. This is called an *arraignment.*

In misdemeanor cases, although there is a right to a jury trial, most defendants who plead not guilty waive a jury and elect a bench trial. This can be heard immediately or on some specially set later date. Should the defendant plead guilty at the arraingment, he usually receives the punishment or fine imposed by the court immediately.

In felony cases, whether by indictment or information, when the defendant pleads guilty, he is usually sentenced forthwith, following argument of his counsel on the question of sentence. His sentence may be deferred pending a presentence investigation by a probation officer of the court. Should the defendant plead not guilty, the case is then calendared for trial at some future date. It is heard by a jury, unless the defendant waives a jury trial.

Criminal trials are similar to civil trials in that the prosecution presents its witnesses and evidence first, subject to cross-examination by defense counsel. Upon the conclusion of the prosecution's case, the defense may present its case, subject to cross-examination by the prosecutor.

The prosecutor gives his opening statement and closing argument first, and the defense second. In addition, the prosecutor has the right of rebuttal, unavailable to the defendant's attorney.

There are certain significant differences between the trial procedures of civil and criminal cases. In a civil case, if a jury is not demanded the matter will be heard as a bench trial. In a criminal case, unless a jury is waived, the matter will be heard by a jury. In a civil case, discovery prior to trial is almost unlimited, so each side is usually as familiar with the opponent's case as with its own. In a criminal case, discovery is severely restricted, and statements of witnesses cannot be examined until they have testified. In a civil case, a party to the suit can call the other party as his witness and question him on direct examination, which opens a broad field of testimony, instead of being limited by cross-examination to the areas covered by direct examination. In a criminal case, a defendant cannot be called as a witness by the prosecution and forced to testify against himself.

Finally, in a civil case the plaintiff must only persuade whoever is to decide the truth that the allegations in his complaint are more probably true than the allegations or denials of the defendant. In a criminal case, however, the prosecutor, whether it be a state attorney, a district attorney, or an assistant United States attorney, must prove the defendant guilty beyond a reasonable doubt of the crime charged. Clearly, the plaintiff may win a civil case merely by presenting his own witnesses if the defendant does not offer rebuttal evidence. In a criminal case, however, if the state cannot prove the defendant guilty with no other alternatives, the defendant must be found not guilty even if he does not present a single witness or piece of evidence.

Upon a finding of not guilty, a criminal matter is ordinarily concluded, the state being permitted to appeal only certain pretrial procedural decisions by the court. Upon a finding of guilty, the defendant has the right to motion for a judgement notwithstanding the verdict or for a new tial or to appeal to courts of appellate jurisdication.

If you are charged with a serious criminal offense but have no money, the court will assign a lawyer to represent you. Such lawyers, usually called public defenders, are available to represent criminal defendants who cannot afford their own lawyers. Public defenders charge little or no fee, depending on the defendant's circumstances.

If your legal troubles are civil, there are in most cities legal aid groups to represent people who cannot afford their own lawyers. These groups are usually financed by the United States government or by law firms in the community or both. Therefore their fees are generally lower than those of unsubsidized lawyers.

3

HOW TO SELECT A LAWYER

Henry Brown walks into the law office of J. Crittendon Greenacre III and retains Mr. Greenacre as his lawyer. Mr. Brown then tells Mr. Greenacre, "You know that bank holdup last week? Well I'm the guy who held up the bank and killed the guard. The police are close to catching me, so I need you as my attorney." Following this conversation, should Mr. Greenacre (*a*) call the police as an officer of the court and tell them he knows who pulled the bank job and where this criminal can be found? (*b*) have lunch with his colleagues and tell them he is representing the guy who robbed the bank last week? or (*c*) that night over dinner tell his wife and family of the day's events, including the exciting conversation he had with Mr. Brown?

If you answered, "None of the above," you would be right. Mr. Greenacre can try to convince Mr. Brown to surrender to the police, or he can withdraw and refuse to represent Mr. Brown. Any conversations between Mr. Brown and his lawyer, however, cannot be repeated by Mr. Greenacre. This is called *privileged communication*. Even if lawyer Greenacre is subpoenaed, placed on the witness stand, sworn on oath to tell the whole truth, threatened with contempt of court and jail, he cannot be compelled to disclose the contents of that priviledged communication between Mr. Brown and himself without Mr. Brown's authorization. Only if Mr. Brown is suing or being sued by Mr. Greenacre or if Mr. Brown falsely accuses Mr. Greenacre of wrongdoing in connection with the matter can this conversation be disclosed.

There is a special relationship between a client and his lawyer and because of this special relationship, it is important that you select the best lawyer you can to represent you in whatever matter concerns you.

Lawyers are licensed by the state or states in which they practice. In addition, they are allowed to practice before most state and federal boards and almost all federal courts only by receiving special permission from those boards or courts.

If a lawyer is admitted to practice before a state court, he is automatically permitted to represent a client before the Internal Revenue Service. However, before discussing a client's matter with a revenue agent, the lawyer must also have a signed power of attorney from the client to represent him.

Once a lawyer has been admitted to practice before a state supreme court, he is automatically permitted to practice before any of the lower courts within that state. However, the lawyer must be admitted to practice by each federal court individually to practice before it.

A lawyer's professional conduct is controlled by a code of ethics developed by the American Bar Association, the state bar associations, and sometimes by local bar associations. Should it be found that a lawyer has violated the codes of ethics, he can be censured and warned not to do it again or he can be disbarred. This means that his license is revoked and he is suspended from the practice of law until he has been reinstated.

Now, how should you select a lawyer? First, most good lawyers build their clientele by reputation. So, it is a good idea to start with friends and relatives who have been involved in matters similar to yours, whether it be divorce, personal injury, selling or buying a house, taxation, or starting a new business. Ask them who represented them, what their experiences were, and how they felt about their representation. If none of your friends or relatives were involved in similar situations or if you do not care to discuss your problem with them, call your county, city, or state bar association. Through its lawyer referral plan, the association will usually recommend a lawyer or lawyers in your area with experience in your field of inquiry.

You can then call one of these lawyers and arrange for a preliminary conference to discuss your matter. These conferences are held either at the bar association office or at the lawyer's own office and usually provide a half-hour conference for a nominal fee the lawyer has agreed with the bar association to charge. If as a result of this initial conference, the lawyer feels you need legal representation and you want that lawyer to provide it, you can make arrangements for further action.

Currently lawyers are permitted to advertise, and some do advertise their services. This can be another source of lawyer's names; but as with all other advertising, the lawyer providing the service rather than the advertising should determine the selection of who will represent you.

In 1978, the American Bar Association prepared and made available to the public an excellent booklet entitled *The American Lawyer: How to Choose and Use One,* which tells you not only what is involved in selecting a lawyer but also what you can expect from your lawyer and how to deal with him. This booklet makes one statement that bears repeating here: accessibility and competence rather than price should be your main concern in selecting a lawyer. The Law has been described as a "living thing"; and like any living thing, it is constantly changing. Therefore a good lawyer keeps up his competence by attending continuing education courses and reading as much of the material published in his field as possible. Ask questions of your lawyer to test his competence.

Not all matters, however, require a lawyer. For example, if the complaint is a small claim or if the defendant does not wish to contest a case, he may only want to consult a lawyer but represent himself in court. Even in such cases, however, a lawyer should at least be consulted. Your lawyer can look at your problem objectively and give good advice without the emotional involvement you bring to it.

SPECIALISTS

Once you've decided that you should have a lawyer, the question becomes, "Do I need a general practitioner or a specialist?" The answer is, "It depends" or "Both."

A lawyer who specializes in only one or two areas of law is usually found in the larger communities or cities, whereas a lawyer with a general practice, familiar with but not expert in most phases of the law, like a country doctor is more likely to be found in the smaller towns. Many problems in our lives do not require specialists. In fact, most specialists have narrowed their scope of expertise to include only one problem or type of problem, whereas general practitioners can usually be consulted on a continuing basis.

One way to avoid trouble is to obtain counsel before taking action, and a general practitioner can give such counsel. Many times we do not need specific representation, but only legal advice. Finally, many matters do not need expert knowledge. Drawing up a simple will or partnership agreement and representation in a simple real estate sale or a traffic or simple misdemeanor case usually do not require a specialist.

Also, your family lawyer and friend, whom you have consulted often on various matters, will probably be aware of how any matter under consideration can affect you or your family in relation to what has happened to you before and to your plans for the future.

If your matter is complex or if it is in a field that requires specialization—taxation; personal injury trial work; criminal law work; condemnation; patent, copyright, and trademark law; trust and estate work; labor law—you will probably need a specialist. If your lawyer feels that this is an area of the law in which he does not have the expertise to handle your matter competently, he is obliged by the code of ethics to refer you to an attorney who does.

Such a referral is not a reflection on your own lawyer's competence. The law can be a tangled web to trap the uninitiated, and special representation under special circumstances protects you and is in your best interest.

When you need someone you can trust, someone who will protect your confidences, someone trained to take an objective view of your problem and exercise independent professional judgment on your behalf, someone who will zealously represent you within the bounds of the law in or out of court, you need a lawyer.

FEES

Setting and charging fees can create difficult problems for both lawyer and client. Some matters are taken by lawyers on a *contingent fee* basis. The client is responsible only for any costs incurred—the costs of filing the lawsuit or the sheriff's costs for serving papers, or possibly the court reporter's costs if depositions are taken. No fee is due to the lawyer unless he is successful on his client's behalf. If he is successful, he charges the client a portion of the amount recovered or saved; if he is unsuccessful, he charges nothing. Contingent fees usually run from 20 percent to 50 percent of the amount recovered or saved.

Under other circumstances, lawyers charge by the hour. Fees are usually calculated in this way when a lawyer cannot reasonably project how much time will be involved in research, investigation, preparation, and perhaps trial of a matter.

Finally, lawyers take some matters on a *fixed fee* basis—they charge a fixed fee for a specific service regardless of the time involved or the results. It is more common for a lawyer to quote a fixed fee if a matter is not contested or if it can be settled within a certain time. If it cannot be disposed of within that time, moreover, he may charge on an hourly basis thereafter.

Before You See a Lawyer

If you sometimes feel that your attorney has charged a higher fee than the time spent with you seemed to justify, consider the following:

1. If your lawyer helped solve your problem quickly, it was not a miracle. Only because of his training in law school, his experiences in practice, and his continuing efforts to keep up with current law by subscribing to books and technical services and by attending seminars (all of which cost money) has he become a reliable professional.

2. If he accepts your case, he is not able to represent someone else during the time he is devoting to it.

3. Most questions or trials are not concluded instantly but require many hours of research, investigation, and trial preparation. Therefore, the time that you spend with your lawyer, like the tip of the iceberg, is probably only a small part of the time he spends on an entire case.

4. In addition to the books, technical services, and seminars mentioned above, a lawyer must also provide an office, a secretary, and other overhead expenses to serve you. After meeting the expenses of all these, he must also earn enough to support himself and his family.

To minimize the problem of fees with your lawyer you should discuss them at your first meeting. You can also help reduce fees in the following ways:

1. Be honest with your attorney and give him all the facts—good or bad.

2. Provide him with as many documents, pictures, names of witnesses, satements, and other data as you can.

3. Respect the fact that your attorney's time and advice are all he has to sell. Avoid telephoning him about trivial matters.

4. Be considerate. If you make an appointment with your lawyer, keep it and be on time; or if you must cancel it, if possible give him enough notice to schedule something else for the time originally set aside for you and set a new time and date for you.

5. Ask questions and be sure you understand what he is doing and what he wants you to do, and do it.

Once you have selected your lawyer and have developed confidence in him, you will find that you have probably developed a good friend and confidant for life. He should not be dismissed unless he turns out to be incompetent or dishonest.

4

CONTRACTS

"Hey Mister, I'll mow your lawn for $15.00." The owner of the property says nothing, but watches while the boy mows his lawn. Does the property owner have to pay the boy when he finishes mowing?

That is a question of *contract*. Contracts are a part of everyday life. Some we enter into knowingly, in purchasing a car or an airline ticket, for example. Others we enter into by our actions. In some contracts, we make the terms very precise; in others we only imply them. In some contracts, we make terms too burdensome for ourselves; in others we accept terms so vague they cannot be determined from the agreement.

Because of the potential complexity of contracts, any contract involving a substantial amount of money, enforceable over a long period of time, or dealing with personal rights should be prepared and reviewed by lawyers for all parties.

Let us first define a contract, so you will know when you are involved with one: A contract is an agreement between two or more competent people to do, or not do, some legal and possible thing for a consideration.

From the definition, you can see that a number of elements must be satisfied before there is a valid, enforceable contract. We will analyze these elements in a moment, but first let us describe the classification of contracts.

CLASSIFICATION OF CONTRACTS

Valid vs Void

A contract can be *valid,* which means it satisfies all legal requirements, or it can be *void,* which means it has no legal effect and cannot be enforced by either party. For example, a contract to commit a crime cannot be legally enforced and is therefore void.

Voidable Contracts

A contract may also be *voidable.* Under a voidable contract, some legal requirement is not met by one party, so the other party has the option of performing or not performing his obligation under that agreement. For example, if an agreement specifies that Mr. Smith must pay before Mr. Jones cuts down his tree and if the agreement specifies that Mr. Smith must pay by a certain time and if that time passes before Mr. Smith has paid, Mr. Jones may, at his option, void the contract or extend the time for Mr. Smith to pay or cut down the tree first and permit Mr. Smith to pay later.

In general, when a contract does not specify how long it will remain performable, if the period of the contract can be implied from its nature that is the period in which the contract must be performed. For example, a contract to deliver fresh fruit or vegetables must be performed within a short enough period to prevent the food from spoiling.

Enforceable vs Unenforceable

An *enforceable* contract is valid and can be enforced by the courts. An *unenforceable* contract is either void from the beginning or voidable and made void by the party who has the option to do so.

Oral vs Written

With certain exceptions prescribed by law and falling within the *statute of fraud,* which will be explained later, a contract can be as informal as an oral agreement between the parties, even without a handshake; or so formal and written as even to be placed under seal. Although few contracts need be so formal as to be under seal, a written agreement offers better protection. First, a written contract is documentary evidence of the agreement. Second, if the written contract is prepared by a competent person, it will clearly set out all the terms agreed to by the parties and there will be no question of ambiguity or disagreement. Finally, where there is a written agreement signed by the parties, neither party can successfully deny that he agreed to its terms.

Executory vs Executed

Under an *executory* contract, the obligations of the parties have not yet been fully completed. Under an *executed* contract, all obligations have been fully performed and nothing more need be done.

Express vs Implied

An *express* contract is an oral or written contract in which all of the terms have been stated. An *implied* contract is one in which the terms are implied by the actions of the parties. For example, in the illustration at the beginning of this chapter, since the property owner heard the boy offer to mow his lawn, and the price for this mowing and did nothing to object or stop the boy (in fact, watched him do it) the property owner implied that he accepted the boy's offer and became legally obligated to pay the $15 after the lawn has been mowed.

Bilateral vs Unilateral

Under a *bilateral* contract, each party promises the other that he will perform. Under a *unilateral* (one-sided) contract, the exchange for the promise is something other than a promise. In our example, the property owner promised nothing, but the boy unilaterally performed under his offer and the property owner accepted the benefits of that performance. Therefore, there was an enforceable obligation on the property owner to pay the boy for his work.

ELEMENTS OF A VALID CONTRACT

Agreement

For there to be a valid agreement, the parties must be in complete agreement as to what is being offered and what is being accepted. This is called a *meeting of the minds*. For example, if I offer to sell you "my car for $5,000," and I own a 1977 Cadillac and a 1979 Plymouth, we must agree on which car is being sold, or there is no meeting of the minds and no contract.

An agreement is sometimes defined as mutual promises by the parties to do or refrain from doing some legally binding thing.

Offer

An offer is a promise by one party, called the *offeror*, to another party, called the *offeree*, to create some legal obligation. The offeree must know that the offer is being made to him, although the offer may be made through an agent of the offeror. The offer must create an obligation to do or not do some thing, which the offeror is not legally bound to do or not do. For example, if one promises to go swimming every day this week, this is not a legal offer, since it is not legally binding. Your mailman cannot legally offer to deliver your mail if you pay him $20.00, because he is already obligated to deliver your mail. However, if someone offers to sell to another a certain specified book for $10.00, this is a legally enforceable offer.

Offers made in jest or requiring performance in the future as part of negotiations or stated in vague or ambiguous terms are not legal. Some examples of these are

1. A writes a letter to B as follows: "Please let me know if you would like to buy concrete from me at $.35 per yard." This is not an offer but an invitation to commence negotiation.
2. C tells D: "If you come to work for me, I'll pay you a fair salary and even a share of the profits, depending on what I can afford." This is not an offer, because it is too vague and uncertain. However, if there is an ascertainable standard (such as a minimum wage), this is a legal offer—even if the contract is to be performed in the future—if the minimum wage on that future date is set as the standard.

An advertisement to pay $25 for every 1913 Indian-head penny sent to the offeror is a legal offer until revoked.

Advertising offering certain merchandise at a specified price is not an offer to sell but an invitation to the public to come and buy.

Acceptance

An offer is not binding until it has been accepted by the offeree. An unaccepted offer, however, continues until it is rejected by the offeree or revoked by the offeror or allowed to lapse by the passage of time, the death or destruction of a person or thing essential for its performance or invalidated by some law that makes the proposed performance illegal.

If an offer specifies a date by which it must be accepted, it is automatically revoked if it is not accepted by that date, unless the parties agree to extend the time. Sometimes this extension of time is done through an option. When an option is used, the offeree pays the offeror a certain sum to keep the offer open for an additional fixed period of time. If the offeree does not accept the offer within that period, the offer terminates and the offeror keeps the money paid to him for keeping the option open.

If an offer does not specify a date by which it must be accepted, the offer terminates (as the courts have held) after a reasonable time, which reasonable time is determined by the nature of the contract, business usage, and other circumstances.

Unless otherwise stated an offer must be accepted by the medium by which it was made or by a faster medium. An offer made by letter can be accepted by letter or by wire. An offer made by wire can be accepted only by wire unless the parties agree on acceptance by some other means.

If an offer is made by mail, the date the acceptance is mailed, as determined by the postmark or a post office receipt, becomes the date of the acceptance, not the date when the acceptance is received by the offeror.

Although mere silence can constitute a rejection of an offer, the offeror cannot construe silence by the offeree as acceptance except when the offeree knowingly accepts the benefits of performance by the offeror and these benefits cannot be returned.

Two or More Competent People

Because there must be mutual promises for there to be a valid contract, there must be at least two or more parties to any agreement. However, there need not be an equal number of parties on each side: One person may make a promise to one other; or two people may make a promise to one another; or one person may make several promises to one person or to several people; or several people may join in a single promise to one person.

As you can see, the number of people involved, so long as there are two or more, is unimportant. It is important, however, that the people who make these promises be *legally competent*—that they have the legal capacity to enter into a contract. Certain people cannot enter into binding contracts. However, such contracts are voidable only on their part—they have the option whether to perform their obligations or not. Therefore, anyone who deals with an incompetent person does so at his own risk, since he cannot enforce any contract if the incompetent party chooses to repudiate it. Moreover, an incompetent can recover whatever money he paid for goods or services whenever he repudiates a contract. The people given this protection by law comprise *infants, intoxicated persons,* and *insane persons.*

Infants. This term refers not to babies in their mothers' arms but to those the law considers too immature to be held fully responsible for their acts. In some states, children under the age of eighteen are considered infants. In other states, children are infants until they reach twenty-one. The statutes of each state specify when an infant ceases to be a minor and attains his or her majority.

An infant's right to void a contract is not lost even if his or her parent or parents joined in the contract or he entered into the contract with the approval of his parents or guardian or adult spouse. It should be further noted, however, that when a minor reaches his majority, he must repudiate any contract he entered into as a minor that he has not previously repudiated or the contract will become binding.

There are also certain contracts for which a minor is liable, even though they were entered into while he was an infant. These are contracts for necessaries—food, clothing, shelter, medicine and medical care, and an elementary or vocational education. How much of these a minor will be liable for is determined by his economic situation. Even in the case of necessaries, however, an infant is not liable for the full retail price but only for the reasonable value of the goods or services provided.

If a minor lives with a guardian or parent, he cannot bind himself for necessaries unless it can be proven that the guardian or parent is unable or unwilling to provide them. Anything more than the items listed above are usually not considered a necessary, even if the infant can show that he needs the item (such as a car) in his business and depends on the business for his support.

Finally, if a minor can return or restore any part of what he has received, he must do so before he can recover what he paid on any contract he repudiates. However, if an infant has lost the property purchased or disposed of it or permitted it to waste away, he may still recover the amount paid when he repudiates the contract.

Should a minor repudiate a contract under which he sold property, the party who purchased it must return it or face suit, not only for the contract but also for a tort. For example, someone who purchases real estate from a minor becomes a trespasser if he fails to vacate and return the property after the infant has repudiated the sale.

If a minor misrepresents his age, he can still repudiate a contract and recover the money he paid. However, the adult seller may at least have a claim against the minor for damages for deceit.

Intoxicated persons. Contracts entered into by a person intoxicated by alcohol or drugs are voidable by him, because a person in an intoxicated condition cannot understand the nature and effect of a contract. However, upon recovery of his judgment, he must promptly affirm or repudiate the contract.

Insane persons. If anyone enters into a contract with an insane person in good faith and without notice of the incompetency, the courts will generally uphold the contract, except where the consideration is inadequate. Generally, intoxicated persons and insane persons must return any consideration paid by the other party to void a contract. Unless a person is adjudged insane and a guardian is appointed, any contracts made by the insane person are voidable and must be repudiated. There is a disagreement among authorities as to whether contracts made by an insane person are void once a guardian has been appointed.

In states where such contracts are void, it is argued that the appointment of a guardian has removed by law the incompetent's power to make contracts until the guardianship is terminated. This rule is applied in those states even to contracts entered into during periods when the incompetent behaves sanely. In other states, the courts hold that the adjudication of insanity gives only an appearance of incompetency. Unless the other party to a contract personally knew of the adjudication, the contract will be upheld if it can be shown that the alleged insane person was of sound mind at the time the contract was made.

The test for insanity is the same as that for intoxication—was the party in question able to understand the character of the transaction. If so, the contract is valid. If not, it is void or voidable.

Old age, failing health, eccentricity, abnormal conduct, or partial impairment of thought processes do not necessarily make one incompetent.

To Do or Not Do Some Legal and Possible Thing

While you may have heard an agreement where one person kills another in exchange for money from a third person called a *contract*, such a contract is clearly illegal and void. So are all other contracts to commit illegal acts. As a result, gambling contracts, except in states where gambling is permitted, are void. In addition, contracts against public policy, however valid they may otherwise be, are nevertheless unenforceable because they damage the public health, safety, or morals. For example, a gambling contract which may be valid in Nevada is not enforceable in New York because it is against the public morals of New York citizens. Contracts that are against the public interest fall in the same category. For example, some people have tried to agree to divorce at the end of each year and remarry at the beginning of the following year thus taking advantage of the reduced income tax rates for single people without giving up their marriages. Such contracts are void.

In addition, a contract must pertain to a possible act. If the acts to be performed are impossible or it is clear that the contract is made in jest, the contract is void. For example, I cannot agree to sell you my wife for $1,000. This is impossible act, and it should be obvious that it is offered in jest.

Ordinarily, representations as to value, as well as opinions or exaggerations or recommendations of an article offered for sale, will not avoid a contract. If an automobile salesman tells you, "This car is worth several thousand dollars more than you're paying for it," and you find that it is worth less than you paid, you're stuck! The salesman's opinion is mere "sales puffery" and is not actionable.

For a Consideration

The final requirement for a valid and binding contract is that there be consideration; that is, a benefit to both of the parties that arises from doing or refraining from doing the acts contracted for. The considerations flowing to both parties need not be equal, but a benefit must pass to both parties. If I offer you $2,000 for your auto (for which you paid only $1,000), we have a valid, enforceable contract; and if you deliver your car to me, I must pay you $2,000 or you can sue me for breach of contract. The only exception to this occurs if the consideration is so unequal that it is unconscionable—that is, the difference would shock the conscience of the court. For example, an offer of $10 for a ring worth $100,000 could not be enforced even if accepted.

The consideration can also be offered to stop doing something you have a legal right to do. For example, I can offer you $1,500 for permitting me to use part of your property to enlarge my driveway. You are not required to do this; but if you accept my offer, we have a valid, enforceable contract.

The promise of a gift is not a contract because there is no consideration flowing to both parties. Therefore, one cannot enforce such a promise. However, once a gift is given, the giver cannot change his mind and recover it.

CONTRACTS THAT MUST BE IN WRITING

Earlier we mentioned the statute of frauds. This law requires that certain contracts be in writing in order to be enforceable. These contracts include

1. An agreement that is not to be performed within one year from the date of making. Assume that an employee retires from a company for which he worked for fifty years and that the company, to induce this retirement, orally agrees to pay his estate upon his death $1,000 per month for twenty years. Now suppose that when employee dies the company refuses to pay the monthly stipend. Can the employee's heirs sue to enforce the contract? No, because this agreement was oral, and not made in writing as required by the statute of frauds.

2. Any contract for the sale of land or any interest therein or a lease of real estate for more than one year. Suppose you agree to buy someone's house and lot. Before his lawyer prepares the contract, however, he sells the property to someone else. Can you sue to cancel the second contract and make him sell the property to you as promised? No, because the contract wasn't in writing.

3. Agreements made upon consideration of marriage. Premarital agreements are discussed in the chapter on marriage. Unless these property settlement agreements are in writing, they are unenforceable.

4. A contract wherein you agree to pay someone else's debt. Suppose a friend with whom you carpool has his car financed and finds he cannot make the payments. Because the car is necessary for you to get to work, you tell the finance company you will make the payments for your friend. Is this promise enforceable? Not unless it is in writing.

5. A contract for the sale of personal property exceeding $5,000 in amount or value. Under the uniform commercial code, such a contract is unenforceable except for a contract for the sale of goods, securities, or security agreements, unless some writing indicates that a contract for sale has been made between the parties at a specific price that reasonably identifies the property being sold and is signed by the party against whom enforcement is sought or by his authorized agent. Notice that this does not require a written contract, but only "some writing." The evidence of the contract can be a purchase order, the confirmation of a purchase order, or even a memo of the transaction, so long as it meets the other identifying requirements and is signed by the party or his agent.

ASSIGNMENTS AND PERSONAL SERVICE CONTRACTS

Generally, all contracts except those that involve the personal skill of one of the parties may be assigned to a third person for performance. For example, if you buy a car and finance a part of the purchase price, the car dealer may have you sign a note payable to him. He can then assign the note to a bank or finance company. Thereafter, your payments will be made to the bank or finance company, even though you never did business with them.

If your contract depends on the skill or talent of the other party, however, you have a right to expect that party to perform. If you hire a famous artist to paint your portrait, for example, *he* must paint your portrait. He cannot assign the contract to someone else, even to someone in his studio, without your permission. Because of the nature of personal service contracts, two factors should be kept in mind:

First, if the person on whose skill or talent you are relying dies or becomes incapable of performing, the contract is terminated, unless the contract can be performed as well by the personal representative of the deceased or incompetent promisor.

Second, if a personal service contract contains the phrase, "satisfaction guaranteed," it means just that! In most contracts, the performance must be good and workmanlike, and the promisee must only expect reasonable performance. When this phrase is put into the contract, however, the promisee must be satisfied—even though the contract involves personal taste, judgment or fancy—before he is required to perform. In the case of the portrait painter, if his contract provides that the satisfaction of the other party is guaranteed, that party must be satisfied before he need pay, and the reasonableness of his demand is immaterial.

TERMINATION AND ENFORCEMENT OF CONTRACTS

Ordinarily a contract must be fully performed by the party seeking to be paid before he can recover for his work. Where one party prevents the other from completing his work, however, the performing party can recover for that portion of the work he did complete. If one party fails to perform (such failure is called a *breach of contract*), when the breach is only slight, inadvertent, and unimportant, the performing party can force the other party to perform his promises.

When a contract provides that "time is of the essence," the party who fails to perform within the specified time is liable to the other party for any damages resulting from the delay, unless the delay was caused by the other party.

When there is a dispute about work performed or the amount of a bill and a party sends a check in an amount less than the contract price, marking it "paid in full," if the performing party keeps the check or cashes it, the contract dispute is settled and there is no cause of action for the unpaid balance. This applies only to a dispute, not to a partial payment for completed performance for an agreed price.

Where a contract is breached, the injured party may

1. Sue for any actual damages he can prove resulted from this breach.

2. Sue for the reasonable value of labor and material provided to the date of the breach.

3. Sue for specific performance. Where there is a contract to sell unique personal property or real estate, which merely by being real estate is considered unique, the buyer can use court action to force the seller to go through with the sale instead of paying money damages. This is called a suit for specific performance.

4. In certain situations, it is possible to enjoin or stop another from working for someone else, where the employee has breached an employment contract. Such injunction suits are generally used against a person with certain skills or talents, like an entertainer, or someone who has acquired certain knowledge, like a patent or secret process, from his employer.

As you can see, contracts can be complex and disagreements about them can cause serious results. Therefore one is well advised to use legal counsel *before* entering into a contract rather than after in an attempt to avoid the duties required by the contract or to seek a remedy for the other party's breach. Also, remember that if someone tells you, "This document is not a contract, but only an offer to purchase," when you accept that offer, the document with all of its terms becomes a binding, enforceable contract. Don't be misled!

5

TORTS, NEGLIGENCE, AND AUTOMOBILE ACCIDENTS

John and Harry have an argument, and John threatens to punch Harry in the nose. George and Bill have an argument, and Bill does punch George in the nose. Jim doesn't like Jack because Jack, as president of the local bank, refused to make Jim a loan; Jim writes the newspaper and tells everyone he meets, "Jack is a thief and an embezzler and spent ten years in jail for these crimes," even though Jim knows these statements are false. Henry needs a place to store his car, and Bob has a garage; so Henry parks his car in Bob's garage without Bob's permission and refuses to remove it. You are stopped at a red light, waiting for the light to change, when Chuck driving another car runs into the back of your car, damaging the car and injuring you. A lady crossing the street is hit by a car driven by Marion. These are just some examples of *torts*. A tort is a wrong that arises apart from a contract but is not a crime under statute or common law.

A tort is always a wrong by an individual against another individual, and the purpose of bringing suit for this wrong is the collection of money for the injury suffered. Such injuries, called *damages,* can be injuries to a person or damage to property.

TORT VS ACCIDENT

One of two essential elements must be proven in order to recover for damages from a tort. The person committing the tort called the defendant must have acted either *intentionally* or *negligently*. If either of these can be proven, the defendant is said to be at *fault,* and the plaintiff the injured party can recover for damages suffered. If it cannot be proven that the defendant was at fault, then the injury to the plaintiff is said to be an accident, and no damages are awarded to the plaintiff.

TORT VS CRIMINAL LAW

In tort law as well as criminal law, the one bringing suit (the plaintiff in tort law, the prosecutor in criminal law) must prove that the defendant committed the wrong. The defendant does not have to prove that he did not commit the wrong. In criminal law, the prosecutor must prove the defendant guilty "beyond a reasonable doubt." In tort law, the plaintiff must prove only that the "greater preponderance of the evidence" is on his side. This is a lesser measure of proof than that required in a criminal case.

DAMAGES

Obviously, if someone is punched in the nose or if his reputation is defamed, or if he suffers pain because his car was struck by another, it is impossible to take back the pain, suffering, and/or humiliation he had to bear. As a result, the law allows additional money for such injuries. In a tort case, therefore, if the plaintiff wins, he is awarded both his actual damages and additional damages for pain and suffering. In some cases, the court, in order to discourage such acts as libel and slander, will award punitive damages, as well as actual damages, as a warning to others.

Suppose that while Mr. Proper is driving his car it is struck by Mr. Careless's car because of the negligent manner in which Mr. Careless is driving. Mr. Proper can recover the cost of repairing his car, the amount of his medical bills, and the amount of wages he lost because of time away from work resulting from the accident. In addition, the judge or jury may award Mr. Proper an additional amount of money because of the pain and suffering he endured as a result of Mr. Careless's negligence.

However, it is worth repeating that *there is no liability without fault.* If Mr. Careless is not found to have operated his car in a negligent manner, Mr. Proper can recover nothing from him.

Three kinds of damages can be awarded:

1. *Nominal damages.* To be awarded nominal damages, a plaintiff must have lost an important right rather than suffering actual losses. Damages can run from one dollar to ten dollars. Suits for nominal damages are obviously brought to defend a principle.

2. *Compensatory or actual damages.* These damages are awarded to return the injured party to his former position by the payment of money.

3. *Punitive or exemplary damages.* This is additional money added to an award as punishment because the act of the defendant was malicious.

WHO IS LIABLE?

Generally, each individual is liable for his own torts. Therefore, a husband is liable for his torts and a wife for hers. A parent is liable for his torts and a child for his. An insane person and a drunken person are held to the same standards of care as a normal person and a sober person.

Although a child is liable for his torts, the standard of care he must exercise may be less than that of an adult. That is, in determining if a child acted with care or with negligence, it must be shown how other children of the defendant's age, understanding, experience, and mental capacity would act in the same circumstances. If the defendant acted with less care, he was negligent and is liable. If he acted with as much or more care, he is not liable, despite the injury to the plaintiff and despite the fact that an adult would have been liable. In addition, certain acts, such as malicious prosecution, require intent. If a child is too young to form this intent, he is not liable.

A person who blacks out because of an organic disorder or illness cannot be liable because he was unable to exercise care. Finally, a person expert in some field of endeavor or profession is held to a higher standard of care than an average person in determining liability for negligence in a matter involving his expertise.

If an employee commits a tort during the course and in the scope of his employment, his employer is also liable for the tort. For example, if a truck driver making a delivery for his employer drives into a pedestrian crossing the street, he and his employer are both liable to the pedestrian. The same is true in a partnership: All partners are liable for the tort of any one partner done in the course of partnership business.

DEFENSES

Five different defenses can be raised to certain alleged tortious acts.

Consent

If a landowner has given you permission, either actual or implied, to hunt on his land, he cannot charge you with trespass if you do so. In this area, most problems have to do with implied consent because it depends on one individual's interpretation of another's intentions. Certain accepted principles have nevertheless been established:

1. *Conduct.* For example, if a vaccination is required before entering a country and a person offers her arm to a doctor for the vaccination, she does not have to say she is giving her consent; her conduct implies it.

2. *Voluntary action.* Someone who voluntarily engages in a sport, game, or activity cannot complain if there is bodily contact during the course of that activity.

3. *An emergency situation.* If someone is in an accident and there is a doctor present, the doctor can take the emergency medical action necessary to save the victim's life without the verbal consent of the injured person.

Consent obtained by duress or fraud is no consent, and the consenting party has a right of action for tort against the acting party. For instance, suppose Frank Faker tells Gertrude Gullible he is a doctor and takes indecent liberties in the pretense of healing or treating her. Miss Gullible can sue Faker even though she gave her consent to the so-called treatment.

What happens if a prostitute's customer pays her for services rendered with counterfeit money? In this case, both are in the wrong, and neither has a right of action against the other. This is called *pari delicto.* Likewise, a person who is part of a group protected by statute cannot give valid consent. For example, intercourse with an underage girl is rape, with or without her consent.

Self-Defense

A person may use a reasonable amount of force to defend himself when there is no time to resort to law. However, the person attacked may use only the degree of force that reasonably appears necessary to overcome the force of the threat. Once the threat is passed, force used against it ceases to be self-defense and the person continuing to use it is liable. Words, no matter how vile or insulting, never justify the use of force. There must be at least a physical threat of attack.

In most states, if you are threatened with deadly force, you may stand your ground and use deadly force to protect yourself. In some states, however, you must try to retreat from deadly force; and only when your back is to the wall can you respond with deadly force. Threatened with deadly force in your home, you do not have to retreat before using deadly force in response.

If a third person is attacked, you can render such aid to the person attacked as would be sanctioned by recognized social custom. For example, if a little girl is attacked by a group of large boys, you can use force in coming to her aid.

In defense of property, a reasonable amount of force may be used, but only by the owner of the property, to protect it. One may never use deadly force to protect property.

Necessity

If certain acts are necessary to protect the public, they may be done without liability. For instance, if you must blow up someone's house to stop the spread of a fire and save the whole community, you can do so without liability for destroying the house. Likewise, if a sudden storm comes up while you are sailing a boat, you can moor your boat to someone else's dock, if it is necessary to save a life, without becoming a trespasser.

Recovery of Property

If property is taken unlawfully, the property owner pursuing the taker may use a reasonable amount of force to recover his property. If the property has been taken legally, however, the owner cannot use force to recover it—he must use legal means. For example, if someone steals your car, you can chase him and use a reasonable amount of force to recover it. If you finance the purchase of a car and then default in payments, however, neither the person who sold you the car nor the finance company can forceably remove it from your possession. This is true even if the conditional sales contract says that force may be used to recover the property.

Legal Authority

If a judge with jurisdiction over an offense issues a proper warrant under that jurisdiction and a police officer duly arrests the person named in that warrant, both the judge and the police officer are acting within their legal authority and neither can be liable for false arrest. If an arrested person resists the police officer, the officer has the right to increase the amount of force he uses to make the arrest. Therefore, should you ever be arrested, even if you think the arrest is unlawful, it is more prudent to cooperate and make your case in court than to resist a police officer.

A parent has the legal authority to use a reasonable amount of force to discipline his or her child; and a teacher may use a reasonable amount of force to maintain decorum in the classroom. Because parents and teachers are dealing with children, the following conditions are considered in measuring "reasonable force:"

1. Age of the child
2. Sex of the child
3. Physical characteristics of the child
4. Acts of the child, and
5. Relationship of force to attaining the objective.

Kinds of Torts

As noted earlier, torts are either intentional wrongs or acts caused by careless behavior, called *negligence.* Certain activities or products are also considered so hazardous that liability arises from injuries caused by these activities or products, even without fault. This is called the law of *strict liability.* Before turning to strict liability, however, let us consider some of the other common torts.

Assault

An *assault* is threatened contact with the person of another sufficient to cause in the mind of a reasonable person an apprehension of contact. Words alone are not enough—there must be a physical offer of contact and an apparent intention to bring it about. The person making the threat must also have the present ability to make contact. Thus if a man shakes his fist at a person passing by in a train, it is not assault. Although there must be an apprehension of contact, apprehension is not fear—fear is not necessary for an assault to occur.

A threat with a pistol, whether loaded or not, is an assault, so long as there was an apprehension in the mind of the person assaulted and an apparent intention and ability on the part of the person with the gun to commit the act. An attacker's secret intention does not matter.

Battery

Any unprivileged or unpermitted contact with a person, or anything so closely associated with that person as to be considered part of that person, is a *battery.* For instance, if one grabs a cigarette from someone's mouth, touches his clothing, or snatches a piece of paper from his hand, the act is a battery.

It is not necessary to use force; it is not necessary to cause damages; it is not necessary even to cause harm. In fact, the contact may even be enjoyable or a joke; but it is still a battery. If a person intentionally strikes at, throws an object at, or shoots at someone and unintentionally hits a third person, he is not excused on the ground that it is an accident. It is an assault and battery on the third person.

Mental Disturbance

If someone intending to cause mental anguish, even as a joke, tells another an untruth and as a result of that statement the misinformed person suffers mental anguish or physical injury, an action is available for the tort of mental disturbance. For example, William wants to play a practical joke on Betty and tells her that her husband was involved in a terrible accident. Betty faints, breaking her arm in the fall. She has a cause of action against William for mental disturbance.

False Imprisonment

False imprisonment is the complete and total confinement of one person by another. The person must be barred in all directions. If there is a reasonable means of exit, there is no false imprisonment. There are four ways to bring about confinement:

1. Restraint or confinement within physical barriers—locking someone in a room.
2. The use of force—holding someone or tying him to a chair.
3. The threat of force, a case in which words are enough to constitute the threat of force.
4. A show of legal authority. If a person voluntarily accompanies the police officer, it is not an arrest. The person must submit to a show of force or legal authority.

Trespass to Land

Any unauthorized, direct voluntary entry on, over, or under the land in possession of another is a *trespass*. In an action for this tort, damages need not be proven, they are inferred. If the actual damages are small, a landowner can collect nominal damages for them, as well as compensatory damages for interference with his reasonable enjoyment of the land.

The question often comes up, "Can airplanes fly over my land?" Although the owner of the land owns the airspace to the heavens, his airspace is subject to navigable rights by planes. Therefore the answer is, "Yes, planes can fly over your land, so long as they do not interfere with your use, occupation, or enjoyment of the land."

If someone is on another's land with permission, there is no trespass. But if that permission is withdrawn, the person occupying the land must vacate it and remove all the things he brought onto that land. If he leaves any property behind, he is continuing to trespass, even though he himself has departed.

Conversion

If someone makes an adverse claim against property of another that affects the use (called *dominion*) and control over this property by the owner, it is called *conversion*. There is a conversion even if the assertion of a claim is made innocently. A conversion is made by unlawful taking, unlawful disposition, unlawful detention, or unlawful use.

1. An unlawful taking. This includes theft, fraud, or trespass.

2. An unlawful disposition. This refers to property that was acquired lawfully but disposed of unlawfully. For example, Mrs. Rich brings her mink coat to Mr. Bear, the furrier, for cleaning and storage. Mr. Bear sells the coat and keeps the proceeds. This is an unlawful disposition.

3. An unlawful detention. This means property lawfully acquired but never returned. Suppose Jack borrows some money from Jill. As collateral he gives Jill his car and its title; but after the loan is repaid, Jill refuses to return them. She is making an unlawful detention.

4. An unlawful use. If someone acquires property lawfully but uses it in an unauthorized way that results in substantial damage or destruction of the property; his use is unlawful. For instance, Tom asks Dick if he can store his car in Dick's garage while he goes on vacation. Dick agrees, but one day he takes Tom's car on a joy ride, has an accident, and completely destroys it. Tom has a cause of action against Dick for conversion because of unlawful use.

Fraud and Deceit

Fraud and deceit is one of the hardest torts to prove. Remember, the plaintiff must prove all of the elements in any suit he files. If the defendant can disprove just one element, the plaintiff will lose his case. In a fraud and deceit case, the plaintiff must prove:

1. That there was a misrepresentation of a material existing fact. An existing fact means a present or past fact. The promise of a future act is not actionable, and the misrepresentation must be one of fact, not of an opinion.

2. That misrepresentation was made with the knowledge that it was false.

3. That misrepresentation was made with the intent that the plaintiff would act on it.

4. That the plaintiff relied on the statement.

5. That the reliance was reasonable. Reliance on a salesman's puffery is not reasonable.

6. That the plaintiff suffered an actual damage from this reliance.

As you can see, many of the elements require proof of what the defendant intended. This is what makes proof of this tort so difficult.

It should also be noted that if there is a defect in a product and the seller actively conceals the defect from the buyer, this concealment is actionable in fraud. The seller does not have to voluntarily disclose a defect or point out a defect if the knowledge of that defect is equally available to both parties. However, if the seller has special knowledge of a latent defect, and the transaction is one in which the buyer would expect full disclosure, the seller has a duty to disclose the defect. Knowledge used with intent to deceive is called *scienter.* Without scienter there can be no action for fraud and deceit, even if there is negligence, because negligence is not a basis for a fraud and deceit action.

Misrepresentation

Misrepresentation amounts to negligent conduct. If a person reasonably believes that what he says is true, there is no misrepresentation if it later turns out to be untrue. However, if someone states that something is true when he hasn't taken the trouble to determine whether or not it is true, it is misrepresentation—he cannot be acting in good faith if he has not attempted to determine the validity of his own statement. For example, if George, without verifying the fact, assures Pete that a danger does not exist and Pete is injured, this is misrepresentation. If someone fails to disclose a latent (hidden) defect where there is a duty to disclose it, this too is misrepresentation. Most action where there has been misrepresentation are brought for breach of contract or negligence or with some other tort.

Defamation

Defamation is divided into two kinds:

1. *Libel,* which is defamation by written word, picture, or drawing.
2. *Slander,* which is defamation by the spoken word.

What is defamation? *Defamation* is anything calculated to hold a person up to ridicule, contempt, or distrust. In addition, it is usually required that it be false. However, the current trend of law in the state statutes is to hold even truthful words actionable unless they are made for some justifiable purpose or end. For example, if Gene gratuitously tells Mel that Ed is a crook, Ed may have an action against Gene for slander, even if it is true. However, if Mel is considering hiring Ed as a teller in his bank, and he asks Gene what he knows about Ed, and Gene says "Ed is a crook," and it is true, then the truth is a defense if Ed sues Gene for slander.

In order for it to be considered defamation, a statement must be made with *malice.* There must be an intent to publish this material—to communicate it to someone other than the person defamed, and in fact, it must be so communicated. For instance, Paul writes to Peter, "I know you're a thief and liar, and you're sleeping with several women around town." If Paul sends the letter to Peter's office with the intent that Peter's secretary will open and read it and if she does so, Peter has grounds for suing Paul for libel. However, if Paul comes in early that morning and picks up and opens his own mail, no one but he reads the letter and there is no libel.

Finally, the defamed person must suffer damages. There are two classes of damages:

1. *General damages* are those that would necessarily, usually, and customarily follow from the defamation. These damages, because they customarily will follow, may be proved without being pleaded.
2. *Special damages* are damages that would not necessarily, usually, and customarily follow. They cannot be proven at trial without first being pleaded, except in the case of libel. In all cases of libel, the court allows the plaintiff to prove special damages as general damages because the defamatory material is written and published. Therefore, in cases of libel, special damages need not be pleaded to be proven.

In slander cases, because the spoken word is such a fleeting thing, special damages must usually be pleaded to be proven, but there is an exception to this rule in cases of *slander per se.*

Slander per se is a statement that imputes to the plaintiff commission of a crime involving moral turpitude, or imputes to the plaintiff the suffering of a loathsome communicable disease, or imputes unchastity to a woman, or would directly affect a person in his business or profession.

There is also *libel per se,* but it is not the same as slander per se. The measure of whether the writing or picture is libelous is whether the language or drawing can be construed as libelous on its face without reference to anything outside the document. For example, if one publishes an advertisement advising voters not to vote for a certain candidate because "all his children are illegitimate bastards," this is libel per se.

If a group as a whole is defamed, whether or not the defamation is actionable depends on the size of the group. If the group is large; for example, "all men," there is no cause for action. If, however, the group is small enough so the libel or slander can be construed as applying to each individual member for example, "the family that lives at 1234 River Road" an action may be brought for any defamatory statement written or spoken about that family or an identifiable member.

Not all defamatory statements are subject to suit for libel or slander. Some are privileged—that is, they can be made with immunity from suit. These privileges are classified as *absolute* and *qualified.*

During a trial, the judge, parties, witnesses, and lawyers may make defamatory and even malicious statements. So long as these statements are pertinent or relevant to the trial, they are privileged from a slander suit.

Statements made during the course of legislative proceedings are also absolutely privileged, as are statements made by high ranking officers in the executive department of a government (mayor, governor, president, cabinet officer, etc.) during the course of business.

Qualified privilege applies to events under specific circumstances. If one must publish a defamatory remark to protect his own interest after a defamatory remark has been made about him, the statement is privileged. For example, Ron says to Don, "You're a thief." If Don answers, "You're a damn liar," this is a qualified privileged statement.

Defamatory material may be published by written or oral expression to protect the interest of a third party. Defamatory material may also be published to protect a common interest, but it may be published only in writing in a common publication. For instance, if a labor union or church publishes material to protect itself, publication can be made only in the union or church bulletin.

There is also a privilege to make reports of matters concerning public interests or of news matters of public interest. However, the material published must be fair, full, and impartial, even if it is only a synopsis. Finally there is a qualified privilege to publish an opinion of fair comment and criticism. This privilege is limited to criticism of a book, actor, play, or the like as it occurred, and not to the private lives of the individuals involved.

If a retraction is made, it is not an excuse from liability, but it will tend to reduce the amount of any recoverable damages.

Invasion of Right of Privacy

This tort covers statements that are not defamatory (they may in fact be flattering) but amount to an invasion of privacy. The material element that must be proven is absence of consent by the person whose privacy is involved. These cases usually are

1. Invasion of the right of solitude. Walking into a girl's bedroom, being present during childbirth, following someone, or wire-tapping his phone are examples of invasion of a right of solitude.

2. Publication of a likeness which is violative of the common decency of mankind. If a matter is newsworthy, then it is privileged. Examples of this kind of invasion includes placing an individual's picture in a rogues' gallery before the individual is convicted, publishing the picture of a reformed prostitute, or publishing the picture of a deformed child for no particular purpose or reason.

3. Appropriation of a person's name and likeness for a commercial purpose. Usually appropriation of the name without the picture is not enough, unless the name is so well known that it would immediately be associated with the person.

Malicious Prosecution and Abuse of Process

Malicious prosecution and abuse of process fall in a group of torts difficult for a plaintiff to win. Because there is and must be an obvious policy of permitting honest men to bring criminals to justice and to settle their differences before an impartial tribunal—the court—it is not easy to show misuse of this policy.

Malicious prosecution is broader than defamation. It involves the interference with a person's liberty by arresting him and putting him to the expense of defending himself against a charge. It has also been extended to cover interference with property, as in the case of malicious attachment.

Four elements must be present before there can be a suit for malicious prosecution:

1. A criminal proceeding must be instituted or continued by the defendant against the plaintiff.

2. That proceeding must be terminated in favor of the plaintiff.

3. There must have been an absence of probable cause for the proceeding.

4. The defendant must be guilty of malice or have a primary purpose other than that of bringing an offender to justice.

A judicial officer and certain other public officials, such as fire marshalls, building inspectors, investigators of a state fish and game commission, are almost never liable for a suit for malicious action.

Before You See a Lawyer

In a criminal case, a police offier usually investigates a citizen's complaint and a prosecuting attorney reviews the facts and makes a determination whether to prosecute. Therefore, if a complaining witness lays the facts before the prosecuting attorney and relies on his decision that they constitute probable cause that a crime has been committed, no action will lie against the citizen from any prosecution resulting from his statements.

In a civil case, the repeated refiling of a complaint against another after the original case has been dismissed or a verdict has been rendered in favor of the accused is malicious prosecution. Appealing an adverse decision by a court is not malicious prosecution.

Abuse of process is the use of legal process, criminal or civil, against another to accomplish a purpose for which it is not designed; and the abuser is liable to the other for any loss suffered. *Misuse* of the process is the element of this tort. It is immaterial that the process was properly issued, that it was obtained in a proper court with probable cause, or even that the case ended in favor of the person who brought the action. The subsequent perverted misuse is the offense.

Interference with Economic Relations

This cause of action goes back to early Roman law, where the head of a household was permitted to bring an action for violence or insults committed on his wife, his children, his slaves, or other members of his family, on the theory that the wrong was to the householder himself. By the thirteenth century, this law was modified to permit action by a master because of loss of service of a slave through violence inflicted on him. In 1349, the Black Plague left England with a shortage of labor, and a penalty was therefore provided to prevent laborers from running away. An action was also given to an employer against anyone who received and kept a runaway laborer in his service.

In the United States, this action was extended to permit anyone who has a contract with another to sue anyone else who induces the other party to break the contract, unless the contract is for an illegal purpose or against the public interest. This principle has been applied even when the contract is unenforceable.

Absolute Liability

In some activities, there is liability whether or not there is fault. Most of these cases involve animals and trespass. As a general rule, if a person keeps a wild animal as a pet and the animal strays (it being the nature of a wild animal to stray), the owner will be absolutely liable for any damage caused by the animal's trespass. Domestic animals such as cattle, sheep, horses, or hogs also have a natural inclination to stray, so their owner is absolutely liable for any damage they cause by straying. However, there is little chance that a domestic animal such as a dog or cat will cause much damage if it strays, so there is not absolute liability. The release of animals to trespass by some third person or by an act of God is a defense to a claim of absolute liability.

If a domestic animal has exhibited viscious characteristics of which the owner has notice or knowledge and the animal strays and causes injury, such as a dog bite, in most states the owner has absolute liability.

Product Liability

A current body of law has been developing with respect to product liability. This theory places liability on the producer, retailer, or intermediary for injuries to a buyer or a third person caused by the use of their product.

The manufacturer is said to owe the duty of employing care, skill, and diligence in seeing that his product is reasonably fit for its intended purpose. For example, a stepladder should have rungs strong and secure enough to support a person. The manufacturer is held to the degree of skill and knowledge of an expert in the making of his product and must keep abreast and informed of any new developments in his field, including new safety devices and equipment.

The seller, by selling the product, warrants to the buyer either expressly or by implication that the goods are fit for the use to which the buyer intends to put them and that he has no knowledge of any danger of which the buyer is unaware that can arise from the use of the product. For instance, the seller warrents that the trousers to be worn by a small boy are not flammable.

The sale of certain products has placed on sellers, distributors, and manufacturers the burden of *strict liability*—they are liable for injuries suffered, even if they were not negligent in the manufacture or sale of the product. Originally this theory applied only to food products, but since 1964 it has been extended to tractors, cars, tires, brakes, steering columns, aerosol cans, and numerous other manufactured products. In fact, product liability law has developed into a whole specialized field. Recoveries have been made because a product was determined to be unreasonably dangerous or its design or manufacture were defective or the manufacturer failed to give warning about a danger he failed to forsee. The area of product liability continues to expand. Anyone in business should investigate whether or not his operation should be protected by product liability insurance.

NEGLIGENCE

Negligence is a "kind of tort." It is the most common type of tort action, and the law of negligence is so extensive that an entire chapter could be devoted to it. Its presentation here, however, must necessarily be brief.

Basically, *negligence* is the failure to do something when one owes a duty to do it or the act of doing something when one owes a duty to refrain from doing it.

Whenever someone engaged in an activity as a reasonable person can forsee harm as a result of this activity, it is the duty of the person so engaged to use care in doing this activity. For example, a reasonable person driving in a residential area full of young children can see that a young child might run out from between parked cars into the path of his or her car. Therefore, the driver owes a duty to use extra care in operating the car in that area. If the driver's car actually strikes a child, that driver may eventually need to defend a suit for negligence.

Notice that the duty of care must be a duty from the defendant to the plaintiff, even though in this case the car operator does not know who the plaintiff will be until the occurrence. Notice also that the degree of foreseeability is generally measured by what harm can be anticipated by a "reasonable person."

Since negligence really amounts to falling below a standard of care in the circumstances, it becomes necessary to determine the standard. Five standards are generally used to measure a defendant's care, depending on which category applies to the defendant.

1. *Sane adult.* The standard of care in this category is based on the question: "What would a reasonably prudent person do or refrain from doing under all of the same or similar circumstances?"

2. *Aged or physically incapacitated adult.* The majority of courts hold that people in this category are judged by the same standards as a sane adult. However, some courts hold that because these people are older or incapacitated they must exercise more effort. For example, if a blind man wants to cross the street safely, it is not enough for him to face both directions before crossing; he must use his other senses as well to determine when it is safe to cross.

3. *Child.* Since a child has not lived long enough to develop the capacity of an adult, the measure of a child's care is both subjective and objective.

Subjectively, we must determine the child's age, experience, understanding, and capacity. Then we objectively try to determine what most children in that category would do in the same situation. This last determination is usually left for a jury to decide.

4. *Insane adult.* In the majority of courts, an insane person is held to the same standard of care as a sane person. However, if a person has a sudden blackout because of an organic disorder or illness, there can be no liability because he has no control over his actions and cannot therefore meet the standards of anyone.

5. *Expert.* Because an expert has special training and knowledge, he is held to higher standards than the average person. He must exercise the same skills and care as other experts who practice the same profession in the same locality. Proof of negligence in the case of an expert depends upon the testimony of another expert from the same profession and locality who can show that another way is the proper way to perform the act and that the defendant either did not possess the required knowledge and skills or did not use them in doing what he did.

In an emergency situation that requires an urgent need for sudden action, the acts of a defendant cannot be measured against those of a person able to exercise deliberation or reflection. In other words, a mere mistake in judgment by someone acting in an emergency is not negligence unless the action is rash. For example, a driver who abandons a truck full of gasoline when it suddenly catches on fire is not negligent when the truck explodes. He had to act quickly and did not have time to think about how to go about putting out the fire.

Being under the influence of alcohol or other drugs does not reduce the required standard of care. The standard remains the same for whatever category of individual the defendant belongs to.

If a person acts in a wilful and wanton manner—that is, in a reckless manner and with utter disregard for the safety of others—then he faces both compensatory and punitive damages if liability can be proven.

A person guilty of violating a statute or ordinance can be found liable for neglecting the duty owed because of the ordinance or statute. If the speed limit is 35 miles per hour and Helen, driving her car at 50 miles per hour, is involved in an accident, her violation of the speed limit may make her liable in a lawsuit for negligence.

Duty to Act

In the previous sections, we discussed how a person must act if he takes some action. However, when someone has a duty to act but fails to act, can he be liable for negligence? The answer depends on the relationship of the parties.

There are three types of action or nonaction.

1. *Nonfeasance.* This is doing nothing at all.
2. *Misfeasance.* This is doing something but doing it negligently.
3. *Malfeasance.* This is doing something but doing it wrong.

Under the common law, there is no liability for a nonfeasance, but there is liability for a misfeasance. For example, suppose that when a person is injured in an accident there is a doctor in the crowd. If the doctor just stands there and does nothing, there can be no legal liability on the doctor because of his failure to act. However, if the doctor takes it upon himself to act and then treats the victim in a negligent manner, he can be liable for aggravating the injury.

There are, however, exceptions to this nonliability for nonfeasance rule. These exceptions arise out of the special relationship between the parties.

A common carrier (bus, train, plane, subway) owes a duty to protect its passengers from injury. Therefore, if a passenger is assaulted on a train, the conductor owes a duty to the passenger to come to his aid.

A naval officer owes a duty to come to the aid of a seaman in trouble. The duty runs from the master to the seaman, but the aid is rendered through the officers.

In other employer-employee situations, if the employee is in a dangerous situation or is seriously injured as a result of his employment, the employer owes a duty to him to come to his aid.

If a defendant's negligence caused the original injury, the defendant has a duty to act so as to prevent aggravation of the injury.

If the occupier of land invites someone onto the land and that individual is injured, the occupier owes him a duty to come to his aid.

If someone is injured because of his own negligence, there is no duty to assist. If there is no duty to assist but one nevertheless comes to the aid of another, he must use care and continue to use care until the danger is passed or until the injured person is deposited in a safe position. For instance, if you come upon a drunk lying in the street and carry him to the top of the subway stairs where you abandon him, you are liable if he falls and becomes injured. He must be deposited in a safe place.

Along with the duty to act, there are certain times in which there is a duty to control the conduct of others. For instance: A common carrier has a duty to control passengers from injuring or bothering other passengers; a car owner who allows someone else to drive his car must control that driver from driving negligently; a parent must control his child—if the parent knows of the child's prior misbehavior and the child again misbehaves in a similar way and by doing so causes an injury, the parent may be liable; and a doctor must exercise control over his assistants.

Liability for Torts

Special institutions, relationships, and situations are considered in determining liability for torts.

1. *Governmental liability.* Generally, the United States government and the states without their consent are immune from any tort liability. However, by setting up a court of claims they have in effect given such consent. They can, however, limit their liability. The trend of recent cases holds that if a state carries insurance, its liability is limited to the face amount of the policy. A municipality is immune from tort liability (except to the extent of any insurance carried) for any injuries resulting from the performance of governmental functions. However, if injuries occur when the municipality is acting in its proprietary function (for example, selling water), there is negligence liability.

2. *Husband and wife.* Generally there can be no action between husband and wife for a purely personal tort, except assault and battery. There can be an action for torts that are not personal, such as trespass or conversion.

3. *Parent and child.* There is no action for a personal tort between an unemancipated child and his or her parent.

4. *Charitable institutions.* Currently, the trend of court decisions holds that the institutions will be liable for torts committed by their agents if the damages can be paid out of money (such as insurance) other than trust funds.

5. *Prenatal injury.* If medical testimony is presented that an unborn infant was a living thing, that is, able to draw sustenance of iself, there can be recovery for prenatal injuries.

The latin phrase, *res ipsa loquitur,* which literally means, "The thing speaks for itself," is used as a theory of negligence where there is no direct proof of negligence although an accident occurred. In order to make a case under this theory, the plaintiff must prove at least two difficult elements:

1. That the injury would not occur in the normal course of events. For example, being struck by a brick falling from a building is not something that would normally occur.

2. That the instrument causing the injury was in the exclusive control of the defendant. Suppose a person is injured by a tack found in a piece of delivered fruit pie he ate in the defendant's restaurant. Can the defendant be liable under res ipsa loquitur? No. The fruit was packed in boxes that have

tacks. The pie was baked off the premises. The pies were delivered in a truck that could have contained the tack. Therefore, the pie was not in the exclusive control of the defendant.

In some states, the plaintiff must further prove that there was no contributory negligence on the part of the plaintiff. For instance, suppose a man is working around machinery and despite warnings to the contrary he wears loose-fitting clothes. One day his uncuffed sleeve gets caught in the machinery, and he is pulled into a machine and injured. Can he successfully raise the theory of res ipsa loquitur? No, because he contributed to the accident by his own negligence.

Causation

Finally, in a suit based on negligence, the plaintiff must prove that the negligence of the defendant caused his injury. Without this link, called *proximate cause,* there may be negligence but there can be no recovery. Thus, there can be no recovery in the case of an accident where there is no cause and no negligence by the defendant, and there can be no recovery if someone other than the defendant was the negligent party. In some states, a plaintiff must allege in his complaint that no contributory negligence on his part caused the injury.

Proximate cause is defined as "that which in a continuous sequence uninterrupted by any efficient intervening cause produces an injury." Suppose that Gus, a gas station attendant, was smoking a cigarette while filling a customer's tank. While the car was being filled, a bolt of lightning struck the gas, and the car exploded. Can the customer recover from Gus because he was negligently smoking while filling the car with gas? No, because an efficient intervening cause produced the injury and damage.

APPORTIONMENT OF DAMAGES

When two or more persons work in concert to commit a tort or when there is a common duty from them or when there is a master and servant or principal and agent relationship, the court will always, where there is a logical basis for doing so, apportion the damages between these people. They are called *joint tortfeasors.*

Suppose Mr. Roundy manufactured a tar-filled ball and sold it to Mr. Mumm to display in his toy store. Both men knew the ball leaked, but they did not tell that to Mrs. Tizzy, who bought the ball for her little daughter, Lizzie. When Lizzie rolled the new ball across their white carpeting, it left tar spots throughout the room. Mr. Roundy and Mr. Mumm were both found guilty of the tort and both had to share the cost of new carpeting for Mrs. Tizzy.

In a joint action against several tortfeasors, when one of them satisfies the judgment (that is, pays the amount of damages to the satisfaction of the plaintiff either in full or in a negotiated amount), then all the other tortfeasors are discharged from any judgment obtained against them. Thus, if Mr. Mumm had paid for Mrs. Tizzy's new carpeting himself, both he and Mr. Roundy would have been released from the judgment.

If a *release,* a document giving up a cause of action, is given to one joint tortfeasor, all other tortfeasors are also released. When a judgment is not paid in full, a release can be given to one joint tortfeasor that specifically reserves the right to recover against the other tortfeasors. Most courts will go along with this expressed intention of the plaintiff.

In some states, a *covenant not to sue* is used to release one joint tortfeasor without releasing the others. In a covenant not to sue, nothing is given up. The plaintiff merely contracts with one of the defendants not to sue in exchange for some consideration. This is a valid contract.

As a general rule, there is no contribution among joint tortfeasors. That is, if one joint tortfeasor pays a judgment, he is not legally entitled to contribution from the others.

Wrongful Death

Wrongful death is a completely statutory cause of action. It did not exist in the common law. If a defendant commits a wrongful act (a tort that results in the death of an individual), that individual's widow, widower, or next of kin, suing in the name of the personal representative of the deceased executor or administrator, can sue the perpetrator of the wrongful act for damages.

All wrongful-death actions must be brought within a time limit, and some states limit the amount that can be recovered and the kinds of damages for which recovery may be had.

OCCUPIER OF LAND

Someone who occupies land owes a duty to outsiders who come on the land. The extent of the duty is determined by who comes on the land.

1. *Trespasser.* Since the occupier has no reason to expect that a trespasser

will be there, he owes the trespasser no duty to maintain the premises in any specific condition. Nor does he owe any duty as to the activity performed on the land. He must exercise reasonable care in the operation of any activity on the land, but he needs only to refrain from engaging in wilful and wanton misconduct, such as laying traps or spring guns for trespassers.

2. *Attractive nuisance.* If someone keeps an object on his land that he knows or should know is attractive to children but harmful to them and if this thing is kept where he knows children of tender age will be, he must exercise reasonable care and reasonable caution to protect the children from injury. As a general rule, this caution does not apply to natural conditions but to an object, like a mechanical device, put on the land.

3. *Licensee.* A licensee is someone who comes on the land with the permission of the occupier but transacts no business there. The occupier's only duty is to warn the licensee of any latent condition of which he is aware or any change in condition. Otherwise, the licensee takes the premises as they are and assumes any risk for his own safety. The occupier does owe a duty to use reasonable care in the conduct of any activity near the licensee.

4. *Business invitee.* A person who comes on the land to actually or potentially transact business; a shopper, for example, is a business invitee. To him the occupier owes a duty to maintain the premises in reasonably safe condition. The occupier must inspect the premises, and if he discovers any dangerous condition, he must either warn the business invitee or correct the condition. If the business invitee is injured from a condition that could have been discovered by inspection, the occupier is liable.

Policemen and firemen usually are classified as licensees, but the postman, milkman, and garbageman usually are classified as business invitees. A door to door salesman is a licensee at best and may be a trespasser, particularly if a notice of no peddling is posted.

AUTOMOBILE ACCIDENT

No chapter covering torts would be complete without some discussion regarding automobile accidents. If an action is brought against you as a result of an accident, it will be brought under one of the theories discussed above.

What to Do

If you are involved in an accident, you should get the name and address of the other driver, as well as the license plate number and description of the car. You should also get the names and addresses of all witnesses, whether in your car, in the other car, or elsewhere.

You should notify your insurance agency and your lawyer as soon as possible, so they may investigate to protect your interest. If you are injured, you should arrange to see your doctor as soon as possible.

If possible, you should get photographs of the cars involved in the accident, the scene where the accident took place, including skid marks, obstructions, the area around the point of impact, and any other physical evidence. It is better to have too many photographs than too few. You can always eliminate the unnecessary.

If someone has been injured or the police have been called, be sure to stay with the injured person until help arrives or until the policeman arrives. If a policeman has been called, do not move your vehicle until he arrives and can inspect the scene.

Liability

If you are injured as a result of the other party's negligence, you are entitled to recover the expenses of any medical treatment and of wages or salary lost because of the accident; the cost of repairing your car; and some amount for the pain and suffering you had to endure because of the accident. Do not be in any hurry to settle with, talk to, or sign any document for any insurance or claims adjuster. Speak to your attorney before doing any of these things.

If you lend your car to a friend and he is involved in an automobile accident, in some states you are liable and in other states you are not. Check your state statute yourself or through your lawyer and examine your insurance to verify your coverage.

You should make sure your automobile insurance includes "uninsured motorists" coverage in case you are involved in an accident with someone who does not have insurance. Such coverage is usually available for a small premium, and with it you may be able to recover all your damages from your own company. It is dangerous, and may be cause for the suspension of your driving privileges in some states, to drive without adequate insurance.

If an employee is involved in an accident while on business for his employer, the employer is liable for any damages caused by his negligence.

If you park you car with the keys in the ignition and someone steals it and has an accident, you could be liable, because you were contributorily negligent. In such cases, insurance companies have been known to terminate further coverage, and some have refused to represent the insured, claiming his actions were gross negligence.

If you park your car illegally and another driver runs into your car, he is still liable, even though you violated the parking ordinance, because he was negligent.

If you attempt either to proceed after stopping for a stop sign, or to enter a highway protected by a yield the right of way sign, or to turn left where there is oncoming traffic, you should do so only after the traffic has cleared and you can take your action with safety. Failure to do otherwise could make you liable for any injuries caused by your action.

Finally, if you are leaving the country and intend to drive in another country, check with your insurance company to see if you are covered there. Generally you are not and should obtain temporary coverage while driving in that country. If you have an accident while driving there, your failure to have insurance can result in some very severe penalties.

6

SMALL CLAIMS COURT

Suppose you buy a lamp at a local store and have them ship it to your home. When it arrives, you find that it is chipped, or worse, that it doesn't even work. When you try to return the lamp, the store refuses to replace it, exchange it, or refund your money. The lamp cost only $75, and the store knows you will not hire a lawyer for a matter that small, so they say, "Sue us!" What do you do? You do just that! You sue them in small claims court.

In many jurisdictions, a simple and inexpensive procedure has been set up to help people with relatively small claims to have their day in court without the expense of a lawyer or the time-consuming requirements of a complex law suit. These cases are heard in a court with limited jurisdiction, called a small claims court, that hears matters involving claims for automobile accidents, complaints by or against tradesmen, consumer complaints as in the example given above, landlord and tenant disagreements, and other civil matters.

Here are some examples of the kinds of cases heard in a small claims court:

1. Someone backs into your car, denting the door, and then refuses to pay for its repair because he says you backed your car into his. You can file a small claim and have the court decide whether the other driver is liable for the damage, and if so, how much he has to pay for the repair.

2. A plumber does certain repair work at the request of a homeowner. The homeowner is dissatisfied with the work or the price and refuses to pay. The plumber can file a small claim against the homeowner for the amount of the bill.

3. A landlord has a tenant who cannot or will not pay his rent and refuses to move. The landlord can file a small claim to recover the unpaid rent and to have the tenant evicted.

4. Your neighbor's dog runs loose and bites you on the leg. You need several stitches to close the wound. You can file a small claim against your neighbor to recover the amount of your medical bills.

The only limit on the jurisdiction of a small claims court is the amount of money involved. Some states limit the amount to $100 or less, while others permit suits up to $1,000.

To file a claim, you go to the clerk of the court in the jurisdiction where this claim arose and get the required number of copies of a complaint form and a summons form. The clerk will tell you how many you need. Then you fill in your claim on the complaint in simple language, and the clerk will help you prepare the summons.

The summons advises the defendant where the court is located, where he must appear, on what date, and at what time to answer the complaint. You pay a small fee to the clerk to file the complaint, and you then take the complaint and summons to the sheriff for service on the defendant. In some jurisdictions, you may if you desire have the complaint and summons served on the defendant by certified mail instead of by the sheriff.

If you are the defendant, on or before the date on which you must appear called the *return date* you fill out a form called an *appearance*, which you get from the clerk of the court. The clerk files this along with an answer to the complaint, if one is necessary. As defendant, you will have to pay a small fee with your appearance. On the return date, the court will set a date within a very short time for trial to hear the matter in dispute.

When the case is called for trial, each party tells his side to the judge and presents any witnesses and evidence he feels will support his argument. Usually this is done with less formality and without the strict rules of evidence required in more complex trials. In most cases, lawyers are not needed to represent the parties, and some judges have refused to permit lawyers to represent clients in their small claims courts. The only exception to this rule is in a case where a corporation is involved. A corporation is different from an individual; it cannot practice law and must be represented by a lawyer.

Usually the trial lasts less than an hour, and it is heard by a judge without a jury in what is called a *bench trial*. The judge usually renders his decision immediately; and on the basis of his judgment, the parties ordinarily settle their differences or make arrangements to settle their differences then and there. The purpose of the court is to provide a simple vehicle for average people to have their disputes heard and decided in a judicial manner.

If the defendant fails to appear to answer the complaint on the date indicated in the summons, the plaintiff will get judgment against the defendant automatically. This is called *judgment by default.*

It should be noted that when the court gives judgment it may also include as part of that judgment the costs paid to bring or defend the lawsuit. So when we speak of "collecting the judgment," we usually mean the amount of the judgment plus costs.

In some cases, judgment may be rendered by the court against a defendant who still refuse to pay. In such a situation, the plaintiff, also called the *complainant,* can take certain legal remedies to collect this judgment.

First, if the plaintiff knows where the defendant is employed, he can garnish his wages. This means that the defendant's employer is served with a court order requiring him to withhold a portion of the defendant's wages and turn it over to the plaintiff until the judgment is paid.

Second, if he knows where the defendant banks or has any money due from anyone, the plaintiff may garnish that money until the judgment is paid.

Third, if the plaintiff knows about any other assets the defendant owns—such as a car, truck, tools, or inventory—he may obtain a court order directing the sheriff or bailiff to take possession of those assets and sell them at a public auction—the proceeds, after the costs of the sheriff and the auction are paid, being used to pay the judgment. This is called a *levy and attachment.*

owes him money or what assets he owns, he can have the defendant brought into court with all his books and records to be questioned about what he owns and his sources of income. The court order requiring a defendant to come to court and be questioned under oath is called a *Citation to Discover Assets.* Using the information he gets from this court hearing, the plaintiff can then proceed with the garnishments or levy and attachment as outlined above. If the defendant lies in response to the questions, he is guilty of perjury. If he fails to come to court when ordered by a citation to discover assets, he is in contempt of court and can be sentenced to jail until he complies.

Also, as indicated in Chapter 1, if a trial is held and a party is dissatisfied with the decision of the trial judge, the decision may be appealed. However, an appeal is a complex procedure with strictly enforced rules and limitations. If you fail to follow these rules or limitations for any reason, your appeal may be dismissed and you will be bound by the decision of the trial court. Therefore, it is suggested that you use a lawyer to proceed with your appeal.

7

BANKRUPTCY

In earlier times in Europe, people were thought to be poor because they were lazy and unwilling to work. It was also thought that if a person engaged in a trade or business was unable to pay his debts, he was dishonest and intended to cheat those who loaned him money or sold him goods or services on credit. Those to whom the money is owed are called *creditors.* Those who owe the money are called *debtors.* Because of these ideas about the honesty of debtors in earlier times, those unable to pay their debts were imprisoned in debtors' prisons as if they had committed crimes. These ideas about debtors continued in this country until 1841 when a bankruptcy act was passed.

The bankruptcy act embodied the theory that a debtor might be honest but unfortunate. This act was later repealed; and several other acts were passed, amended, and repealed until the Great Depression of 1929 and its aftermath. In 1933, 1934, and 1935, amendments to the act adopted the philosophy that the debtor was honest and that it was better to rehabilitate him and give him a fresh start than to permit him to be harrassed and punished for his economic mistakes. A major revision of the bankruptcy act enacted in 1938 remained substantive law, with certain added amendments, until November 6, 1978, when the act was again substantially changed, effective October 1, 1979.

BANKRUPTCY COURT

A bankruptcy court is a federal court. Each federal district, besides having a district court, now also has a United States bankruptcy court. Each bankruptcy court is presided over by a bankruptcy judge, who is appointed by the president for a term of fourteen years. He may continue to serve beyond that time if no successor is appointed. A bankruptcy judge can be removed from office during his term only for incompetence, misconduct, neglect of duty, or physical or mental disability.

WHO MAY BE A DEBTOR

One of the changes made by the 1978 revision is that the person who files a petition in bankruptcy is no longer called a *bankrupt.* He is now called a *debtor.*

Only a person who lives or has a home or a place of business or property in the United States may be a debtor. A municipality may also be a debtor.

TYPES OF BANKRUPTCY PLANS

Chapter 7 Plan

If a debtor wishes to completely liquidate his assets and completely eliminate his debts, he files a petition under Chapter 7 of the bankruptcy act.

Any person may be a debtor under Chapter 7, except

1. A railroad.
2. A domestic insurance company, bank, savings bank, cooperative bank, savings and loan association, homestead association, or credit union.
3. A foreign insurance company, bank, savings bank, cooperative bank, savings and loan association, building and loan association, homestead association, or credit union, engaged in such business in the United States.

To start bankruptcy proceedings, a debtor must file a petition to do so in the bankrupty court. After he has filed his petition, the judge of the bankruptcy court may appoint a disinterested person from a panel of private trustees to act as trustee. Although this trustee is called an *interim trustee,* unless the creditors elect a permanent trustee at a later meeting, he will serve until the debtor has been discharged. A *discharge* is a court order releasing the debtor from all further responsibility for his debts, except those which cannot be discharged by bankruptcy.

If a trustee is appointed or elected, it is his duty to

1. Collect and liquidate that property of the debtor which the law permits him to collect.

2. Account for the property received.

3. Investigate the financial affairs of the debtor.

4. Examine proof of claims filed by creditors and contest those that are improper.

5. If advisable, oppose the discharge of the debtor.

6. Unless the court orders otherwise, furnish such information concerning the debtor's estate and the estate's administration as is requested by a party in interest.

7. If the business of the debtor is authorized to be operated, file with the court periodic reports, and with governmental units tax returns.

8. Make a final report and file a final account of the administration of the estate with the court.

Not all debtors' estates require trustees. In fact only where the debtor is operating a business or has substantial assets that must be collected and sold is a trustee appointed or elected.

After the assets of the debtor's estate have been collected and sold, the debtor's creditors are paid in their order of preference as provided by law. When all of the assets have been distributed, the debtor is given an order of discharge by the court, unless

1. The debtor is not an individual. In other words, only an individual can be discharged and permitted to start fresh again. A corporation or partnership may be released from further liability, but the corporation or partnership cannot start over again in the same name.

2. The debtor, with intent to hinder, delay, or defraud a creditor or an officer of the estate charged with custody of the property, has transferred, removed, destroyed, mutilated or concealed, or permitted to be transferred, removed, destroyed, mutilated, or concealed either property of the debtor, within one year before the date of the filing of the petition; or property of the estate, after the date of the filing of the petition.

3. The debtor has concealed, destroyed, mutilated, falsified, or failed to keep or preserve any recorded information, including books, documents, records, and papers, from which the debtor's financial condition or business transactions might be ascertained, unless such act or failure to act was justified under all of the circumstances of the case.

4. The debtor knowingly and fraudulently, in or in connection with the case made a false oath or account; presented or used a false claim; gave, offered, received, or attempted to obtain money, property, or advantage, or a promise of money, property, or advantage, for acting or forbearing to act; or

withheld from an officer of the estate entitled to possession any recorded information relating to the debtor's property or financial affairs.

5. The debtor has failed to explain satisfactorily any loss of assets or deficiency of assets to meet the debtor's liabilities.

6. The debtor has refused to obey any lawful order of the court, other than an order to respond to a material question or to testify; on the ground of privilege against self-incrimination, to respond to a material question approved by the court or to testify, after the debtor has been granted immunity with respect to the matter concerning which such privilege was invoked; or on a ground other than the properly invoked privilege against self-incrimination, to respond to a material question approved by the court or to testify.

7. The debtor has committed any act specified in paragraphs 2, 3, 4, 5, or 6 within one year before the date of the filing of the petition, or during the case, in connection with another case concerning an insider.

8. The debtor has been granted a discharge in bankruptcy within six years before the filing of the petition.

Once a debtor is discharged, he is discharged from all debts listed in his petition, whether the creditors file claims or not.

Reorganization under Chapter 11

Excluding a stockbroker or a commodity broker but including a railroad, any debtor who may file under Chapter 7 may be a debtor under a Chapter 11 reorganization. Such a reorganization permits the debtor to develop a plan that permits him to continue operating his business free of harassment, so that his creditors may receive some, if not all, the money due them.

Shortly after a debtor files his petition with the bankruptcy court, the court will appoint a committee of creditors to help the debtor formulate a plan of reorganization. This committee is usually made up of the seven largest creditors holding unsecured claims against the debtor's estate. The size or membership of the committee can be changed if it is not representative of the different kinds of claims or interests to be represented. The committee may authorize the employment of attorneys, accountants, or others to help them. The committee may also

1. Consult with any trustee appointed by the court to operate the business or with the debtor if he is still in possession of the business.

2. Investigate the acts, conduct, assets, liabilities, and financial condition of the debtor, the operation of the debtor's business and the desirability of the continuance of such business, and any other matter relevant to the case or to the formulation of a plan.

3. Participate in forming a plan, advise the creditors of its recommendations, and collect and file with the court acceptances of the plan.

4. Request the appointment of a trustee if one has not already been appointed.

The trustee then files the plan with the court. If a plan cannot be worked out, he must report to the court why a plan cannot be formulated, after which he can recommend conversion to a liquidation under Chapter 7 or to an individual repayment plan under Chapter 13 or suggest dismissal of the petition as not being justified.

The debtor himself, of course, may also submit a plan of reorganization to the court. The plan must classify claims, specify the treatment of the claims, and provide adequate means to carry out the payment under the plan. The holders of claims (the creditors) may accept or reject the proposed plan. If creditors holding claims at least two-thirds in amount and more than one-half in number of the allowed claims accept the plan, it is confirmed by the court and put into operation.

Wage Earner Plans under Chapter 13

A wage earner or a self-employed individual (except a stockbroker or commodity broker) by himself or together with his wife, owing a total of less than $100,000 in unsecured debts and $350,000 in secured debts, can file as a debtor under Chapter 13 of the bankruptcy act.

A plan under Chapter 13 permits a wage earner who does not want to file a Chapter 7 liquidation to submit to a plan of repayment of his debts.

Once a Chapter 13 wage earner plan is filed, creditors are not only barred from taking any further legal action against the debtor but also enjoined from taking any legal action against any cosigner with the debtor of any note, unless the cosigner became liable in the ordinary course of his business, or the case is closed, dismissed or converted to a Chapter 7 or Chapter 11 proceeding. In addition, the creditor is permitted to present a negotiable instrument for payment and give notice of dishonor, where such proceedure is necessary to protect the creditor's legal rights. Also, the injunction can be vacated and the creditor permitted to proceed when

1. The creditor can prove that the cosigner received consideration for the claim. For example, if John Smith and Mary Smith borrow money from a bank to buy a car and Mary Smith cosigns on the note but in reality takes title and possession of the car, the bank can proceed against Mary if John declares Chapter 13 bankruptcy; or

2. The wage earner's plan proposes not to pay the creditor's claim. Tom Brown borrows money and John Brown cosigns the note. If Tom Brown

files a petition for a Chapter 13 bankruptcy and agrees to pay 80 percent of the debt they owe under his plan, the creditor can pursue John for the other 20 percent. However, if Tom defaults on any scheduled payment under his plan, the creditor cannot pursue John for the defaulted amount.

3. The creditor's interest would be irreparably harmed by such a bar to his action. If the cosigner filed bankruptcy himself or threatened to leave the area or lost his job, the creditor could get court permission to pursue the cosigner so his assets would not disappear before the creditor could act.

After a petition for a Chapter 13 bankruptcy is filed, a trustee is appointed by the bankruptcy judge to gather the assets of the debtor; if the debtor is in business, consider the further operation of the business; and sell the assets and disburse the proceeds under a plan of repayment. In addition, the trustee may also

1. Appear and be heard at any hearing that concerns the value of property subject to a lien; confirmation of a plan; or modification of a plan after confirmation.

2. Advise, other than on legal matters, and assist the debtor in performance under the plan.

After the trustee has been appointed, the debtor may aside from the trustee use, lease, or sell any property of the estate other than in the ordinary course of business, so long as the creditors' interests are protected.

A self-employed debtor may continue his business after filing a petition under Chapter 13. He may also keep possession of his property. Nevertheless, all of his property and any earnings from services performed after the petition is filed but before the case is closed become part of the bankruptcy estate.

Under Chapter 13, a debtor can convert to a Chapter 7 liquidation or dismiss the case at any time. If the debtor for some reason signed an agreement not to convert to a Chapter 7 liquidation or dismiss the case, it is not enforceable.

Upon the request of any creditor, after notice and hearing except in the case of a farmer, the court may either convert a case under Chapter 13 to a case under Chapter 7 or Chapter 11 or dismiss it, whichever is in the best interests of the creditors and the estate, for cause, including

1. Unreasonable delay by the debtor that is prejudicial to creditors.

2. Nonpayment of required fees and charges.

3. Failure to file a plan on time.

4. Denial of confirmation of a plan and denial of additional time for filing another plan or a modification of a plan.

5. Material default by the debtor with respect to a term of a confirmed plan.

6. Revocation of the order of confirmation of the plan and denial of confirmation of a modified plan.

7. Termination of a confirmed plan by reason of some condition specified in the plan.

A Chapter 13 Plan

1. The plan shall provide the payment of all or so much of future earnings of the debtor to the supervision and control of the trustee as is necessary to carry out the plan; provide for the full payment, in deferred cash payments of all claims entitled to priority; if the plan classifies claims, provide the same treatment for each claim within a particular class.

2. The plan may not provide for payments over a period longer than three years, unless the court for cause approves a longer period; but the court may not approve a plan for a period longer than five years.

3. The plan will be confirmed by the court if it conforms to these provisions; all required fees and charges have been paid; the plan has been proposed in good faith and not by any means forbidden by law; unsecured creditors will not get less than they would under a Chapter 7 filing; with respect to each allowed secured claim: the holder of the claim has accepted the plan, the plan provides that the holder of such claim retain the lien securing such claim, and the value of the property to be distributed is not less than the allowed amount of the claim, or the debtor surrenders the property securing such claim to such holder; and the debtor will be able to make all payments under the plan and to comply with the plan.

4. If the plan is confirmed by the court, this confirmation binds the debtor and each creditor, whether or not the claim of such creditor is provided for by the plan, and whether or not such creditor has objected to, accepted, or rejected the plan. In other words, all creditors must accept the payments provided in the plan, whether or not they accepted the plan itself and even if it does not provide for payment of the creditor's claim.

5. In addition, unless otherwise provided in the plan, all property goes to the debtor's estate, and it goes free and clear of any claim or interest of any creditor.

6. After all payments have been made under the plan, the court will order a discharge of all debts provided for by the plan.

The court may also grant a hardship discharge to the debtor if he fails to complete the payments, if the failure was due to circumstances for which the debtor should not justly be accountable.

INVOLUNTARY BANKRUPTCY

The preceding sections describe bankruptcy petitions a debtor may file when he needs relief from the efforts of his creditors to collect money they allege is due to them. Before October 1979, if a husband and wife had to file for relief under the bankruptcy act, each had to file his or her own petition; but husband and wife can now file a joint petition. Because this procedure is less complicated and makes the administration of the estate easier, it is also cheaper. A joint petition may be filed under any appropriate chapter.

In addition to voluntary bankruptcy, a debtor who is generally not paying his debts as they become due or within 120 days can be forced into bankruptcy by his creditors by their filing an involuntary petition. If this is done, a custodian is appointed to take charge of the debtor's property. However, an involuntary case may be filed only under Chapter 7 or Chapter 11 and only against a person (except a farmer) or an institution such as a church, school, charitable organization, or foundation.

Who May File an Involuntary Case

Three or more creditors who have claims totaling $5,000 or more; or if there are fewer than twelve creditors, any one or more creditors having claims totaling $5,000 or more may file an involuntary case.

Contest by a Debtor

After an involuntary case has been filed, the debtor may file an answer denying the allegations in the creditors' petition. There will then be a trial by judge or jury as to the issues.

If, the judge dismisses the creditors' petition after the trial, the court may grant judgment against the creditors for costs, a reasonable attorney's fee and any damages the debtor suffered because a trustee took possession of his property. A judgment may also be granted against any creditor who filed the petition in bad faith for any damages caused to the debtor by such filing (such as loss of business during and after the case) or for punitive damages.

UNDISCHARGED DEBTS AND EXEMPT PROPERTY

Not all debts are discharged by an order of discharge in a bankruptcy. Some debts survive such an order and can be discharged only through payment. They include the following:

1. A tax or customs duty.
2. Money or services obtained by false pretenses.
3. A debt due to a creditor that was not scheduled in time to permit the creditor to file a claim.

4. A debt from fraud, defalcation while acting in a fiduciary capacity, embezzlement, or larceny.
5. Alimony and/or child support.
6. Judgment, resulting from wilful and malicious injury to another.
7. A fine, penalty, or forfeiture payable to a governmental unit.
8. An educational loan due less than five years before the filing of the petition.
9. Debts of previous bankruptcy that were not discharged by that bankruptcy.

When a debtor files a petition, his assets and debts are scheduled and the assets are used by the trustee to pay the debts. However, not all assets of the debtor can be used—some are exempt from this use and returned to the debtor. In fact, the debtor may choose to exempt assets either under the federal laws or under the laws of the state where he lives. If the exempt property is subject to a lien, only the unencumbered amount is exempt. For example, if a debtor owns an automobile worth $1500 but owes $500 for the car, he can exempt only $1,000. Although statutory exemptions differ from state to state, the federal exemptions include

1. Up to $7,500 of real or personal property that a debtor or a dependent of the debtor uses as a residence or as a burial plot for a debtor or a dependent of the debtor.
2. Up to $1,200 in value in one motor vehicle.
3. The debtor's interest, (not to exceed $200 in value in any particular item) in household furnishings, household goods, wearing apparel, appliances, books, animals, crops, or musical instruments that are held primarily for the personal, family, or household use of the debtor or a dependent of the debtor.
4. Up to $500 in jewelry held primarily for the personal, family, or household use of the debtor or his dependent.
5. $400 in any property.
6. $750 in implements, professional books, or tools of the trade of the debtor or the trade of his dependent.
7. Any unmatured life insurance contract owned by the debtor other than a credit life insurance contract.
8. $4,000 in loan value in any life insurance policy.
9. Professionally prescribed health aids for the debtor or his dependent.
10. The debtor's right to receive the following
    a. A social security benefit, unemployment compensation, or a local public assistance benefit.
    b. A veteran's benefit.
    c. A disability, illness, or unemployment benefit.

d. Alimony, support, or separate maintenance, to the extent reasonably necessary for the support of the debtor or a dependent of the debtor.

e. Benefits under certain stock bonus, pension, profit sharing, annuity, or similar plan based on illness, disability, death, age, or length of service.

11. The debtor's right to receive compensation for losses from crime, up to $7,500 in personal injury compensation (not including pain and suffering), wrongful death benefits, life insurance proceeds, and loss of future earnings payments.

PRIORITIES OF CREDITORS' CLAIMS

Creditors do not share equally in the estate of debtor. Some claims are paid before others, according to the following priorities:

1. Costs of administering a debtor's bankruptcy estate.
2. Unsecured claims that arose in the normal course of the debtor's business between the time a petition in bankruptcy was filed and the time a trustee was appointed.
3. Unsecured claims for wages, salaries, or commissions, including vacation, severance, and sick leave pay earned by an employee within 90 days before the filing of the petition, up to $2,000 for each employee.
4. Allowed unsecured claims for contributions to employee benefit plans for services rendered within 180 days before the date of the filing of the petition, up to $2,000 per covered employee.
5. Up to $900 from deposits in connection with the purchase, lease, or rental of property or the purchase of services for personal, family, or household use.
6. Taxes due a governmental unit.
7. Claims of creditors secured by a lien on property of the estate to the extent of the value of the collateral.
8. Other unsecured claims.

PROCEDURE FOR A VOLUNTARY PETITION

In order to proceed with a voluntary petition for discharge as a debtor, the procedure is as follows:

The debtor purchases preprinted petition forms from a legal supply store and completes the petition, listing his creditors in the order of their priority by name, address, manner in which the debt arose, amount due, and where applicable any collateral securing the debt and the value of that collateral.

The debtor then lists his assets and schedules those that he claims are exempt from claims of creditors.

This petition, with the number of copies required by the district court where it is filed, together with a statement of affairs, with copies, is signed by the debtor, notarized, and filed with the clerk of the bankruptcy court for the district where the debtor resides or does business. The statement of affairs is also a preprinted form, with questions relating to the affairs of the debtor depending on whether he is in business or not. Chapter 7 and Chapter 13 cases usually require an original and three copies of the petition and statement of affairs; a Chapter 11 case requires an original and six copies. In a Chapter 11 case, the debtor may also be required to file a list of the names and addresses of his ten largest unsecured creditors with his petition. The proper filing fee is paid to the clerk of the court: $60 for a Chapter 7 or 13 case and $300 for a Chapter 11 case. The case is immediately given a case number and assigned to one of the bankruptcy judges for the district.

After the petition is filed, the debtor may mail a restraining order bearing the judge's name to each of his creditors, ordering them to restrain from taking any further action against the debtor or his property and any codebtor or his property.

The court sends notice of a first meeting of creditors to each creditor. This meeting is usually held not less that twenty nor more than forty days after the petition or order for relief is entered. The debtor must be present to be examined at this meeting, where a trustee is elected to administer the estate of the debtor and if appropriate, a creditor's committee is also elected. Until a trustee is elected, the clerk of the bankruptcy court is designated to preside over the meeting.

The notice of the first meeting of creditors also sets a date by which all creditors must file their proofs of claim. This also is a form that may be obtained at most legal supply stores. If there is an objection to any claim filed, there must be a hearing; and the hearing becomes an adversary proceeding.

When the debtor remains in possession of his estate, as in a Chapter 11 or Chapter 13 case, he must file a plan of repayment within 120 days after the order of relief. If he does not file such a plan, or if the plan filed is rejected, a plan may be filed thereafter by the debtor, by a creditors' committee, by a secured holders' committee, by a creditor, by a secured holder, or by a trustee.

After a Chapter 11 or 13 plan has been approved, the debtor performs in accordance with its terms until it is fully complied with or the estate is transferred to Chapter 7 liquidation.

In the case of a Chapter 7 liquidation, the court sets a date on which the debtor will be discharged from his debts. The notice also sets a date by which those objecting to the discharge must file their objections. The grounds for objecting to the discharge are described earlier in the section on Chapter 7 plans. If no objections are filed, or if after an adversary hearing it is determined that a discharge should be given to the debtor, the court will order the debtor discharged, and no further action may be taken or continued against the debtor, except in those matters not barred by discharge.

Before discharge, however, if a debtor wants to keep certain assets or pay certain debts that would otherwise be discharged, he may advise the court that he wishes to *reaffirm the debt.* If the debtor is an individual, the court must advise him at a hearing of the various effects of the reaffirmation and approve the reaffirmation for it to be enforceable. Any debtor may rescind a reaffirmation within thirty days after it becomes enforceable.

Once a debtor has received his discharge, he is barred from filing any other petition for relief as a bankrupt for a period of six years from the date of his discharge.

8

SALES

John Smith telephones an order to Harry Brown for 300 hairbrushes at $2 each. Before they are delivered, Harry gets an offer from Bill Jones to buy them for $2.50 each. Harry sells the brushes to Bill. John sues Harry, alleging his oral contract, and Harry says the contract was not enforceable. Can John win his lawsuit?

Frank telephones an order to Sam for 100,000 cameras, each bearing Frank's tradename, at 50 cents each. Sam manufactures these cameras to Frank's specification, but when they are delivered, Frank refuses them. Sam threatens to sue, and Frank says the contract is unenforceable. If Sam sues, who should win?

These matters are covered by the law of sales. As mentioned in Chapter 5, certain orders must be placed in writing to comply with the statute of fraud and be enforceable—a provision that applies to the sale of goods for $500 or more. In the case of John Smith and Harry Brown, therefore, since the contract for the hairbrushes involved $600 and was made by telephone, the sales contract is not enforceable by Smith.

However, there is an exception to this requirement: If goods are to be specially manufactured for the buyer and are not suitable for sale to others in the ordinary course of the seller's business, and before notice of repudiation is received, the seller has made either a substantial beginning of their manufacture or commitments for their purchase, the contract of sale is enforceable by either party, even if it is oral. In the case between Frank and Sam, the cameras were specially manufactured for Frank with his trade-name. Therefore they were not suitable for sale in the ordinary course of Sam's business and the contract is enforceable by Sam. Frank must pay for the cameras.

THE WRITING

How formal does "some writing" have to be to comply with the statute of frauds? So long as there is some writing sufficient to indicate that a contract for sale has been made between the parties and this writing is signed by the party against whom enforcement is sought or his agent and it states a quantity, it is enforceable. If there is an error in the quantity stated, the contract cannot be enforced beyond the quantity stated. If any other terms are omitted or misstated, the contract will not become unenforceable, since these can be determined. This is discussed later.

If there is an oral sales contract between two merchants, either party can bring it within the statute of frauds by sending the other party a written confirmation of the contract. If the other party receives the memo of confirmation, knows its contents, and does not send the sending party written objection within ten days after he receives it, this memo will make the oral contract of sale enforceable.

OTHER EXCEPTIONS

What else makes an otherwise unenforceable oral contract enforceable? In addition to the exception for specially manufactured goods, two other exceptions are enforceable. If the party against whom enforcement is sought admits in his pleading or testimony that a contract for sale was made, it is enforceable up to the quantity of goods admitted. If some goods have been accepted and paid for, or received and accepted, the contract is enforceable up to the amount of the partial delivery.

What constitutes receipt and acceptance? Acceptance of goods occurs when the buyer

1. After a reasonable opportunity to inspect the goods, signifies to the seller that the goods conform to his order or that he will accept them in spite of their nonconformity.
2. After a reasonable opportunity to inspect the goods, fails to make a timely rejection to the seller.

3. Does any act inconsistent with the seller's ownership. For example, if the buyer, despite his notice of rejection, uses the goods or sells them or includes them in a proof of loss filed with an insurance company, his acts are inconsistent with the seller's ownership.

FIRM OFFERS

If a merchant in a signed writing offers to buy or sell goods and if the writing gives assurance that the offer will be held open for a certain period of time, the offer cannot be revoked within the time stated. If no time is stated, the offer cannot be revoked for a reasonable period, not to exceed three months.

SUPPLYING MISSING TERMS

The writing required to make an oral contract enforceable, in addition to being signed, needs only to state a quantity. The other terms can be determined in various ways:

1. If no price is stated, a reasonable price at the time of delivery becomes the selling price.
2. Unless otherwise agreed, the place for delivery of goods is the seller's place of business, or if he has none, his residence; but in a contract for the sale of goods that can be identified which both parties know are in some other place, that place is the place for their delivery; and documents of title may be delivered through customary banking channels.
3. The time for shipment or delivery shall reasonable. What is reasonable is determined by the nature of the goods (for example, fruit or vegetables must be delivered more quickly than a product that will not spoil), the use to which they are being put (Christmas toys are needed in time to sell for Christmas), and other circumstances.
4. Unless otherwise agreed, payment is due at the time and place at which the buyer is to receive the goods, even if the place of delivery is the place of shipment.

WARRANTIES

Express Warranties

An express warranty is any statement of fact or promise that relates to the goods and becomes part of the basis of bargain. For example, if a seller represents to the buyer that the barrels of apples stacked at a railway depot are good, hand-picked fruit of the same quality as previously purchased by the buyer and shipped by this seller, and on the basis of this representation and an inspection of some of the apples, the buyer buys them, the seller's representations are an express warranty.

If goods are sold by description, and this description forms part of the bargain (that is, the buyer wants the items described), this also is an express warranty that the goods shall conform to the description. The same rule applies to goods sold from a sample or a model. That is, if the buyer relied on the sample or model when he made this decision to buy the goods, there is an express warranty that the goods sold shall conform to the sample or model.

The seller does not have to use formal words like *warrant* or *guarantee.* It is enough that he affirm the value of the goods. However, a seller's opinion or commendation of the goods does not create a warranty. For example, suppose you are shopping in an appliance store. You want to buy a vaporizer. The sales clerk tells you that a particular vaporizer will hold enough water to last at least two hours. This is a warranty. Then you look at a clothes dryer. The sales clerk tells you, "This is the best dryer money can buy." This is sales talk, called "puffing"; it is not a warranty.

Implied Warranties

Under the uniform commercial code, there is an implied warranty made by a merchant who sells specific goods that the goods sold are *merchantable.* In order for goods to be merchantable, they must meet a numer of criteria. This must be able to pass without objection in the trade as the goods described in the contract. Goods that can be mixed together, such as grains of wheat, must be of fair average quality; that is, not the best and not the worst of goods of that description. In addition, they must be fit for the ordinary purposes for which such goods are used and be within the variations permitted by a contract of the same kind, quality, and quantity. Finally, they must be adequately packaged and labeled and conform to the promises or affirmations of fact made on the container or label.

A person making an isolated sale is not a merchant. However, serving food or drink for value, whether to be consumed on the premises or elsewhere, is a sale and binds the seller as a merchant to the implied warranty of merchantability.

The courts have also held that if a manufacturer knows or should know that danger may result from a particular use of his product, the product may be considered defective if it is sold without adequate warnings. If the goods are defective, the purchaser may recover the purchase price paid under the theory of breach of implied warranty of merchantability.

Suppose Fred buys a "good" used car. Seven days after he takes it home, the transmission falls out and the brakes fail. Fred returns the car to the dealer, who keeps it for three weeks but fails to fix it. Can Fred revoke his purchase and get his money back? The courts have held that he can, under a breach of implied warranty of merchantability, even though it was a used car and he himself used it for seven days.

Under the implied warranty of fitness for a particular purpose, if the seller at the time of contracting has reason to know that the buyer is buying the goods to use for a particular purpose and that the buyer is relying on the seller's skill or judgment to select or furnish suitable goods, there is an implied warranty that the goods sold shall be fit for such purpose. It is not enough that the seller knows that the buyer needs the goods for a particular purpose; the buyer must also rely on the seller's skill or judgment to select suitable goods. This means that if the buyer comes in and makes his own selection without relying on the seller, there is no implied warranty of fitness for a particular purpose.

Exclusions of Warranties

By proper labeling or by acts of the buyer, warranties can be excluded or modified. To exclude or modify the implied warranty of merchantability, the exclusion must mention merchantability and if in writing it must be conspicuous. To exclude or modify an implied warranty of fitness, the exclusion must be by a writing and conspicuous.

Of course, expressions like "as is," "with all faults," or other such commonly understood language will also exclude all implied warranties. So, if Henry sells Tom a car and the sales contract specifies he is selling it "as is," Tom cannot later complain if the brakes fail or the radiator leaks that there was a breach of the implied warranty of merchantability or fitness for a particular purpose.

Also, under the uniform commercial code, if the buyer has examined the goods or sample or model as much as he wanted before he entered into the contract, or if he refused to examine them, there is no implied warranty with regard to defects that an examination would have revealed.

Finally, an implied warranty can be excluded or modified by a course of dealing or a course of performance, by usage of trade. For instance, in the grape trade, it is the custom that a buyer take grapes at the time of sale; and if they are in a different condition at the time of arrival at their destination, this is not a breach of warranty of merchantability for not conforming to sample.

A seller's warranty, whether express or implied, extends to any natural person in the family or household of the buyer and to a guest in the buyer's home if it is reasonable to expect that such person may use, consume, or be affected by the goods. For example, if a mother buys milk, there is an implied warranty that the milk is fit for human consumption. If this milk is tainted and makes the woman's infant ill, she can bring a cause of action against the seller on behalf of the infant.

SHIPPING TERMS

F.O.B. and F.A.S.

F.O.B. means "free on board." It is usually followed by either "shipment" or "destination." If goods are shipped "F.O.B. Shipment," the seller has the responsibility of getting the goods to the named place of shipment bearing the expense of getting them on the carrier (truck, train, plane) at that shipping point. His responsibility then ends, and the responsibility for the safe delivery of the goods switches to the buyer.

"F.O.B. Destination" means that the seller is responsible for getting the goods to the ultimate destination named in the sales or purchase documents. Until the goods reach that point, the risk of loss is on the seller and he must bear the cost and responsibility for any such loss.

F.A.S. means "free alongside." If goods are shipped "F.A.S. Vessel," the seller must, at his own expense and risk, deliver the goods alongside the vessel in the manner usual in that port, or on a dock designated and provided by the buyer, and obtain and tender a receipt for the goods.

C.I.F. and C. & F.

The term *"C.I.F."* means that the price includes not only the cost of the goods but also the insurance and freight to the named destination. The term *"C. & F."* means the price includes only cost and freight.

A C.I.F. contract is not a destination but a shipment contract. The risk of loss or damage passes to the buyer upon shipment if the seller has properly performed all his obligations with respect to the goods. Delivery to the carrier is delivery to the buyer for purposes of risk and title. Delivery of possession of the goods is accomplished by delivery of the bill of lading. A *bill of lading* is a document providing evidence of the receipt of goods for shipment issued by a person engaged in the business of transporting or forwarding goods.

Upon tender of the required documents, the buyer must pay the agreed price without awaiting the arrival of the goods. If the goods have been lost or damaged after proper shipment, the buyer must seek his remedy against the carrier or insurer, and not against the seller. The buyer has no right of inspection before payment or acceptance of the documents.

Under both C. & F. and C.I.F., title and risk of loss pass to the buyer on shipment. Therefore, the buyer must provide his own insurance to protect against risk of loss.

SALE ON APPROVAL, SALE OR RETURN, AND CONSIGNMENT SALES.

In *sale on approval,* the buyer wants to inspect and test the goods before he buys them. Therefore, title to the goods remains in the seller until the buyer has signaled his acceptance.

A *sale or return* is a transaction where the goods are delivered primarily for resale. If they are not sold, they may be returned to the deliverer. While these goods are in the buyer's possession they are subject to claims by his creditors.

Goods delivered to a buyer *on consignment* are treated as sale-or-return goods unless the buyer places a sign indicating the seller's interest in the goods (in states that provide for such a practice), or establishes to a court or jury that he is generally known by his creditors to be substantially in the business of selling goods of others; the filing provisions of the article on secured transactions are complied with. This alternative is probably the easiest and safest way for a seller to protect himself. He has only to file the appropriate form with the proper recording office, so that his interest is public knowledge, and he is protected.

TRANSFER OF TITLE

A sale is complete only after title has passed from the seller to the buyer, Therefore, if some conditions must be fulfilled, there is no title to the goods in the buyer until those conditions have been completed. However, a buyer gets only the same title his transferor (the seller) had. If Lorenzo steals a car and sells it to Adrian, because Lorenzo did not have title, neither does Adrian. In that case, the real title owner can recover his car and Adrian will lose both the money he paid and the car he thought he was buying.

There are certain exceptions to this rule. If the buyer has a *voidable title,* he has the power to transfer a good title to a good faith purchaser for value. A good faith purchaser is one who buys without any knowledge of wrongdoing on the part of the seller. A purchaser has a voidable title, if the transferor (original seller) was deceived as to the identity of the first purchaser; or delivery was made in exchange for a check that was later dishonored; or the delivery was procured through fraud punishable as larcenous under the criminal law.

Unless otherwise agreed, the seller does not have to complete delivery until he has been paid. Because payment by check is conditional, delivery does not have to be made until the check is honored. However, if a seller accepts a note or a check postdated by even one day, the seller's acceptance amounts to a delivery on credit. A buyer has the right, except in C.O.D. deliveries, to inspect the delivered goods in any reasonable place, time, and manner before payment is made. When the seller is required or authorized to send the goods to the buyer, the buyer may inspect them after their arrival.

BUYER'S RIGHTS

If the goods delivered fail to conform in any way to the contract, the buyer may either reject the whole shipment or accept the whole shipment, or accept some goods and reject the rest. Any rejection must be made within a reasonable time after delivery, and the seller must be notified. What is a reasonable time depends upon the nature of the goods. For example, if the goods are perishable, like fresh flowers, the rejection must be immediate. If the goods are manufactured items or the like, rejection in sixty days is not unreasonable.

After goods have been rejected, the buyer who has them in his possession must reasonably protect them for a sufficient time to permit the seller to remove them. Once goods have been rejected, the buyer cannot exercise any ownership over them. A merchant buyer, after rejection of any goods in his possession, must follow any reasonable instructions from the seller in respect to the goods. If he demands it, the buyer must receive expense reimbursement before acting on these instructions. If the goods are perishable or threaten to decline in value speedily, in the absence of instructions from the seller, the buyer may make reasonable efforts to sell the goods for the seller and may take reimbursement out of the proceeds for the expenses of caring for and selling the goods, as well as the usual sales commission in the trade.

If the goods are not perishable and the buyer receives no instuctions from the seller, the buyer may return them to the seller, store them at the expense of the seller, or sell them and deduct expenses and commissions from the proceeds.

If goods are delivered in separate lots (by *installment contract),* the buyer may reject any nonconforming installment unless the seller gives adequate assurance that he will cure the defect, in which case the buyer must accept the installment. If the nonconformity or default of one or more installments impairs the whole contract, the buyer may consider the whole contract breached and cancel the contract and/or sue for damages.

If a seller fails to make delivery or repudiates or the buyer rightfully rejects the goods, the buyer may cancel the contract and purchase substitute goods to cover for the goods not delivered by the seller. The buyer can then recover the difference in cost between the cost of the "cover" goods and the contract price from the seller.

If the goods are unique, the buyer can sue to have the seller perform as he contracted to perform. For example, Joe agrees to sell Vera stock in a corporation not listed on the open market at a certain price. Before Joe delivers the stock, Mack offers him more money than Vera did, so Joe refuses to sell to Vera. Vera can sue for "specific performance," asking the court to order Joe to comply with the terms of their contract, because the stock is unique and therefore damages cannot be determined.

SELLER'S RIGHTS

If a seller discovers that the buyer is insolvent, he may refuse delivery except for cash, including payment for goods already delivered. He may also stop delivery to the buyer of goods in the possession of a carrier. If the seller discovers that the buyer has received goods on credit while insolvent, he may reclaim the goods upon demand within ten days after the goods were received. However, if misrepresentation of solvency has been made in writing within three months prior to delivery, the ten-day demand requirement is waived.

If a buyer wrongfully rejects goods or revokes their acceptance or fails to make a payment, the seller may withhold delivery of the goods; stop delivery by any carrier; if the goods are unfinished, either complete their manufacture or cease manufacture and resell the material for its scrap or salvage value; resell the goods at public or private sale and recover the difference between the sale price and the contract price from the buyer; sue for damages; or cancel the contract.

TIME TO SUE

So that rights to sue do not remain open forever, the law provides certain time limits within which suits must be brought. This is called the *statute of limitations.* The statute of limitations for breach of any contract of sale is four years. A suit for such an action must be filed within four years after the breach; and this limitation runs from the time the breach occurs, even if the injured party does not discover it until later. For example, Joan buys a chair to give her husband Peter on his fiftieth birthday. Peter is only forty-five when Joan buys and takes delivery of the chair. She hides the chair in a box for five years; and when she gives it to Peter, she discovers that it is defective and unusable. She brings suit, alleging breach of warranty of merchantability. The suit will be dismissed because the four years have passed. A buyer and a seller can by agreement reduce the limitation period within which to bring suit, but they cannot extend the period.

9

NEGOTIABLE INSTRUMENTS

Most sales, particularly those involving substantial amounts, are made on credit. Bills or invoices from these sales are later paid by check or evidenced by a promissory note. Checks and promissory notes are kinds of *negotiable instruments*.

Which of the following are negotiable instruments?

1. Seymour borrows $50 from Les and promises to pay him back next Wednesday.

2. Mel Brown borrows $100 from Henry. As evidence of the debt, Mel writes on a piece of paper, "January 28, 1982. I, Melvin Brown, promise to pay Henry Hoover $100 on March 28, 1982. [Signed] Melvin Brown."

3. Betty borrows $500 from Gertie. Betty writes on a piece of paper, "I promise to pay to Gertie Gelt on her order $500 as soon as I can. [Signed] Betty Poor."

4. A writing that says, "I.O.U. $30 [Signed] Jack Spratt."

5. A writing that states, "I promise to pay $50 to Bearer."

If you answered, "None of the above are negotiable instruments," you would have been correct.

In order to be negotiable, an instrument, must

1. Be in writing. [1] above is oral.

2. Be signed by the maker or drawer. A *maker* is one who issues a promissory note. A *drawer* is one who issues a check. [5] above is unsigned.

3. Contain an unconditional promise or order to pay a sum certain in money and no other promise, order, or obligation or power given by the

maker or drawer, except as discussed in [4] below. Since in [3] repayment is conditional on Betty being able to repay Gertie, this note is nonnegotiable. [4] is not negotiable either because it is only an acknowledgement of a debt, not an unconditional promise to pay.

4. Be payable on demand or at a definite time. [3] fails this requirement too, because it is payable only when Betty "can."

5. Be payable to order or to bearer. In the examples, [2] fails this requirement. Mel's note is payable to Henry Hoover only, and not to the order of Henry Hoover or bearer.

WHAT WRITINGS ARE NEGOTIABLE?

The following comply with the above requirements. They are negotiable.

1. A *draft* or *bill exchange*, which is a direction in writing, by the person who signs it, to another, to whom it is addressed, to pay to a third person a definite sum of money at a specified time.
2. A *check* if it is drawn on a bank and payable on demand.
3. A *certificate of deposit* if it is an acknowledgement by a bank of receipt of money with a promise to repay it.
4. A *note* if it is a promise other than a certificate of deposit. An unconditional written promise does not become nonnegotiable because it states the consideration that gave rise to the instrument or refers to a separate agreement or states that it is drawn under a letter of credit or states that it is secured by a mortgage or indicates a particular account or source from which reimbursement is expected. If, however, the written promise says it is governed by the terms of another agreement or that it is payable only out of a particular fund or source (unless issued by a government or governmental agency or unit), it is not unconditional; and it is therefore not negotiable.
5. A *letter of credit* is also a negotiable instrument. A letter of credit is issued by a bank. In it, the bank promises to pay all drafts drawn by the beneficiary of the letter, provided proper documents accompany the draft. Since letters of credit are usually used for making foreign purchases, they often require that the drafts be accompanied by bills of lading or warehouse receipts.

INCOMPLETE INSTRUMENTS

If an instrument is signed while it is still incomplete in any necessary respect, such as payee, amount, or due date, it cannot be enforced until it is completed. If it is completed in an unauthorized way, the original maker is discharged from liability to the holder who made the unauthorized change or to one who knows of the unauthorized change. However, the maker is not discharged from liability to an innocent person to whom the instrument has been negotiated for value who took it in good faith. Such an innocent person is called a *holder in due course*.

INSTRUMENTS PAYABLE TO TWO OR MORE PERSONS

If an instrument is payable to two or more people in the alternative (for example, Arnold Marx *or* Bernard Marx *or* Carl Marx), it may be negotiated, discharged, or enforced by any one of those people to whom it is payable. However, if the instrument is payable to all of them (Arnold Marx *and* Bernard Marx *and* Carl Marx) all of them must jointly negotiate, discharge, or enforce the instrument.

INSTRUMENTS PAYABLE TO A PERSON WITH DESCRIPTION

If an instrument is made payable to "Donald Doe, Recorder of Salt County," Mr. Doe is named only for identification and he takes the instrument only as an agent of Salt County. Thus, if the maker of the instrument does not know there had been an election in Salt County and Paul Pepper is the new recorder, Mr. Pepper can negotiate the instrument. The maker is actually paying Salt County and the identity of the recorder, whoever he is, is immaterial.

However, if an instrument is made payable to "Edward Easy, Executor of Estate of Franklin Filmore," only Mr. Easy may endorse, discharge, or negotiate it. In this case, the instrument is made payable to an officer, not to his office. Mr. Easy remains subject to any liability for a breach of his obligation as an executor and cannot divert the instrument to his own use.

This brings us to an instrument made payable to someone described not as an agent or fiduciary. This person is the unconditional owner. For example, an instrument made payable to "Robert Weber, Attorney" may be negotiated, discharged, or endorsed by Robert Weber personally. The description "attorney" adds no condition to the payment. It is only identification.

An instrument payable "at" or "through" a bank does not authorize the bank to pay it. The bank's only function is to advise the maker that the instrument has been presented for payment and to request instructions.

TITLE THROUGH TRANSFER

When an instrument is transferred to another person, the new owner, called the *transferee*, receives the same rights as the old owner, called the *transferor*. However, if someone has been a party to any fraud or illegality affecting the instrument or if as a prior holder he had notice of a defense, he cannot improve his position by taking from a holder in due course.

For instance, suppose Gilda Glutton fraudulently induces Dora Dumb to give her a note for $1,000. Gilda knows that if she tries to enforce the note against Dora, Dora will refuse to pay it and raise Gilda's fraud as her defense. However, if Gilda sells the note to Freda Fine, a good faith purchaser and holder in due course, Freda can enforce the note against Dora. If Gilda repurchases the note from Freda, however, she retains her former position—she does not become a holder in due course through Freda.

NEGOTIATION

Negotiation is the transfer of an instrument in such form that the transferee becomes a holder. If the instrument is payable to order, it is negotiated by delivery and indorsement. If it is payable to bearer, it is negotiated by delivery only.

An indorsement may be written on the instrument itself or on a paper so firmly attached that it becomes a part of the instrument. This attached paper is called an *allonge*.

An indorsement must convey the entire instrument or unpaid residue. Anything less is an assignment. A writing that says, "Pay *A* one-half of the balance due," is a partial assignment, not an indorsement, and the laws covering partial assignments are governed by the statutes of each state. Even an indorsement which reads "Pay A and B" is valid because it transfers the entire instrument.

Negotiation is effective even when it is made by an infant; or made by a corporation exceeding its powers; or made by any other person without capacity; or obtained by fraud, duress, or mistake of any kind; or part of an illegal transaction; or made in breach of duty.

INDORSEMENTS

Wrong or Misspelled Name

If an instrument is made payable to a person under a misspelled name or one other than his own, he may indorse it by using the wrong name or by using his own name or by using both names.

Special Indorsement

A special indorsement specifies the person to whom or to whose order it makes the instrument payable. It can be further negotiated only by his indorsement. For example, if a check is made payable to the order of Herman House and Herman indorses the check to Jerry Jackson with the words, "Pay to the order of Jerry Jackson, [signed] Herman House," only Jerry Jackson can negotiate the check further.

Blank Indorsement

An indorsement in blank does not specify a particular person and may consist of only a signature. Such an indorsement makes the instrument payable to bearer, so it can be negotiated by delivery alone. In the above example, if Herman had indorsed the check with his signature only, anyone, even someone who found it or stole it, could negotiate it further.

The holder may convert a blank indorsement into a special indorsement by writing over the signature of the indorser in blank any consistent special indorsement.

Restrictive Indorsement

An indorsement on an instrument is restrictive if it is conditional, such as "Pay only after notification of delivery"; or purports to prohibit further transfer as in "Pay to Mary Smith only"; or includes the words "for collection," "for deposit," "pay any bank," or other such terms signifying deposit or collection; or otherwise states that it is for the benefit of the indorser or another person.

Holder vs Holder in Due Course

A *holder in due course* is a holder who takes the instrument for value, in good faith, and without notice that it is overdue or has been dishonored or of any defense against or claim to it on the part of any person.

Someone who is aware of or has participated in some defect in the instrument is a holder, but not a holder in due course. A holder merely has possession of the instrument.

1. To the extent that a holder is a holder in due course, he takes the instrument

a. Free from all claims to it on the part of any person.

b. Free from all defenses of any party to the instrument with whom the holder has not dealt, except

[1] Infancy, to the extent that it is a defense to a simple contract as determined by local law

[2] Such other incapacity or duress or illegality of the transaction as renders the obligation of the party a nullity.

[3] Such misrepresentation as has induced the party to sign the instrument with neither knowledge nor reasonable opportunity to obtain knowledge of its character or its essential terms.

[4] Discharge in bankruptcy.

[5] Any other discharge of which the holder has notice when he takes the instrument. If he knows that the note has already been paid, for example, but the maker did not get it back. This is a caution to any maker of a note. When a note is finally paid in full, the maker should make sure it is marked *paid* or otherwise cancelled and returned to him. Otherwise, it could be negotiated to a third-party holder, and the maker could find himself paying the note all over again.

2. Unless he has the rights of a holder in due course, a person takes the instrument subject to

a. All valid claims to it on the part of any person.

b. All defenses of any party that would be available in an action on a simple contract.

c. The defenses of no consideration, no performance of a required condition, nondelivery or delivery for a special purpose.

d. The defense that the holder or a person through whom he holds the instrument acquired it by theft or that payment or satisfaction to such holder would be inconsistent with the terms of a restrictive indorsement.

LIABILITY OF PARTIES

No person is liable on an instrument unless his signature appears on it. A signature can be a name, a trade or assumed name, or any word or mark used as a signature. Unless the instrument clearly indicates that a signature is made in some other capacity, it is an indorsement. This means that the courts will look at the instrument primarily to determine the capacity of the signer. For instance, if Ian Shannon signs after "I, Ian Shannon promise to pay," he is a maker. If he signs after, "Ian Shannon, witness," he is not liable at all.

If an authorized representative signs his name, unless it is clearly shown that he signed in his representative capacity, he will be personally liable. For example, suppose ABC Corporation borrows money. If Sherwin Stanley, treasurer of ABC Corporation, signs the note "Sherwin Stanley," he will be personally liable because ABC Corporation is not identified as the debtor. If he signs "Sherwin Stanley, Treasurer," he is still personally liable because "treasurer" only further identifies him. If, however, he signs "ABC Corporation, by Sherwin Stanley, Treasurer," ABC Corporation is liable because it is apparent that Sherwin Stanley signed only in his representative capacity.

If a note or check is materially altered, and the alteration takes place because of the maker's negligence, the maker is liable to anyone who relies in good faith on the altered instrument. Larry Loser gives Terry Taylor a check for $1,000. He makes the check out in pencil or leaves a large space between the figure $1 and the three zeros and another space in the written amount. Terry then changes the check by erasing the pencil-written figure or inserting another numeral, changing the amount of the check to $11,000, and indorses the check to Norman Nonot who in good faith gives him $11,000. Larry will have to pay Norman $11,000, because his negligence permitted Terry to alter the check.

Certification of a check by a bank means that the bank agrees to hold sufficient funds from the drawer of the check to honor and pay the draft when it is presented.

An indorser of a check, unless he specifies by words like "without recourse," agrees that if the maker does not pay the check when it is presented, he will. Indorsers are liable in the order in which they signed. That is, the first indorser is liable if the maker dishonors the instrument (cannot or will not pay). If the first indorser cannot pay, the second indorser is liable, and after him the next indorser, and so on to the last indorser.

Every indorser says by his indorsement that he has good title to the instrument, and all signatures are genuine or authorized, the instrument has not been materially altered, no defense of any party is good against him, and he has no knowledge of any insolvency proceeding instituted by the maker.

If an indorsement is without recourse, the indorser warrants only that he has no knowledge of any defense that could be raised against him. Therefore, if any of the other defects occur, a holder who goes after an indorser without recourse cannot recover from that indorser.

DISCHARGE

Allen borrows money from Ed and gives Ed his note as evidence of the debt. The note bears interest at 10 percent and is due in six months. When the six months are up, however, and Allen tries to pay Ed the amount of the note plus the six months interest, Ed likes the interest rate so well that he refuses payment, expecting to get more interest. Can he charge Allen more interest? No. If payment is tendered to a holder when or after a note is due, the offering party [Allen] is discharged to the extent of any further liability for interest, costs, and attorney's fees.

A holder also discharges any party to the extent that without such party's consent, the holder, without express reservation of right, releases any person or agrees not to sue any person against whom the party has a cause of action if this right of cause of action is known to the holder.

A holder also discharges any party to the extent that he impairs any collateral securing the instrument. For example, Merrill borrows money from Mark, and Mark requires that Merrill pledge his truck and get a cosigner as additional security for the loan. Under these circumstances, Dan cosigns for Merrill. Without Dan's consent, Mark then returns the truck to Merrill who disposes of it. Dan is discharged as cosigner to the extent of the fair market value of the truck returned to Merrill.

BANK DEPOSITS AND COLLECTIONS

For the purpose of allowing time to process items, prove balances, and make the necessary entries on its books to determine its position for the day, a bank may fix an afternoon hour of 2:00 P.M. or later as a cut-off hour for handling money and items and making entries on its books. Any item or deposit of money received on any day after the cut-off hour may be treated as being received on the next business day.

Unless a contrary intent clearly appears, a collecting bank acts only as the agent of the owner of the item. If Sandy deposits a check from Jeff in an account in Central Bank, Central Bank forwards the check to Jeff's bank for collection. Even though Central Bank credits Sandy's account with the deposit, Sandy cannot write a check against Jeff's check until Jeff's bank has cleared [paid] the check given to Sandy.

A collecting bank must use ordinary care in presenting an item or sending it for collection and sending notice of dishonor and for settling an item when the bank receives final settlement.

A depository bank [the first bank to which an item is transferred for collection] that has taken an item for collection may supply any indorsement of the customer that is necessary. This may be done by placing a statement on the item to the effect that the item was deposited by a customer or credited to his account.

A bank may charge against the account of its customer any item properly payable from that account, even though the charge creates an overdraft. By issuing the check that will cause the overdraft, the customer impliedly promises to reimburse the bank for any overdraft. It should also be noted that a payor bank is liable to a customer for any damages caused directly to the customer, such as a penalty for a late payment of tax or an arrest or prosecution that results from the wrongful dishonor of an item.

10

PARTNERSHIPS

DEFINITION OF A PARTNERSHIP

A partnership is an association between two or more persons to operate a business for a profit as co-owners. Not all associations between two or more persons are partnerships: For instance, if two people get together to complete a single transaction, it is called a *joint venture*. Whereas a joint venture contemplates a single transaction, a partnership contemplates a continuous business. In the same way, if two or more people own property as co-owners, as in joint tenancy, they are not necessarily partners unless they own the property for the purpose of carrying on a trade or business for their common benefit and profit.

SHARING OF PROFITS

The essential test for determining the existence of a partnership is whether the parties intend to *share profits* from the operation of the business. For example, a salesman entitled to commissions from sales he makes is not a partner, even though his income and the profits of the business are determined by those sales. In fact, he is entitled to his commissions whether or not the business realizes a profit. A partner would be entitled to share only in any profits.

OTHER ELEMENTS OF A PARTNERSHIP

A partnership agreement is a contract. Like any other contract, it can be oral or written. Likewise, the parties must have the capacity to contract. A partnership agreement with a minor, for example, can be voided by the minor at any time until he reaches adulthood.

Forming a partnership requires the consent of all the partners. It also requires a contribution of capital by the partners. *Capital* is the money, property, and/or service each partner is contributing to the business to get it started. Thus, because of this investment, one cannot be forced to be a partner with others. Although a partner may "assign his interest" in the partnership to an outsider, all he is really assigning is his right to share in the profits. He cannot assign his right to manage the business. The assignee of a partner's interest can share in the management of the business only with the consent of the other partners.

Since a partnership requires constant competency on the part of each of the partners, if a partner dies or becomes insane, he is no longer competent and the partnership is automatically ended.

Although it must be determined if a person has an owner's interest in the profits of a business to determine if he is a partner, it is not necessary that he share in the losses for there to be a partnership; nor is it necessary that each partner share equally in the profits. For example, if Aaron, Baker, and Charles agree to form a partnership, they may agree that Aaron gets 60 percent of the of the profits, Baker 30 percent and Charles 10 percent. They may also agree that only Aaron and Baker share any losses equally. Partners may thus share profits in different proportions and losses in different proportions or not at all. However, if there is no agreement as to losses, the partners must share them in the same proportion as they share profits. If there is no agreements as to how profits will be shared, they are shared equally.

Finally, and probably most important, a partner dealing with outsiders in the usual way of carrying on the business acts as an agent for the firm and the other partners. Therefore his acts can bind the partnership and the other partners. It should be noted at this point that the liability of individual partners for the firm's debts is unlimited. If the partnership incurs debts and there are not sufficient assets in the firm to pay these debts, each partner is individually liable for them, and creditors may choose which partner to proceed against. The debts do not have to be allocated proportionately among the partners. It is because of this potential for unlimited liability for firm debts that a partnership can be formed only by the voluntary agreement of all the partners.

The only exceptions to this rule occur when a partner's acts are not apparently for carrying on the business of the partnership in the usual way or when in fact the partner has no authority to act for the partnership in a particular matter *and* the person with whom he is dealing knows about his lack of authority. In those cases, the partner's acts do not bind the partnership and the other partners. Here are some examples.

Delbert and Egbert are partners in the operation of a farm. If Delbert goes to an auction and contracts to buy five horses for the farm, the partnership could be liable for the purchase price of the five horses.

If, however, Delbert goes to a machine auction and buys three printing presses and a truck for delivering concrete in the name of the partnership, the partnership would probably not be liable for the purchase price because these are outside the usual business of farming. Delbert personally would be liable for his purchases.

Finally, if Egbert tells Delbert that he may never borrow money in the partnership name and also tells the local banker about this lack of authority by Delbert, if Delbert goes into the bank and the banker lends him in the partnership name the money to purchase the five horses, the partnership is not liable for this debt. Delbert lacked the authority to borrow and the banker knew of this lack of authority.

It is also the rule of law that if a partner commits any wrongful act, including fraud, while acting in the ordinary course of the business of the partnership or with the authority of his copartners, the partnership is liable for any injury or loss caused to a person not a copartner by these acts, to the same extent as the partner committing the wrongful act.

As to anyone dealing with a partnership, if one partner receives any notice or knowledge concerning a particular transaction, it is considered notice or knowledge to all the partners. Also, if a partnership is sued in its firm name, the partnership is considered as being served with a copy of the summons and other process if a copy is given to any one partner personally or to an agent of the partnership.

The one exception to the rule of partnership liability for the wrongdoing of a partner lies in the area of criminal law. Generally, neither the partnership nor any partner is liable for the criminal acts of a copartner merely by reason of the partnership relation. In order to show liability, it must be proved that the partner possessed guilty knowledge of the criminal act of his copartner or was an accessory before or after the fact.

PAYMENTS TO CREDITORS

Since a partner can by his acts within the apparent scope of his authority bind the firm and his copartners for debts, it is well to see how creditors are paid.

When the firm has debts, its assets are used to pay these debts. If a partner has individual debts, his personal assets are used to pay his individual debts. If the partnership assets are not sufficient to pay the firm's debts, the individual assets of the partners can be used for this purpose. If a partner's personal assets are not enough to pay his individual debts, his creditors can seek payment out of the partnership assets; but creditors of individual partners can get payment from partnership assets only after the firm's creditors have been paid.

Retirement and Admission of Partners

When a partner retires or a new partner is admitted to a firm, the old partnership is dissolved and a new one created with the consent of all partners of the new partnership. Generally, when a partner retires he remains liable to creditors for debts of the partnership until the time of his retirement. The incoming partner, unless he assumes such a liability, is not liable for debts of the partnership incurred before he became a partner.

After a partnership is dissolved, the business is continued only to conclude the business of the partnership, and liabilities of the firm are paid in the following order:

1. Those due to creditors other than partners.
2. Those due to partners for loans or other debts from the firm to them.
3. Those due to partners for the balance in their partnership capital account.
4. Those due to partners for their share of profits. On settlement after the dissolution, if one partner is found to owe another, the second partner can sue the first for the amount due.

LIMITED PARTNERSHIP

In a *limited partnership*, there must be at least one general partner and one or more limited partners, who are not bound by the obligations of the partnership. Such a partnership is usually formed to accomplish a specific speculative purpose with limited liability. For example, such a partnership is often used to obtain investors in a movie: the limited partners share in any profits but limit their liability. To be a valid operation, a limited partnership must be formed in compliance with the Uniform Limited Partnership Act.

A limited partnership can carry on any legitimate business, except banking, insurance, or the operation of a railroad.

In a limited partnership, the general partners are personally responsible for the debts and obligations of the firm, without regard to amount, as in the case of an ordinary partnership. Limited partners have no liability for debts, except to the amount of their capital contributions. Once those contributions have been used to pay creditors, they have no further obligation.

WRITTEN GENERAL-PARTNERSHIP AGREEMENT

Although a partnership may be formed by the oral agreement of the parties, or even by their acts, complex and potentially expensive problems often arise from a partnership; and it is a good idea to put any partnership agreement in writing and have it signed by the partners. Such an agreement should include the following twenty-one items.

1. The name of the firm.
2. The address of the firm's place of business.
3. The purpose of the partnership.
4. The date the partnership is to become effective.
5. The names and addresses of the partners.
6. The length of time the partnership is to last.
7. How profits and losses are to be shared.
8. What capital each partner is contributing, and whether this is a contribution of money, equipment, supplies, services.
9. Whether or not interest is to be paid on invested capital.
10. What salaries or drawing accounts are to be provided each partner.
11. How much time each partner is to devote to partnership business.
12. The authority of each partner, particularly the power to sign checks, make loans, buy goods, or enter into contracts or leases.
13. How and by whom the business is to be managed and controlled.
14. Provision for accounting and the preparation of financial statements.
15. Provisions for the retirement of each partner.
16. Agreements to set up any tax deductible retirement plan.
17. Provision for the dissolution of the partnership and the right to continue the business should a partner withdraw.
18. How any surplus will be distributed upon dissolution.
19. What provision, if any, is to be made for use of the firm's name or goodwill after dissolution.
20. Provision for arbitration in case of disputes between partners.
21. Provision in regard to continuing the business upon the death or insanity of a partner and whether or not the legal representative of such a former partner shall have access to the books and records of the firm.

LIMITED PARTNERSHIP AGREEMENT

Since a limited partnership must be formed in compliance with the Uniform Limited Partnership Act, that act should be consulted; and any limited partnership agreement should include at least the following items.

1. The name of the partnership.
2. The nature of the business.
3. The location of the principal place of business.
4. The name and address of each partner and whether each is a general or limited partner.
5. The term of the partnership.
6. The amount of cash or the value of other property contributed by each limited partner. (A limited partner may contribute cash or property as his capital contribution, but not services.)
7. The additional contributions, if any, to be made by each limited partner and when they are to be made.
8. Whether any contribution of each limited partner is to be returned.
9. The share of the profits each limited partner shall receive.
10. The right to admit additional limited partners.
11. Any priorities given to one or more limited partners over other limited partners.
12. The right of any remaining general partners to continue the business on the death, retirement, or insanity of a general partner.
13. The right, if any, of a limited partner to receive property instead of cash in return for his contribution.
14. The right, if any and under what conditions, of a limited partner to substitute another in his place.

11

CORPORATIONS

A corporation is an artificial being composed of one or more individuals and created under the authority of law as an independent being separate from its several members with the capacity of continuous existence.

CHARACTERISTICS OF A CORPORATION

A corporation has the following characteristics that differentiate it from a partnership. First, no matter how the membership changes as to shareholders, directors, or officers, it continues in existence, whereas a partnership dissolves with any change in the members. It may sue or be sued in its own name, whereas only the partners of a partnership may sue—not the partnership itself. Contracts, leases, bank accounts, loans, and the like may be made by the corporation; in a partnership, only the partners may do these things.

Ownership in the corporation may be transferred without the consent of the other members, unless such consent is specifically required by the articles of incorporation or the by-laws. In a partnership, a partner's interest in profits or assets may be transferred, but not his ownership interest.

The shareholders have no personal liability for the debts of the corporation, except to the amount of their investment in their respective shares. If the corporation has debts and lacks sufficient assets to pay them, the shareholders cannot personally be required to pay. All a shareholder would lose in such a case is his investment in the stock of the corporation. Along these same lines, a member of a corporation is not liable for the unauthorized acts of his associates. Although the acting member and the corporation may be liable, this liability does not extend to the other members.

FORMATION OF A CORPORATION

A corporation can be created and exist only as permitted by statute; and a number of formalities must be observed and a number of fees and taxes paid in order to start and keep a corporation. For this reason, many incorporators examine the statutes of various states to determine which state will give the corporation its greatest advantage.

To incorporate, the incorporators usually meet with their lawyer and explain what they would like to accomplish with the corporation. After determining where they should incorporate, the lawyer prepares the articles of incorporation. This is done on a form provided by the state of incorporation on which the following information is recorded.

1. *The name of the corporation.* The name cannot be the same as that of a corporation presently doing business in that state or so similar as to be deceiving. It is also required that the corporate name include the word *incorporated, inc., company, co., limited,* or *ltd.* to be sure that those dealing with the corporation know that it is a corporation and not a partnership or a sole proprietorship. If the company is to do business in states other than the state of incorporation, the name must be cleared in those states too.
2. The names and addresses of the incorporators.
3. The location of the principal office of the corporation in that state.
4. How long the corporation will be in existence. Unless the corporation is set up for some specific purpose or purposes so that it will close operations after that purpose is accomplished, most corporations are set up to have a perpetual life.
5. The total number of shares of capital stock authorized and the par value, if any, of this stock.
6. The classes of stock. For example, common stock, preferred stock, etc.
7. The number of shares of each class to be issued and the amount to be received from subscribers for these shares.
8. The purpose of the corporation. This is a most important clause. Since a corporation is a creature of statute, it can do only those things permitted by statute. Therefore, the purpose clause sets out what type of business the corporation can engage in, and the corporation is limited to those purposes. If the purpose clause is too narrow, the corporation could be restricted in its operations. If the purpose clause is too vague, the state may not grant the charter to do business.

9. Many incorporators also put any restrictions or preferences or privileges they desire on the sale or transference of the stock, the voting of the stock, or the power or authority of the shareholders into the articles of incorporation.

10. The states usually require that at least $300 to $1000, depending on the state, be received for the stock before the company can do business.

11. Some states also require an indication of how many directors the company will have. Only one director is required in some states, while others require three or more.

After this form is completed, with the required number of copies, and signed by the required people, it is sent to the secretary of state of the state of incorporation along with the proper recording fees and pro-rated franchise taxes to the date of incorporation.

The *franchise tax* is levied by the state on the right and privilege of carrying on business in the state. The tax is usually assessed annually and based on the amount of capital received for the stock issued.

If all fees and taxes are paid, if there is no conflict in name or purpose, and if the articles of incorporation are properly filled out, the secretary of state will issue a charter to the corporation to do business. These articles usually then must be recorded where the company is going to do business.

SHAREHOLDERS

The *shareholders* are the ones who own the stock in the corporation. They purchase this stock from the corporation or from an agent authorized to act for the corporation. After the charter has been issued, the shareholders meet, adopt the by-laws of the corporation, and elect the company directors. The *by-laws* are the rules and regulations by which the officers and members will manage the affairs of the company among themselves.

Unless otherwise provided or unless there is a special reason to do so more often, the shareholders meet annually. At that time, financial operations of the year past and for the projected future are discussed. The board of directors for the coming year is also elected.

Because the shareholders risked their money by investing in the corporation, they usually are entitled to some payment out of the profits of the corporation in the form of *dividends*. Because the dividends represent taxable income to the shareholders, it is said they are subject to double taxation: They are taxed once as part of the corporation's profit and again when they are paid to the shareholders. Dividends are paid from income, and they are not deductible from taxable income as is interest when it is paid out.

Evidence of each shareholder's interest in the corporation is represented by a *stock certificate* signed by the proper officers and bearing the corporate seal. The certificate shows the company name, the number of shares represented by the certificate, and the name of the shareholder.

Not all shares of stock are entitled to dividends, which are paid only on issued and outstanding shares. The total number of shares which the corporation is permitted by its charter to issue are called the *authorized shares*. The total number of authorized shares actually given to shareholders in exchange for money, services, or property are called *issued shares*. When issued shares are repurchased by the corporation, they become *treasury shares*. Authorized and issued shares that have not been repurchased are called *outstanding shares*.

DIRECTORS

A shareholder in a corporation agrees that his interests as such shall be managed by the corporation, and direct participation in corporate management is not a right a shareholder may properly claim. The corporation, however, is controlled for the shareholders by the directors.

The directors have the following powers, duties, and prerogatives: They elect the officers of the corporation, such as the president, the vice presidents, the secretary, and the treasurer; they are the trustees of the corporation's business and property; they administer corporate affairs; they are entitled to salaries for acting as directors; they can be personally liable for corporate debts or contracts when they are guilty of certain official neglect or misconduct; and they declare dividends.

A shareholder is not entitled to a dividend until it has been declared by the directors. Whether a dividend should be declared and in what amount usually rests in the sound discretion of the directors. Unless the directors act fraudulently or unreasonably, the shareholders cannot force the directors to declare a dividend.

However, before dividends can be declared the corporation must be *solvent* (that is, able to meet its debts as they mature). If any directors vote for or assent to the declaration of any dividend or other distribution of assets when the company is insolvent or its net assets are less than its stated capital, they are jointly or severally liable for the amount of the dividends paid or the value of the assets distributed.

Any directors who vote for or assent to the declaration of any dividend or other distribution of assets that renders the corporation insolvent or reduces its net assets below its stated capital are jointly and severally liable for the amount of the dividends paid or the value of such assets distributed, to the extent that the company is rendered insolvent or its net assets are reduced below its stated capital.

Stated value is the par value of all shares then issued having a par value, or the consideration received by the corporation for all shares issued without par value.

COMMON STOCK VS PREFERRED STOCK

Until the directors decide to declare a dividend, no shareholder is entitled to receive one. Therefore, if a business year goes by and no dividend is declared, unless a shareholder is somehow preferred over other shareholders he loses his right to any dividends for that year. The directors also determine the dividends to be paid for each share of stock. Therefore, unless a shareholder is preferred over other shareholders, he can receive only whatever dividends the directors decide upon. Shareholders who have no say in their dividends are usually holders of *common stock*, and shareholders who receive preferred treatment when dividends are declared are usually owners of *preferred stock*. For example, if there is 8 percent preferred stock outstanding, the shareholders who own this stock must be paid 8 percent of their shares' total par value before the holders of common stock can be paid. If there are 5000 shares of 8 percent preferred stock outstanding at a par value of $100 each, $40,000 will have to be paid to the preferred share holders before the common-stock shareholders can receive dividends.

Some preferred stock may also be *cumulative preferred stock*. Noncumulative preferred stock is like common stock in that if a dividend is not declared, the preferred-stock shareholder loses his right to the dividend. With cumulative preferred stock, that right is deferred until a dividend is declared. In the above example, if the 8 percent stock were cumulative, and the directors declared no dividends for two successive years but declared dividends for a third, the cumulative preferred shareholders would have to be paid $120,000 for three years before the common-stock shareholders could receive any dividends.

There are other ways of distinguishing preferred stock. In case of liquidation of the corporation, certain shareholders would be paid first. Another preference can permit preferred shareholders to share dividends equally with common-stock shareholders in any additional dividends paid after the preferred stockholders receive their guaranteed percentage.

Because of these advantages, preferred stock usually costs more than common stock; but in some states, only common-stock shareholders can vote at shareholders' meetings.

MINUTES AND MEETINGS

One of the biggest disadvantages to a corporation is its formality. Someone who owns his own business makes his own decisions on the spot; a partnership is usually operated with the same informality. A corporation, however, unless it is owned and operated by only one person, must have meetings to make business decisions; and each of these meetings must be recorded in a corporate minute book. Annual shareholders' meetings and annual directors' meetings are provided for in the corporate by-laws. In addition, when other major decisions must be made during the year, a special meeting must be held; and a notice of this meeting must be sent either to all of the shareholders or to all of the directors, requesting their presence. A shareholder who cannot attend the shareholders' meeting can designate in writing someone to vote on the issues for him. He does this by giving this person a written authorization, called a *proxy*.

TAXATION

Another disadvantage of a corporation is that it is subject to an income tax separate and apart from that assessed against the shareholders, directors, officers, or other employees. This income tax is levied in addition to the original charter fee and the annual franchise tax. A man in business for himself who makes a profit or suffers a loss includes them in his personal income tax returns. The proceeds of a partnership are pro-rated among the partners in accordance with their partnership agreement, and each includes his share in his personal income tax returns. A corporation, however, pays its own tax on any income earned by it. If the corporation suffers a loss in any year, that loss can be carried forward or back to reduce taxable income of a future or past year.

If the corporation is able to meet certain requirements as to the number and kind of shareholders and if the election is made by the proper time, a corporation may receive permission from the Internal Revenue Service to report its taxable income or losses as a *Sub Chapter S* or *psuedo corporation*. This permits the shareholders to include the corporation's profit or loss each year on their personal tax returns as if the corporation were a partnership, while retaining the other benefits of a corporation—continuity of life, limited liability, and ease of transference of ownership. In other words, the shareholders can have the best of both worlds.

CORPORATE CAPITAL

The owners equity in a corporation is commonly called *net worth* or *stockholders' equity* or *capital*. The two principal sources of corporate capital are

1. Investments contributed by the stockholders
2. Profits retained in the business.

The investments from the stockholders are usually stated separately by the class of stock purchased. At the end of each business year, net income after taxes is recorded in an account called *retained earnings* or *surplus*. This account reflects the company's years of operation: A profit increases it; a loss decreases it. Declared dividends also reduce this account. If at some stage this account has a negative balance, that is, more losses and dividends than income were added to the account, this balance is called a *deficit*.

MARKET TRADES

The price of stock sold on the open market, through the New York Stock Exchange, the American Stock Exchange, or some other exchange, is called its *market value*. It bears no relationship to the par value or the book value of the stock. *Par value* is an arbitrary value placed on the stock by the incorporators when the stock is authorized. It has no source of reference except the minds of the incorporators. *Book value* indicates what the stock is worth on the company's books: The stockholders' investments plus surplus divided by the number of shares outstanding gives the book value per share. However, market value is determined in the marketplace. It is based on what a buyer is willing to pay for the stock and what a seller is willing to take for it. This price, like the price of anything else in a free market, is determined by what buyers and sellers think about the future of the company and the country. Since it is based on speculation on a grand scale, it is difficult to forecast how the stock market will behave.

12

SOCIAL SECURITY

The *Social Security Handbook*, sixth edition, published by the United States Department of Health, Education, and Welfare, Social Security Administration, in July 1978, says that the objectives of the Social Security Act and related laws are to provide for "the natural needs of individuals and families, protecting aged and disabled persons against the expenses of illnesses that could otherwise exhaust their savings, keeping families together, and giving children the opportunity to grow up in health and security."

Retirement, survivors, and disability insurance benefits are paid monthly to those qualified. To be qualified for such payments, an individual must be

1. A disabled insured worker under age sixty-five,
2. A retired worker at age sixty-two or older,
3. The spouse of a retired or disabled worker entitled to benefits, who is age 62 or older, or in the case of a wife, has the care of the worker's child who is under age 18 and entitled to social security benefits.
4. The divorced wife (in some cases) of a retired or disabled worker entitled to benefits if age sixty-two or older and married to the worker for at least twenty years. For benefits payable after 1978, the twenty-year requirement is reduced to 10 years.
5. The dependent, unmarried child of a retired or disabled worker entitled to benefits, or of a deceased insured worker if the child is under age eighteen; or eighteen or over but under a disability that began before age twenty-two; or age eighteen to twenty-two and attending school full time.

6. The surviving spouse (including a surviving divorced wife in some cases) of a deceased insured worker, if the widow or widower is age sixty or older.

7. The disabled surviving spouse (including a surviving divorced wife in some cases) of a deceased insured worker if the widow or widower is age fifty to fifty-nine and becomes disabled within a specific period.

8. The surviving spouse (including a surviving divorced wife in some cases) of a deceased insured worker, regardless of age, if caring for an entitled child of the deceased who is under age eighteen or disabled.

9. The dependent parents of a deceased insured worker at age sixty-two or over.

In addition, a lump-sum payment can be made to a widow or widower who was living in the same household as the insured worker at the time of his death. This amount is usually referred to as a "burial benefit," since it is intended to help offset burial expenses.

MEDICARE

Medicare provides comprehensive health insurance protection to the aged, disabled, and those suffering from chronic kidney disease in the form of hospital and medical insurance. This insurance is provided for

1. Persons age sixty-five or over who are entitled to monthly social security benefits.
2. Qualified railroad retirement beneficiaries age sixty-five or over.
3. Certain uninsured persons age sixty-five or over who voluntarily enroll under a special provision requiring the payment of a monthly premium.
4. Certain uninsured persons age sixty-five or over who reached age sixty-five before 1968 or earned a specified number of quarters of coverage in employment or self-employment under the social security program and who meet the requirements of a special transitional provision.
5. Persons under age sixty-five entitled to social security disability benefits (for the previous twenty-four consecutive calendar months) and certain persons entitled to railroad retirement benefits on account of disability.
6. Persons under sixty-five who have end-stage renal disease and require kidney transplant or a course of dialysis.

To receive these benefits, a person must apply for and become entitled to them. One can get hospital insurance protection even though he or she does not wish to receive other monthly benefits or cannot receive them because earnings are too high.

Medicare benefits are of two kinds. The first, called *Part A* benefits, pays for all or part of the hospitalization, for posthospital skilled nursing facility care, for posthospital home health care, and for blood. The second, called

Part B, pays for doctors, for inpatient and outpatient medical services and supplies, for physical and speech therapy, for ambulance service, for home health care whether there was prior hospitalization or not, for outpatient hospital treatment, and for blood.

BENEFITS FOR WORKERS AGE SIXTY-TWO OR OLDER

A worker is entitled to retirement insurance benefits if he or she files an application for retirement benefits and is age 62 and fully insured or age 72. If he or she is age 72 and is not fully insured, the worker may still receive benefits if he or she reached age seventy-two before 1969 and has at least one quarter of employed coverage for each calendar year after 1950 up to age sixty-five for a man and age sixty-two for a woman and has a total of at least three quarters of coverage.

A worker may choose to receive a reduced benefit at age sixty-two or can wait until age sixty-five and receive the full retirement insurance benefit to which he or she is entitled.

If a worker is under age seventy after 1982 and earns over $6,000 annually or $500 monthly, he will not qualify for retirement benefits. A worker is also denied benefits if he is deported, is an alien who has been outside the United States for more than six full consecutive calendar months, is an alien living in a country to which the mailing of United States Government checks is prohibited, or has waived the right to benefits by reason of membership in a recognized religious group which is conscientiously opposed to the acceptance of social security benefits and other types of insurance and has been granted an exemption from paying the self-employment tax contribution.

Any duly ordained, commissioned, or licensed minister of a church, member of a religious order, or Christian Science practitioner who is conscientiously, or because of religious principles, opposed to the acceptance of social security benefits because of services as a minister may file a timely Exemption Form 4361 with the Internal Revenue Service and be granted exemption from social security coverage. This exemption is irrevocable and applies only to net earnings from services in the exercise of the ministry or religious order or on practice as a Christian Scientist.

Retirement benefits end with the beneficiary's death. No retirement insurance benefit can be paid for the month in which he or she died.

A wife is also entitled to insurance benefits on her husband's social security record if her husband is entitled to retirement or disability benefits; she has filed an application for wife's benefits; and she is not entitled to coverage on her own equal to or greater than one-half her husband's insurance benefits.

She must also be over age sixty-two or have in her care a child under age eighteen or over age eighteen and disabled who is entitled to benefits on her husband's social security record.

To qualify, the wife also must have been married to her husband for at least one year just before she filed her application for benefits, or she must be the mother of her husband's son or daughter (though the child need not be still living when she applies for benefits), or she must have been entitled or potentially entitled to wife's, widow's, parent's, or childhood disability benefits in the month before the month she married her husband, or she must have been entitled or potentially entitled to a widow's, parent's or child's annuity under the Railroad Retirement Act in the month before the month she married her husband. A husband may be entitled to insurance benefits on his wife's social security record if he meets the same requirements.

A child is entitled to child's insurance benefits on the social security record of a parent if an application for child's insurance benefit is filed; the child is or was dependent upon the parent; the child is unmarried; the child is under age eighteen, or age eighteen through twenty-one and a full time student, or age eighteen or over and under a disability which must have begun before age twenty-two; and the parent is entitled to disability or retirement insurance benefits or was insured at the time of death.

SURVIVOR'S BENEFITS

When the insured worker dies, cash benefits may be paid to eligible survivors. The benefits may be paid monthly in the case of a widow, widower, surviving child, or surviving parent, or as a lump-sum death payment. Generally, a survivor's benefit rates are figured as a percentage of the deceased worker's primary insurance amount. The lump-sum death payment may be no more than $255, and it may be paid in addition to any monthly survivor's insurance benefits that are due. The application for a lump-sum death payment must be filed within two years of an insured person's death.

If all or part of the burial expenses incurred by or through a funeral home are unpaid, the lump sum will be paid to the funeral home to the extent such burial expenses are unpaid. If these expenses have been paid, the lump sum will be paid to the person or persons equitably entitled to it.

Disability Benefits

The Social Security Act provides benefits for disability as follows:

1. Monthly cash benefits for a disabled worker.
2. Monthly cash benefits for needy disabled individuals.
3. The establishment of a "period of disability" wherein disability or retirement benefits may not be lost or reduced.
4. Monthly cash benefits for a disabled widow, disabled surviving divorced wife, or disabled widower aged fifty to fifty-nine.
5. Monthly cash benefits for a disabled child of a worker.
6. Vocational rehabilitation.
7. Hospital and supplementary medical insurance protection. To qualify for disability benefits a person must not only be unable to do his or her previous work but also be unable—considering age, education, and work experience—to do any other kind of substantial gainful work that exists in the national economy. It is immaterial whether such work exists in the immediate area or whether a specific job vacancy exists or whether the worker would be hired if he or she applied for work.

SUPPLEMENTAL SECURITY INCOME BENEFITS

Supplemental Security is a cash assistance program designed to supplement income for the aged, blind, or disabled who have little or no income or resources. Payments are made after application to an individual who

1. Is age 65 or older, or
2. Is blind (vision no better than 20/200 even with glasses, or tunnel vision, which is limited peripheral vision of 20 degrees or less), or
3. Is disabled, which disablement is expected to last twelve months or more or result in death, and
4. Is a resident of one of the fifty states or the District of Columbia, and
5. Is a citizen of the United States or an alien legally admitted for permanent residence, and
6. Does not have *countable* income in a month of more than $177.80 for an individual or $266.70 for a couple, and
7. Does not have *countable* resources in excess of $1,500 for an individual or $2,250 for a couple, and
8. Is not excepted because of status as an inmate of a public institution and not receiving Medicaid, failure to accept treatment for drug addiction or alcoholism, absence from the United States, refusal to accept vocational rehabilitiation services, failure to apply for other benefits, pensions, and the like to which he is potentially eligible.

The maximum federal payments are

1. $177.80 to an eligible individual considered to be living in his or her own household.

2. $266.70 to an eligible couple considered to be living in their own household. This amount is issued in separate checks, one-half of the amount to each.

3. $118.54 to an individual considered to be living in the household of another.

4. $177.80 to an eligible couple considered to be living in the household of another, issued in separate checks, one-half of the amount to each.

5. $25.00 to an individual who is a patient in a public or private medical treatment facility and receives substantial support from Medicaid.

6. $89—the increment added to the payment of an eligible individual when there is an essential person on the household.

Countable income is basically all income, whether earned or unearned, except assistance payments, tax refunds, and grants, scholarships, and fellowships. Blind individuals may deduct ordinary and necessary expenses attributable to earning an income if they are working. Income of an ineligible spouse or parent of an eligible child is deemed to be available to the eligible individual and may therefore preclude him or her from receiving benefits.

In determining the *countable resources* of an individual, the following are excluded:

1. Home and adjacent land and buildings owned by the eligible individual or spouse.

2. Household goods and personal effects of a reasonable value. One wedding and engagement ring are excluded, regardless of value.

3. Property necessary to operate the individual's trade or business or to produce income.

4. One automobile of reasonable value per individual or couple. An automobile especially equipped for a handicapped individual or needed for employment or for specific or regular medical treatment of the individual or a member of the household is also excluded.

5. Life insurance policies up to $1,500.

6. Proceeds from casualty insurance intended to replace an excludable resource, within three months if personal property or six months if real property.

7. Assets of an eligible individual and/or the eligible spouse that are needed to accomplish an approved plan to achieve self-support.

BLACK LUNG BENEFITS

The black lung benefits program provides for payment of monthly cash benefits to a coal miner totally disabled by pneumoconiosis or the widow, child, parent, brother, or sister of a miner who was entitled to black lung benefits at the time of death or was totally disabled by pneumoconiosis at the time of death or died from pneumoconiosis, or the child of a widow who was entitled to benefits at the time of her death.

To be entitled to black lung benefits, a coal miner must be totally disabled by pneumoconiosis that arose out of employment in the nation's coal mines and file a timely application for benefits.

A miner is under a total disability due to pneumonconiosis if he is suffering or suffered from a chronic dust disease of the lung and is unable to engage in comparable and gainful work by reason of pneumoconiosis, which can be expected to result in death or which has lasted or can be expected to last for a continuous period of not less than twelve months.

Comparable and gainful work is work in the immediate area of residence requiring skill and abilities comparable to those of any work in a mine or mines in which the miner previously engaged with some regularity and over a substantial period of time. Notice how this differs from the requirement to receive *disability benefits* that the applicant cannot do any work of any kind anywhere, whether or not a job vacancy exists.

The existence of pneumoconiosis may be proved by X-ray, autopsy, or biopsy. A miner's benefit is increased by 50 percent if he has a wife or child dependent on him, by 75 percent if he has two dependents, and by 100 percent if he has three dependents. Payments can be reduced if he receives state workmen's compensation, unemployment compensation, or state disability insurance because of the disability due to pneumoconiosis.

OTHER BENEFIT PROGRAMS

Unemployment Insurance

Most states have their own programs to help people who find themselves unemployed through no fault of their own. These programs are funded by taxation of workers' employers. To insure that funds are available for these programs, the federal government also has an unemployment insurance program. This program is also funded solely by taxation of the employer, except for three states in which employees are also taxed. The purposes of the federal program are to provide a program in states that do not have one and provide funds that may be borrowed by a state in the event the state's program runs short of funds.

A state unemployment insurance program must conform to federal requirements, but the state can specify the requirements for getting unemployment compensation, the amount of the compensation, and the number of weeks for which benefits may be paid.

When an employee files a claim for unemployment insurance benefits, the state determines whether or not the employee is entitled to any benefits. The unemployed worker and the former employer each have the right to appeal any decision on unemployment benefit claims. Why the worker would appeal an adverse decision is obvious; but why would an employer appeal a decision granting the claim? The rate at which an employer is taxed for the unemployment fund is determined by the state's experience in providing benefits to that employer's former workers. The more benefits the state must pay out, the higher the tax rate. Conversely, the fewer former employees drawing unemployment benefits, the lower the tax rate. Therefore, it is to the employer's economic benefit to try to keep as many former employees as possible from collecting benefits.

Public Assistance

Public assistance programs provide benefits to those whose other income is inadequate to provide the basic necessities of life. Their purposes are to attain strengthened family life, economic stability, personal independence, and participation in community life. The programs are intended for needy families with dependent children and individuals or families who are medically needy.

Aid to families with dependent children (AFDC) is provided in all fifty states, the District of Columbia, Puerto Rico, Guam, and the Virgin Islands when the father or mother is disabled, absent from home, or dead. It may in some cases be extended to provide assistance to children of unemployed fathers. The child must be living with a close relative or in an approved foster home or institution.

Aid to individuals or families who are medically needy (usually called *Medicaid*) provides direct payments to suppliers of medical care and services to families who receive AFDC and to those who are receiving supplementary security income. In some states, like California, aid is also provided to medically needy persons who are not receiving public assistance or supplemental security income because they have sufficient income and resources for the essentials of living, aside from their medical costs. Medicaid pays for inpatient and outpatient hospital services; other laboratory and X-ray services; skilled nursing home and home health care services for individuals aged twenty-one or over; early and periodic screening, diagnosis, and treatment for individuals under age twenty-one; family planning services, and physician's services. The provision of other medical services is optional with each state. While a state may impose nominal deductible or cost sharing amounts, it cannot impose an enrollment fee, premium, or similar charge for the required services.

The federal and state governments share in financing AFDC and medical assistance. A person usually applies for assistance at a local public welfare office. The Social Security Act requires each state to give an individual the opportunity to apply for assistance under any one of the programs and to provide assistance with reasonable promptness to all eligible persons. General relief and general assistance are also available from states and/or localities to needy individuals or families who do not qualify for help under the federally aided assistance programs.

Children's Services

There are two types of services for children under the Social Security Act.

First, maternal and child health and crippled children's services are provided by each state. The federal government provides funds for the states to use for maternity clinics, family planning services, home visits of public health nurses, well-child clinics, school health programs, pediatric clinics, dental care, mental retardation clinics, and immunizations against preventable diseases.

Funds for crippled children's programs provide for the location, diagnosis medical and surgical treatment, and care of children who are crippled or suffering from conditions that lead to crippling.

Second, child welfare services and AFDC are public social services that supplement or substitute for parental care and supervision. These services are concerned with prevention of child abuse, neglect, exploitation, or delinquency.

Workmen's Compensation Laws

These laws are intended to protect workers. They are mandatory in most states and require that an employer insure with a private insurance company or act as a self-insurer to provide prompt medical care and cash benefits to a worker injured in connection with a job or cash benefits to dependents if the worker is killed. Most laws exclude benefits for injuries attributable to an employee's intoxication, willful misconduct, or gross negligence.

Railroad Retirement Act and Railroad Unemployment Insurance Act

These laws provide protection for people who work for railroads and for certain companies closely connected with the railroad industry. Both programs are administered by the Railroad Retirement Board and have offices in major cities and representatives who regularly visit other locations.

In addition, some disability benefits are administered by the Veterans Administration.

HOW DO WE QUALIFY?

Now that we know what benefits are available, we should know what we have to do to qualify to receive these benefits.

First, every United States resident should have a Social Security number. This can be obtained from any local Social Security office. At a Social Security office, anyone can also check on his earnings record, apply for benefits, enroll for medical insurance, and get full information about individual and family rights and obligations—all without cost.

The applicant receives his Social Security number on a Social Security card. This number is used to report income to the Internal Revenue Service; and it is needed on most job applications or applications for any of the benefits discussed above.

A person who does not receive a benefit when it is due should file a written request for prompt payment. If the request is made within ninety days after the payment is due, benefits found to be due will be paid within fifteen days after the end of the ninety-day period. Where it appears that benefits are probably due, preliminary payments may be made, even though additional evidence may be needed for a final decision.

If a husband or wife request it, separate checks will be sent to them. If they receive a combined check, and if either dies, the combined check for the month in which the death occurred can be made over to the survivor if it is returned to the Social Security office with a request for such a change. The amount not due the survivor will be deducted from subsequent checks.

If a beneficiary cashes a check to which he or she is not entitled, he must refund the money. Social Security benefits cannot be assigned; and except for delinquent federal taxes and child support or alimony required by court order, they are not subject to levy, garnishment, or attachment.

A person must be insured in order to receive retirement, survivors, or disability insurance benefits or have them paid to his or her family. Anyone is insured who has a sufficient number of quarters credited to his or her Social Security earnings record.

A Social Security beneficiary age sixty-five or older is automatically entitled to hospital insurance. In addition, certain disabled persons and persons suffering from chronic kidney disease who are under age sixty-five are entitled to hospital insurance.

In January 1978, both employers and self-employed individuals began reporting their earnings annually. Before that, earnings were reported each calendar quarter. After 1977, if annual earnings divided by four equals $250 or more, an employee or self-employed individual is entitled to a quarter of coverage. The amount necessary to acquire a quarter of coverge is subject to change annually by the secretary of the Department of Health and Human Services. Therefore, anyone who has a question regarding the amount of his or her coverage or quarters of coverage should contact the nearest Social Security office.

13

REAL ESTATE

In the average person's lifetime, his biggest expenditure will be made to buy a house—whether a single detached house or a shared structure like a cooperative apartment, a condominium, or a town house.

In addition, people are buying vacation homes or condominium apartments with more frequency than they did in the past. The trend toward condominiums has spread even to business and office buildings.

In acquiring any property of this type, the buyer is entering into a contract with the seller to purchase real estate. Since many such properties lie in states other than the state of a buyer's residence, he is well advised to seek legal services in the state where the property is located. This is true no matter how well versed and competent the buyer's attorney may be in real estate law in his home state.

WHAT IS REAL ESTATE?

Real estate is land and any structures built on the land and anything attached to the structure or land in a permanent manner. For example, if a stove and refrigerator are placed in a house, they are personal property rather than real estate, unless they are built-in, because they can be moved without damage to the structure. However, if kitchen cabinets are permanently attached to the walls, they are part of the real estate, even though they are not as big, bulky, or heavy as the stove or refrigerator. The cabinets become real estate only when they are attached to the walls. They are personal property before that time. They become part of the real estate because they cannot be removed without damage to the wall, a part of the structure.

HOW IS TITLE TO REAL ESTATE HELD?

Title to real estate can be owned by one person, by two or more people, or in a trust.

Sole Ownership

If a person owns title in his own name, he is said to own *fee simple* title. The property is his and he can use it in any lawful way he wants. He can give it away during his lifetime or bequeath it by will. He can even give it away during his lifetime but retain a *life estate* whereby he retains the right to use the property during his lifetime. Finally, he can sell it at any price a buyer is willing to pay.

Joint Ownership

If the title to real estate is in the names of two or more people, they are joint owners.

One form of joint ownership is called *joint tenancy*. When one of the joint owners dies, title to the property immediately and automatically goes to the other joint owner. For example, John and Mary Black own their home in joint tenancy. If John dies, Mary owns the entire title to the property without anything more having to be done. If John and Mary decide to sell the house, both of them must sign the deed conveying the title to the buyer. If John dies after the contract for sale is signed but before the date title is to be transferred, Mary can convey title herself because she became the sole owner of the title immediately and automatically upon John's death.

A second form of joint ownership is called *tenancy in common*. If people own property as tenants in common, each owns a proportionate interest in the property. Upon the death of one owner, his is devised by will to another or passes to his heirs if there is no will. For example, A, B, and C own real estate as tenants in common. A owns 50 percent, B 30 percent, and C 20 percent. If B dies without a will, his heirs will inherit his 30 percent interest.

A third form of joint ownership is *community property*. In states recognizing the concept of community property, any property purchased by a husband and/or a wife during their marriage is owned by them equally, regardless of which pays for the property or in what manner they take title. Upon the death of either the husband or the wife, the survivor is entitled to one-half of the community property. The other half may be devised by the deceased spouse by will. It should be noted that property acquired by a husband or wife before marriage (or by inheritance or gift after marriage) does not become community property. However, if the owner spouse conveys the property to both spouses during marriage, it becomes community property. For example, suppose Sally Brown buys a condominium in Aspen, Colorado. She later marries Harry Carey; and because of love and for convenience, she conveys the title to the property to Sally Carey and Harry Carey as joint tenants. The condominium is now community property; and upon Sally's death, Harry is entitled to at least one-half—even if the joint tenancy was severed before her death. In the case of divorce, once real estate becomes community property, each spouse is entitled to a half-interest, regardless of which spouse supplied the payment.

Title in a Trust

If title is held in the name of a trust, the names of the individual owners are not a matter of public record. Therefore, if anyone wants to keep his ownership of certain real estate a secret, he sets up a land trust; and title to the property is taken in the name of the trust rather than the name of the owner. Confidentiality is not the only reason to put title to real estate into a land trust. Such a trust has only a bare legal title—the trustee can act only upon the written direction of the one who set up the trust (called the *Settlor* or *Grantor*) or the beneficiary or beneficiaries of the trust. Therefore, if title to real estate is held in a land trust, the settlor names the beneficiaries, but he need only advise the trustee by letter that he wants to change the beneficiaries; and upon the settlor's death, title to the property is given to the new beneficiaries instead of the old. This procedure is much simpler than leaving real estate to someone by bequest. Anyone who changes his mind about a bequest must execute a codicil to his will, with the same formal requisites of witnesses, writings, and the like required for the original will.

In addition, when title to real estate is in the names of two or more people who want to transfer title to someone else by gift or sale, all owners must sign a document called a *deed*, which transfers title. This could be difficult if the owners are in different states or even different countries at the time. If the title is held in a land trust, each person who has the authority can individually advise the trustee to execute the deed of conveyance.

Finally, if title is put in a land trust and the grantor of the trust does not retain any right to the title to his estate upon his death, the property is not subject to probate.

HOW IS TITLE TO REAL ESTATE ACQUIRED?

Sale

People usually transfer title to real estate by sale. The owner enters into a contract to sell his title in certain specified real estate to a buyer at an agreed to price. Remember that a contract to convey title to real estate must be in writing to conform to the statute of frauds, as discussed in Chapter 4.

Law

If a person obtains title to real estate by inheritance or by will (called a *devise*) or through the laws of community property or by a tax or other judicial sale, it is said that he acquired his title by action of law.

If a spouse dies intestate, the surviving spouse is entitled by law to a life interest in the estate of the deceased spouse. This interest amounts to anything from one-third to one-half and includes real estate. The wife's interest in the husband's estate is called *dower*, and the husband's interest in the wife's real estate is called *curtesy*.

Acts of the Parties

Of course, title can be transferred by an act of the owner—making a gift of title to an individual, an institution, or some governmental body. This is called dedicating the property.

Eminent Domain

When a government body condemns a piece of property and takes possession, this action is called acquiring title by *eminent domain*. To do this, the government body must go to court to prove that the public interest in the land is superior to the interest of the individual owner or owners. The owners must also be compensated for the loss of their property. The matter of such compensation is the most common cause of law suits between government bodies and individuals. The individual must be compensated fairly on the basis of the highest and best use that can be made of the property. The questions of what is "fair" and what is the "highest and best use" for which a property can be used are the things of which law suits are made.

Other Acquisition of Title

Title or use of real estate can be acquired by other less common methods.

Tax Sale. The owner of real estate is annually assessed a tax based on the fair market value of his property. If he fails to pay this tax, the taxing body may sell the title to the highest bidder at a public auction. Acting as seller, the court then conveys title to the buyer. The proceeds are used to pay the delinquent taxes, and any excess is paid to the original owner. The previous owner has a right to redeem his property from the buyer within a stipulated period of time, usually a year, by paying him the auction price plus court costs, attorney's fees, any other costs incurred, and interest at the rate provided by statute. After the period, the buyer, unless he engaged in fraudulent acts to acquire the title, cannot be forced to return title to the previous owner.

Homestead. Occasionally, the United States government permits people to settle on public land and own it. This is called *homestead.*

Adverse Possession. If a person uses someone else's land as his own in a manner open, notorious, and adverse to his neighbor for a long period of time, usually fifteen to twenty years, he acquires title. For example, Mr. Smith and Mr. Green own contiguous lots. Against the wishes of Mr. Green, Mr. Smith builds a fence on Mr. Green's land, thereby increasing his lot size and decreasing Mr. Green's. Mr. Smith then plants trees and bushes in that area, mows the lawn in that area and manages to get his tax assessment increased to cover that area. Mr. Green objects to Mr. Smith's acts, complains, and even threatens to take legal action against Mr. Smith for trespassing. If Mr. Green does nothing more to get his property back, after the statutory period has elapsed, Mr. Smith would own that strip of Mr. Green's land.

Prescription. Mr. Jones owns two adjoining lots. There are two buildings on them but one can gain entrance to one of the buildings only over the other lot. If Mr. Jones later subdivides the lots, people are given the right to cross the lot to continue to gain access to the other building. This is called a *prescriptive easement.*

Easement. An *easement* is a right given to someone, to the public, to a government body, or to a utility to cross or go over or under an owner's land. For example, a property owner owns not only the surface area of his land but everything above and below it to a reasonable distance. Since utilities must install wires above or below the land to provide service, they are given an easement by all property owners to place poles and string wires over their land or dig trenches and place wires under their land.

DEEDS

What constitutes evidence of title? After all, real estate consists of land, its improvements, and everything permanently attached to them. When owner ship is transferred, the property cannot physically be transferred, and there must be some way of identifying who owns what real estate and what real estated is owned. Ownership of real estate is transferred by a document, called a *deed*, signed by the sellers and conveying to the buyers their interest in the property. This deed becomes a notice to the public of who owns title to the property when it is recorded in a place where all public documents are officially recorded, such as a county recorder's office. Various kinds of deeds are used to transfer various interests in the real estate.

Warranty Deed. When title is given by a warranty deed, the seller guarantees, or warrants, that he has good title, that there are no undisclosed defects clouding the title, that the seller has the right and the authority to transfer the title, and that he is transferring unreservedly all of that to the buyer.

Quit Claim Deed. A quit claim deed is used when the transferor of the title does not want to make any warranties. By use of a quit claim deed, the transferor tells the new owner, "I'm not sure of what title I have, but I am conveying whatever I have to you." Obviously, this is not a very common document of transference. It usually is used in informal transfers—when joint tenants want to break their joint tenancy into a tenancy in common or when a husband or wife wants to transfer title from his or her own name to both names.

Bargain and Sale Deed. This type of deed is used in the same way as a quit claim deed.

Others. Other deeds are used for specific purposes:

1. *Release Deed,* used by a mortgage company to release its security deed, usually called a *trust deed.*

2. *Tax Sale Deed,* used by a court to convey title to property purchased at a tax sale.

3. *Trustee's Deed,* used by a trustee to convey title out of a trust.
4. *Deed in Trust,* used to convey title into a trust.
5. *Executor's Deed,* used by the executor of an estate to convey out of the estate title previously held by one who died.

LEGAL DESCRIPTIONS

In order to convey title to property, we must describe the property being transferred. This legal description is entered on the deed, so when it is recorded each parcel of real estate can be identified. The property is identified by various methods. Two of the most common are

1. By a system of meridians and parallels extending north and south and east and west. These divide a region into townships. Each township is then divided into thirty-six sections one mile square. Each section is sub-divided into lots. A legal description using this method might read as follows: Lot 24 in John S. Hovland's Subdivision, being a part of the North half of Section 18, Township 23, East of the third principal meridian.
2. By a description by reference to natural objects that are permanent and well known, such as trees, mountain ranges, or rocks. This is called a *metes and bounds* description.

SALES OF REAL ESTATE

People can offer to sell their real estate themselves or use a real estate broker to list it for sale. To sell property without a broker, one should advertise it for sale in local and other newspapers, place *for sale* signs on the property where they can be seen by people driving by, and be available to show their property to prospective buyers.

When property is listed for sale with a broker, the broker does these things. In addition, brokers usually cooperatively list the properties they are showing for their sellers. This is called *multiple listing*. A multiple listing means your property is listed for sale with a number of brokers. This increases the possibility for sale.

To list a property for sale with a broker, the seller signs an exclusive contract with the broker. The contract, which usually runs for sixty to ninety days, provides that if the property is sold during that period through the efforts of the listing broker, a cooperating broker, the owner, or anyone else, the broker will be entitled to a commission. The *commission* is a percentage of the selling price, usually 6 to 8 percent. If the property is sold after the exclusive period expires to someone who investigated it during the exclusive period, the broker is usually still entitled to a commission.

Since a listing agreement is a contract, any of its terms, including the commission rate, can be negotiated. When a broker finds a buyer ready, willing, and able to purchase the property at the asking price, the broker is entitled to the agreed commission—even if the seller changes his mind and refuses to go through with the deal. It should be noted that the seller pays the commission unless the contract of sale provides otherwise.

On the other hand, if the buyer refuses to go through with the sale, the seller is entitled to any forfeited earnest money deposited toward the selling price. In this case, the broker should *not* be entitled to a commission, because if the buyer refuses to proceed, the broker has not performed his duties. Many brokers' listing contracts and contracts of sale, however, provide that forfeited deposits will be paid to the broker. For this reason, a seller should examine all such contracts thoroughly before signing them and negotiate the best possible terms.

After the buyer and seller have agreed orally to the terms of sale, the seller should contact his attorney to have them reduced to a written contract. No other writing should be signed by either buyer or seller, no matter what the document is called; and the buyer should take the contract prepared by the seller's attorney to his own attorney for examination. The participation of attorneys for both seller and buyer is sometimes discouraged by brokers or their agents or by mortgage companies, the reason given being that attorneys unduly complicate or delay a closing by their requests for changes or additions to the contract. Nevertheless, although the broker earns his fee by finding a buyer and the mortgage house earns its money by charging interest on the loan, the lawyer earns his fee by protecting the interests of his client. Therefore, involving a lawyer is inexpensive protection, and any delays or demanded changes or alterations are for the client's interest only.

After the terms of the contract have been approved by the attorneys, the contract is signed by the buyers and the sellers. The contract contains all terms of the sale, the legal description of the property being conveyed, and its selling price. It names the buyers and specifies in what manner they are taking title, whether as joint tenants, tenants in common, or some other way. It describes any personal property being sold and lists any contingencies that could affect the sale. It also lists any conditions to which the title may be subject, such as easements. It states the date by which the sale must be closed, and the kind of deed by which the title is being conveyed.

In signing the contract, the buyer usually deposits with a disinterested party a sum called *earnest money*, which is a deposit—usually 10 percent of the selling price—to insure that the buyer is in earnest in purchasing this property. If the seller can deliver good title and if none of the contingencies named in the contract occur, the buyer must complete the purchase or forfeit his earnest money.

Purchase with a Mortgage

One of the contingencies provided for in the contract of sale, unless the buyer is buying on contract or for cash, is that the buyer be able to obtain a mortgage on terms with which he can live. Therefore, one of the first things such a buyer will do after signing a contract of sale is find a mortgage house that will lend him the money. Mortgage houses include banks, savings and loan associations, and other mortgage finance companies. Within the industry, terms can vary from institution to institution. It is therefore wise to shop around for the best possible terms. A mortgage institution may lend up to 90 percent of the fair market value or cost of the property, whichever is less.

The buyer files an application with the lender. A check is made of his credit worthiness and his ability to repay the loan over the period he is requesting, and an appraisal is made of the property. If the lending officers are satisfied, the loan is approved. The lending institution will charge a fee for making the appraisal and *points*. These points, which are a service charge for handling the paper work in making the loan, can be 1 to 3 or more percent of the amount borrowed, and this amount is deducted from the gross amount of the loan. After the loan is made, it will appear as a lien against the title to the property until it is paid in full. A *lien* is a right against some property as security for a debt.

Purchase for Cash

If a property is purchased entirely for cash, there is no mortgage or lien; and the purchase price is paid at the closing of the deal.

Purchase on Contract

Sometimes, if a buyer is unable or unwilling to obtain a mortgage and does not have enough cash to purchase the property outright, a seller is willing to sell the property *on contract*. This is an installment sale of the property. The buyer makes a down payment and signs a contract wherein he agrees to pay the balance of the selling price directly to the seller in periodic, usually monthly, installments over a period of years. The seller collects interest on the unpaid balance with each installment payment. There is one significant difference between buying with a mortgage and buying on contract: When one buys with a mortgage and the closing takes place, title is conveyed immediately to the buyer by deed, subject to the mortgage. When one buys on contract, title is not conveyed until the contract terms are fulfilled. Therefore, until the contract balance is paid in full, the seller retains the title. If the buyer defaults in any of the terms of the contract before it is completed, he can lose the property to the seller, and with it all the money he has paid up to the date of the default.

For example, Mr. Blue sells 100 acres of land to Mr. Brown for $100,000 on contract. After paying $40,000 in down payment and installments, Mr. Brown defaults in making his next payment. Mr. Blue can declare the contract breached, cancel it, evict Mr. Brown from the property, and keep Mr. Brown's $40,000. This is the danger in a sale on contract.

Evidence of Good Title

The fact that the purported seller is in possession of the property or says he owns it should not satisfy the buyer. The seller must show evidence of good title; and if the conveyance is to be by warranty deed, the seller's ownership must be free of undisclosed encumbrances or clouds on the title. To insure this, the seller has a title search made, sometimes by his attorney, who submits a title report showing ownership and recorded transactions from the first recorded conveyance to the present, at other times by a title company, whose search and report usually reflect only current outstanding clouds on the title and do not give the history of the property.

The Closing

After the buyer arranges financing and the seller shows evidence of good title, the closing is set. At the closing, the seller gives the buyer a deed of the kind contracted for, an affidavit showing he still has good title, and a bill of sale for any personal property sold with the real estate. Such personal property includes carpeting, window shades, range, refrigerator, or the like. The buyer presents the seller with a check for the net proceeds, the sale is closed, and the deed or contract sale agreement is recorded for public notice.

The buyer receives a check for the net proceeds because certain items are pro-rated between buyer and seller at the closing. For example:

1. If the seller still has a mortgage recorded as a lien against the property, the buyer wants to be sure that loan is paid. Therefore, the amount necessary to pay the debt, as determined from a payoff letter obtained from the lender, is deducted from the amount the seller gets and remitted directly to the lender.

2. The seller has to pay for the title search. In addition, the buyer wants to be sure his deed or contract is recorded. There is also a charge for doing this. Generally the same third party or title company does both. Therefore, the buyer, to be sure his deed is recorded, will agree to pay the seller's title search charges at the same time he pays for getting his documents recorded. He then deducts these charges from the amount the seller is entitled to and sends the total amount to the third party.

3. Many places require that a seller pay for revenue stamps before a deed is recorded. This is a source of revenue for the political body that requires these stamps. Generally, the buyer agrees to pay for these stamps to be sure they are purchased and the documents can be recorded, again deducting their cost from the seller's proceeds.

4. Usually the final amount deducted from the seller's proceeds takes care of pro-rated real estate taxes. Because real estate taxes are assessed against a property and not against its owner and are assessed in one year and billed in the next, the seller is liable for his share of those taxes from January 1 until the date of closing. Thus, if the sale is closed on September 30, the seller is liable for three-quarters of the real estate tax and the buyer will be liable for one-quarter.

5. Sometimes the *buyer* has to pay the *seller* for additional items. Some of these might include unused fuel oil left in the tanks at the time of closing or prepaid insurance or prepaid scavenger service the buyer expects to use.

6. If rental property is being conveyed and there are tenants' deposits or prepaid rentals, these items must also be pro-rated between buyer and seller.

These various items usually are listed on a form called a "closing statement" or "pro-ration statement." The items are explained by the attorneys to their clients, and when everyone is satisfied, the buyer and the seller generally sign and exchange copies to show their acceptance of the figures.

After the documents have been signed and the net proceeds have been paid to the seller, the deed or contract is given to the buyer, or to someone acting on his behalf, it is recorded, and the sale is completed.

CONDOMINIUMS AND COOPERATIVE APARTMENTS

Because of smaller families and because people live longer than before, many people are buying condominiums or cooperative apartments rather than single-family or multiple family homes.

In a cooperative apartment building, the individual apartment owners own stock in the cooperative. They share one real estate tax bill, one mortgage payment, and if applicable, one water bill and one fire insurance bill. Each owner has one vote regardless of the size of his unit.

In a condominium, individuals vote on a proportionate basis and individual owners are responsible only for the real estate taxes on their own units. Each condominium owner is responsible only for financing the purchase of his own unit and hence only for the mortgage on his own unit. He may be responsible for a proportionate share of maintenance costs for the whole building, but only if he contracts to be so liable. Generally, in both cooperative and condominium apartment buildings, a unit cannot be sold without the permission of the other owners; but in a condominium, this restriction can be enforced only if the unit owner contracts to be so restricted.

A condominium building is usually operated and maintained by a condominium association. The owner of each unit can vote for the officers of the association, and his vote at association meetings is based upon his proportionate share of ownership in the building. He usually pays a monthly charge for maintenance of the areas of common use. However, except for this association, each unit owner is as independent of any other unit owner as separate homeowners are.

RESTRICTIONS AND NEIGHBOR PROBLEMS

A local government has a right to set certain building standards, so as to maintain the character of the municipality. The only requirement on such building and zoning restrictions is that they be reasonable. A *zoning restriction* might take the form of an ordinance that prohibits building a gas station in the midst of a residential neighborhood. A *building restriction* might determine the maximum height to which a building can be built or the material from which it can be constructed or the amount of open area that must be maintained between buildings on adjoining lots. This last requirement is called a *set back*. Set backs may apply to side yards, front yards, rear yards, or all three. For example, a city's building code may require that "no building may be built closer to the front or rear property line than 50 feet, and no closer to the lot line on either side of the building than 12 feet." These are building restrictions. Building codes may also require that the buildings built in a certain area be "no less than 80 percent brick or stone," or that in a certain area "no building may be built which is more than four stories high." These are also building restrictions.

Occasionally, the owner of an entire area subdivides it into separate lots and sells them to potential home builders. To maintain the character of the subdivision, he may also place building restrictions on those lots. He does this by providing these restrictions in his deed of conveyance. The restriction is then recorded and passed from owner to owner each time the property is conveyed. So long as the restrictions are reasonable and do not conflict with any ordinances or statutes, they may be enforced against any original or subsequent lot purchaser by the original subdivider or his estate or heirs. Restricting sales to people of a certain race or religion is not enforceable, and prohibiting the use of alcoholic beverages on the premises is generally not enforceable.

Except for these restrictions, a homeowner can build on or use his property for any legal purpose, so long as he does not interfere with his neighbor's air or light or quiet enjoyment of his property.

One item that causes controversy is trees. One cannot interfere with the natural growth of trees or shrubbery. Therefore, if a tree growing on your neighbor's property offends you, there is not much you can do about it. However, if the limbs of the tree extend over your lot, you can cut them back to your side of the property line. If a tree or shrub is growing between the two properties, you can unilaterally trim the limbs back, so long as you do not kill the tree. You are prohibited from removing the tree or doing anything to damage or kill it.

Another item of common controversy between property owners is the flow of water from one person's lot to another's. If one person lives on a lot higher than someone else's, his lot is superior; and he needs take no steps to prevent water from draining on to his neighbor's land, no matter how difficult this makes things for his neighbor. However, neither owner can do anything to dam up the water or change its natural flow if this action can damage a neighbor or his property. Should a property owner take these actions, the injured property owner can sue to remove any offending structures and recover any damages suffered.

MECHANICS' LIENS AND JUDGMENTS

When a tradesman does work on a person's land or building, he is entitled to a *mechanic's lien* against that property to insure that he gets paid. When a tradesman wants part payment or full payment for his work, therefore, a property owner should request a *partial waiver of lien* or *final waiver of lien* if the work or money involved is substantial. For example, if you call a plumber to change a washer, you would not ask for a waiver of lien. If, however, the plumber installed a whole plumbing system throughout the building, you would get a waiver.

The right to a mechanic's lien is granted by statute, but the requirements, including time requirements, must be scrupulously followed or the right can be lost. In addition, the enforcement of the lien is complex and should not be attempted without an attorney.

A person can find a lien recorded against his property if someone gets a judgment in court against him. A *judgment* is a declaration in a court of law of the legal rights and obligations of the parties to a suit. If this judgment is not paid, the judgment order may be recorded against the real estate of the losing party; and if the judgment continues to be unpaid, the real estate can be sold to satisfy the judgment.

INCOME TAXATION OF REAL ESTATE TRANSACTIONS

Buying, owning, and selling real estate can have various tax effects. For example, if you itemize your tax deductions, the real estate taxes and mortgage interest you pay are deductible. If you pay a sales tax on the purchase of large appliances (washing machine, dryer, refrigerator, or stove), this tax is deductible.

If a property is used for commercial or investment purposes, all costs of operating the building are deductible: insurance, repairs, utilities, labor, and depreciation. *Depreciation* is an accounting concept which provides that the cost of property purchased or built, called an *asset*, should be applied against the income produced from the use of that asset instead of being charged off entirely in the year of purchase. For example, if a building to be used for office rentals is purchased at a cost of $150,000 and it is anticipated that it will be used for this purpose for fifty years; $3,000 of the cost will be charged against the rental income from that building each year for 50 years.

If you sell your personal residence for more than you paid for it, your gain on the sale is taxable. If you invest the selling price in another personal residence for yourself of the same or greater value, then the gain is deferred and is not taxed in the year of sale. For instance, Mr. Byer bought a house of $20,000 which he sold ten years later for $40,000. He would have $20,000 in taxable gain. If he invests that $40,000 in another house for himself that costs $60,000, however, the gain is not taxable in the year of sale. However, the basis of the new house is reduced by the unrecognized gain to $40,000 ($60,000 minus $20,000), and when the second house is sold, any sale in excess of $40,000 is taxed, unless the selling price is again invested in a personal house of the same or greater cost than the selling price.

One other income tax relief is available to taxpayers fifty-five years of age or older. If a taxpayer in that age category lives in his house for the required time and then sells it, up to $100,000 of a gain from that sale is excluded from his taxable income forever. However, this exclusion can be taken only once, and any unused difference between the gain and $100,000 that cannot be used is also gone and cannot be saved for a subsequent sale.

14

LANDLORD AND TENANT

The previous chapter discussed ownership of real estate. This chapter deals with the rights and obligations of the parties when a property is not owned but rented. The landlord or the owner of the property is called the *lessor*. The tenant or renter is called the *lessee*. The agreement that sets out the rights and obligations of the lessor and the lessee is called a *lease*. Because a lease agreement is a contract, all comments made about contracts in Chapter 4 apply to leases. A lease may be written or oral, it may be express or implied, and the parties must have the capacity to enter into it. In addition, as with any other contract, the terms of a lease are subject to negotiation.

Premises may be leased for any lawful purpose. If legal restrictions make it difficult but not impossible for a tenant to carry on the business for which his premises were leased, he is not relieved from the duty of paying rent. However, if premises are leased for an illegal purpose, no rent may be recovered unless they are so used without the knowledge of the landlord.

A lease may be made for an expressed period of time or it may be at will or it may be at sufferance. A *tenancy at sufferance* is an informal agreement for a lease for an indefinite period. Such an agreement is often called a month-to-month lease, because the tenant and landlord agree that the tenant may remain in possession of the premises unless the lease is terminated by either party by giving the other thirty days notice of the termination.

A tenancy for a fixed period may be terminated during that time only by the landlord, who must give the tenant sixty days notice of the termination. The tenant has no right to terminate a lease until its period is over.

A tenancy for a fixed period of time usually specifies a year or longer. It is made in writing to comply with the statute of frauds, which provides that a contract that cannot be performed in less than one year must be in writing. A year-to-year tenancy also requires that written notice of termination be given to the tenant sixty days before the end of the year in which the lease terminates.

A written lease should contain the following:

1. The names of the landlord and the tenant.
2. The period of the lease.
3. The amount of the rent and whether it is to be paid monthly, annually, or at some other interval.
4. The address of the property.
5. The amount of any security deposit.
6. The purpose for which the property has been leased.
7. The rights and obligations of both the landlord and the tenant.
8. The signatures of both the landlord and the tenant.

Since a lease is a contract, any change in its terms must be supported by some new consideration. Therefore, if a tenant pays a landlord a reduced rent and the landlord accepts it for a period of time, this action is not a permanent change in the lease terms unless the tenant does something for the landlord he is not legally obligated to do. Without such consideration, the landlord can demand at any time that the original rent again be paid. Suppose Mr. Handy leases property from Mrs. Homer for one year at a monthly rental of $500. Mr. Handy has some business setbacks and pays Mrs. Homer $300 per month for four months. The fact that Mrs. Homer accepts $300 per month does not change the rent to $300 per month; after the four months, Mrs. Homer can demand that Mr. Handy again pay $500 or be in breach of the lease. If, however, Mr. Handy offers to repair the roof or pay the real estate taxes or do some other thing he is not required to do in exchange for the reduced rent and Mrs. Homer accepts the offer, the rent is reduced to $300 per month; and it cannot again be returned unilaterally to $500.

A lease differs from other contracts in one major respect. Most contracts require the personal service of the parties, and one party cannot assign his interest without the permission of the other. With a lease, this restriction usually applies only to the tenant. That is, most leases cannot be assigned by a tenant without the express approval of the landlord, but the landlord may assign the lease by selling the building. A purchaser takes title to the building subject to any leases, but as the new owner, he stands precisely in the shoes of the seller. Each tenant must perform his duties to the new landlord under his lease as he did to the old landlord. However, the new landlord has no right to evict any tenant, except for a breach of lease terms, until the period of his lease expires; and he cannot change the terms of an existing lease. Therefore, anyone purchasing a building occupied by tenants should examine any existing leases and in the contract of purchase should prevent any new leases from being executed between the contract date and the closing date.

During the term of a lease, the tenant has a right to the absolute possession of the premises for any lawful purpose without any interference or disturbance from the landlord or from any other tenant. This is called the *right of quiet enjoyment.* The tenant is obligated to pay the rent in the amount and on the day provided in the lease. If the due day for the rent falls on a Sunday or holiday, the rent is due the next business day. If the lease is for a specific period of time, not for month-to-month tenancy, and the tenant remains in possession after the lease expires, the landlord may sue to remove the tenant as a trespasser and to obtain rent for the period of holding over in possession, as well as any damages suffered by the landlord or to the premises. If the landlord chooses, he may elect instead to treat the lease as reexecuted by the tenant for another period the same as the previous term of the lease and hold the tenant liable for rent for that period.

If the tenant moves out before the expiration date of the lease, he is still liable for the rent until the end of the lease period. The landlord, however, is obligated to reasonably try to find another tenant; but if he can find a tenant only at a reduced rental, the old tenant is liable for the difference between the reduced rent and the original rent.

If the premises are destroyed or substantially destroyed so they cannot be occupied or the tenant is evicted or the parties agree to terminate the tenancy, the tenant is relieved of any further obligation to pay rent. If condemnation occurs and all of the property is appropriated by the government, the lease is also terminated. However, if only a part of the premises is taken and a part is left that can be occupied by the tenant, the lease continues.

If the landlord breaches an essential promise made in the lease, the tenant may move out and be relieved from further obligation. For example, suppose that in leasing space in a shopping center to a tenant who sells luggage the landlord promises that he will not accept another tenant who also sells luggage. If the landlord later rents to another luggage dealer, the first tenant may consider this a breach of an essential provision of the lease and move out without liability for future rents.

How may a tenant be evicted? If a tenant breaches some term or terms of a lease, a landlord may declare the lease terminated and require that the tenant move out after reasonable notice. If the tenant does not move out, he becomes a trespasser, and the landlord may take legal action to have him evicted and to recover damages. If a tenant fails to pay his rent or if he consistently pays his rent late or in less than the lease amount, the landlord may terminate the lease. If a tenant responds to a notice of eviction by paying his rent and the landlord accepts the payment, the landlord has waived his right to evict the tenant unless the lease is breached again. Whenever a landlord makes a statutory demand for rent and sets forth a period by which it must be paid, if the tenant tenders the rent during that period, the landlord is prevented from forfeiting the lease. This forfeiture is prevented even if the landlord refuses the tender, because the tender is as legally valid as actual payment.

Another type of eviction is called *constructive eviction.* This occurs when a landlord takes some action that makes the premises uninhabitable. For example, if the landlord turns off the water or the gas or the heat in winter or the air conditioning in summer, the tenant may consider that the lease is terminated and that he has been evicted. He can then move out without any further obligation under the lease. In fact, if the landlord by his action has caused any damage to the tenant or his property or his business, the tenant can also sue the landlord for damages. A mere breakdown of some apparatus, such as the heating equipment, which can be repaired, does not amount to constructive eviction; and in such cases, the lease continues.

Unless the lease provides otherwise, a tenant is required to make repairs to his premises, except for any common areas, which are in control of the landlord. For instance, if a tenant lives in an apartment building where the landlord provides heat to all the apartments, the landlord has the duty to repair the furnace if it breaks down; but if a tenant leases a store with its own heating unit, the tenant is required to fix it if it breaks down. This repair obligation also applies to store windows and roofs. If the rented premises is a house rather than an apartment, the tenant is liable for repairs since he has exclusive control of the premises. The same rules apply to the removal of snow and garbage. In an apartment building, the landlord is responsible for their removal; but in a store or house, the tenant is responsible. If someone falls because of the tenant's failure to remove the snow, the tenant is liable for any damages. If there is damage to the structural part of the premises, such as a wall, ceiling, or floor, the landlord is responsible for the repair. The landlord is not usually responsible for personal injuries sustained by a tenant or those entering for the purpose of dealing with the tenant if such injuries result from a dangerous or defective condition of the premises wholly under the control of the tenant, unless the landlord has been guilty of concealing some latent defects.

When a tenant vacates the premises, he has the duty to return the premises in the condition he received them, normal wear and tear excepted and to remove his belongings as soon as possible. He must replace any fixtures he removed; and if he dug holes in the wall for mounting things, he must refill, replaster, and repaint these holes. If he fails to remove his personal belongings as soon as possible after he vacates, the landlord may remove them and charge the tenant for their storage.

Although most leases provide that a tenant cannot assign his lease without the consent of the landlord, if a lease does not have this prohibition, then under both common law and the statutory laws of most states, the lease may be assigned. Most leases also bear a prohibition against *subleasing*. An *assignment* differs from a *sublease* in that if a lease is assigned, the original tenant is relieved of any further responsibility under the lease and the new tenant has all of the obligation to comply with its terms. If another tenant is substituted for the original tenant by a sublease, however, the second tenant only takes the lease through the first tenant. Should the new tenant breach the lease, the first tenant is still liable. Suppose Mr. Lesser leases an apartment from Mr. Bigg for four years at a monthly rental of $200. After three years, Mr. Lesser sublets the apartment to Miss Skipper and moves out. Miss Skipper is now responsible for complying with the terms of the lease; but if she should fail to make a monthly rental payment, Mr. Bigg could sue Mr. Lesser for any unpaid rent, and Mr. Lesser would have to sue Miss Skipper to recover for any money he had to pay out. On the other hand, if Mr. Lesser was able to assign the lease to Miss Skipper when he moved out, then if Miss Skipper defaults in the rent payments, Mr. Bigg can sue only Miss Skipper, and Mr. Lesser is free and clear of any responsibility for any breach by Miss Skipper.

Because a lease specifies a fixed period of time, many leases provide an *option* for renewal. An option is merely a promise or covenant to renew the lease for an additional definite period with definite terms and conditions. An option to extend or renew a lease must be exercised in accordance with the terms of the option agreement, and the notice that the tenant intends to exercise his option must be given to the landlord some time before the termination date of the original lease.

When a lease covers a certain period and the term expires, the tenant must move out, and no statutory notice is required from the landlord to terminate the lease. However, when default is made in any of the terms of a lease, the landlord must give the tenant up to ten days notice that the breach must be cured within five days or the lease will be terminated and the tenant evicted. This notice should be in writing; it must be clear, intelligible, and definite; and it must be served on the tenant or given to a person above the age of ten years residing in or in possession of the premises. The notice can be as simple as,

To A.B.: You are hereby notified that in consequence of your default in [here insert the character of the default] of the premises now occupied by you, being [here identify the premises], I have elected to terminate your lease, and you are hereby notified to quit and deliver up possession of the same to me within ten days of this date.
Dated this ________ day of ____________, 19 ______.
[Signature of landlord or his agent]

If a landlord orally leases the premises to one tenant and then leases it to another and puts that person in possession before the first tenant takes possession, the first tenant can either sue to eject the second tenant or sue for breach of contract and for any damages he suffered as a result of the landlord's failure to deliver possession. This suit for damages may be maintained even though the tenant has never been in possession. A new tenant may sue to put out a tenant who remains in possession after the expiration of his term.

If a tenant sues for damages, the damages must be proven with a reasonable degree of certainty and cannot be speculative. Ordinarily, the measure of damages for a landlord's failure to give possession is the excess rent the tenant has to pay to rent alternative premises. The loss of probable profits from a business to be operated from the premises is not part of recoverable damages.

If farm lands are rented, there is an implication of law that they shall be used for such purpose and that the soil shall not be unnecessarily exhausted by negligent or improper tillage. A tenant in possession of farm land is entitled to the crops grown during his tenancy, but he is not entitled to crops maturing after the termination of the lease. Those belong to the landlord.

Finally we come to the question of *security deposits.* There is no legal requirement that a tenant make a deposit in order to lease some premises, but a lease may require that he make a security deposit to insure that the rent is paid or the property returned in reasonably good condition when the lease is terminated. The deposit may be applied only to the purpose specified in the lease or any agreement regarding the lease deposit. In other words, if a deposit is intended to insure that the property will be returned in good condition or to repair any damage, it cannot be used to pay the last months' rents. That is, the landlord can still recover the rent while retaining the security deposited for the good condition of the property. Of course, the landlord cannot retain a deposit forever. He must within a reasonable time inspect the premises and repair any damage or return the deposit. Some states also have laws requiring landlords to pay interest on tenants' security deposits.

The owner of property may peaceably enter the premises while they are in possession of the tenant, during the term of the lease or after it has expired, or if they are in the possession of a wrongdoer for an unlawful purpose. For example, if the walls of an apartment are ruined because of rain or snow or fire, the landlord has the right to enter the premises to make them again suitable for occupancy.

If a tenant breaches a provision of the lease causing forfeiture or a landlord discovers that his premises are being used for an illegal purpose, he may enter the premises and take possession of them. However, he cannot use force to enter the premises; and if the tenant refuses to permit him to enter, he can do so only by a civil suit for *forcible entry and detainer.* By this suit, he obtains a court order permitting him to enter, and he can call upon the law enforcement body charged with the responsibility to help him gain access. If the landlord wrongfully takes or attempts to take possession of the premises by force, he can be liable to the tenant for damages.

15

MARRIAGE

WHO CAN MARRY

Marriage is a contract between two people, the terms of which are determined by law. Contemporary marriage laws, except as they have been changed by statute, are part of our common law, which we inherited from England. English matrimonial law in turn came from Medieval canon law as it evolved in the Roman Church. Canon law itself derived from ancient Roman law. All of these have influenced our modern law of marriage.

Because it is public policy to favor the institution of marriage, marriages will be upheld wherever possible, and they will be considered valid unless someone proves that they are not. While marriage is a contract, it is different from usual business contracts in the following ways:

1. The mental capacity required to contract marriage is somewhat less, according to some courts.

2. People can enter into a marriage contract at a younger age than they need attain to make business contracts.

3. The contract of marriage cannot be revoked by the parties to it. Only a competent court acting for society can issue a judgment revoking a marriage.

4. The personal rights or obligations created by marriage cannot be assigned, transferred, or delegated to someone else.

5. The remedies for breach of contract of marriage or for termination of the state of being married are different from the remedies for breaches of ordinary contracts.

Table 1. Marriage Laws As of December 31, 1979*

State or other jurisdiction	Age at which marriage can be contracted without perental consent		Age at which marriage can be contracted with parental consent		Blood tests & other medical requirements		Waiting period		Common law marriage	
	Male	Female	Male	Female	Maximum period between examination & issuance of license (days)	Scope of medical inquiry	Before issuance of license	After issuance of license	May be contracted in state but not valid if attempted after date shown	Recognized if valid at time & place where contracted
Alabama	18	18	17(a)	14(a)	30	(b)	—	—	Yes	Yes
Alaska	18	18	16(c)	16(c)	30	(b)	3 da.	—	1/1/64	Yes
Arizona	18	18	16(c)	16(c)	30	(b)	(d)	—	No	Yes(e)
Arkansas	18	18	17(c)	16(c)	30	(b)	3 da.	—	No	Yes
California	18	18	18(a,c)	16(a,c)	30	(b,f,g,h)	—	—	1895	Yes
Colorado	18	18	16(c)	16(c)	30	(b,g,i)	—	—	Yes	Yes
Connecticut	18	18	16(c)	16(c)	35	(b)	4 da.	—	No	(j)
Delaware	18	18	18(c)	16(c)	30	(b)	—	(k)	No	Yes(e)
Florida	18	18	16(a,c)	16(a,c)	30	(b)	3 da.	—	1/1/68	Yes
Georgia	18(l)	18(l)	16(c,l)	16(c,l)	30	(b,f)	3 da.(m)	—	Yes	Yes
Hawaii	18	18	16	16(c)	30	(b,g)	—	—	(n)	Yes
Idaho	18	18	16(c)	16(c)	—	(g)	(o)	—	Yes	Yes
Illinois	18	18	16(c)	16(c)	15	(b,f)	3 da.	—	6/30/05	(e,j)
Indiana	18	18	17(c)	17(c)	30	(b,f)	3 da.	—	1/1/58	(e,j)
Iowa	18	18	16	16	20	(b)	3 da.	—	Yes	Yes
Kansas	18	18	18(c)	18(c)	30	(b)	3 da.	—	Yes(p)	Yes
Kentucky	18	18	(a,q)	(a,q)	15	(b,f)	3 da.	—	(n)	Yes
Louisiana	18	18	18(c)	16(c)	10	(b)	—	72 hrs.	(n)	(j)
Maine	18	18	16(c)	16(c)	60	(b)	5 da.	—	(j)	(j)
Maryland	18	18	16(c)	16(c)	—	—	48 hrs.	—	No	Yes
Massachusetts	18	18	18(c)	18(c)	30	(b,g)	3 da.	—	No	Yes(e)
Michigan	18	18	(r)	16	33	(b)	3 da.	—	1/1/57	Yes
Minnesota	18	18	18	16(s)	—	—	5 da.	—	4/26/41	Yes
Mississippi	21	21	17(c)	15(c)	30	(b)	3 da.	—	4/5/56	(j)
Missouri	18	18	15(c)	15(c)	15	(b)	3 da.	—	3/3/21	(j)
Montana	18	18	18(c)	18(c)	20	(b)	5 da.	3 da.	Yes	Yes
Nebraska	19	19	17	17	30	(b,g)	2 da.	—	1923	Yes
Nevada	18	18	16(a,c)	16(a,c)	—	—	—	—	3/29/43	Yes
New Hampshire	18	18	14(s)	13(s)	30(t)	(b)	3 da.	—	No	Yes(e)

New Jersey	18	18	16(c)	16(c)	30	(b)	72 hrs.	—	1/12/39	Yes
New Mexico	18	18	16(c)	16(c)	30	(b)	72 hrs.	—	No	Yes
New York	18	18	16	14(u)	30	(b,f)	—	24 da.(v)	4/29/33	Yes
North Carolina	18	18	16	16(c)	30	(b,g,w,x)	—	—	No	Yes
North Dakota	18	18	16	16	30	(b,y)	—	—	No	Yes(e)
Ohio	18	18	18(c)	16(c)	30	(b)	5 da.	—	Yes	Yes
Oklahoma	18	18	16(c)	16(c)	30	(b)	(o)	—	Yes	Yes
Oregon	18	18	17	17	30	(b)	—	(z)	No	Yes
Pennsylvania	18	18	16(c)	16(c)	30	(b,aa)	3 da.	—	Yes	Yes
Rhode Island	18	18	18(c)	16(c)	40	(b,g,x)	—	—	Yes	(j)
South Carolina	18	18	16(c)	14(c)	—	—	24 hrs.	—	Yes	Yes
South Dakota	18	18	16(c)	16(c)	20	(b)	—	—	7/1/59	(j)
Tennessee	18	18	16(c)	16(c)	30	(b)	3 da.(ab)	—	No	Yes
Texas	18	18	14(c)	14(c)	21	(b)	—	—	Yes	Yes
Utah	18	18	16(a)	14(a)	30	(b)	—	—	No	Yes
Vermont	18	18	16(c)	16(c)	30	(b)	—	5 da.	No	(j)
Virginia	18	18	16(a,c)	16(a,c)	30	(b)	—	—	1631	Yes
Washington	18	18	17(c)	17(c)	—	(b,x,ac)	3 da.	—	No	Yes
West Virginia	18	18	(q)	(q)	30	(b)	3 da.	—	No	Yes
Wisconsin	18	18	16	16	20	(b)	5 da.	—	1913	(j)
Wyoming	19	19	17(c)	16(c)	30	(b)	—	—	No	Yes
Dist. of Col.	18	18	16(a)	16(a)	30	(b)	3 da.	—	Yes	Yes
Puerto Rico	21	21	18(c)	16(c)	10(ad)	(b,ac)	—	—	No	(e,j)

*Prepared by the Women's Bureau, U.S. Department of Labor, with the assistance of the attorneys general of the states.

(a) Parental consent not required if previously married.
(b) Venereal diseases.
(c) Legal procedure for younger persons to obtain license.
(d) Blood test must be on record at least 48 hours before issuance of license.
(e) If permanent residents (domiciliaries) attempt to contract a common law marriage in another state, such marriage is not valid in state where domiciled.
(f) Sickle cell anemia.
(g) Rubella immunity.
(h) Tay-Sachs disease.
(i) Rh factor.
(j) Legal status uncertain; will probably recognize marriage if valid where contracted.
(k) Residents, 24 hours: nonresidents, 96 hours.
(l) Parental consent is not needed regardless of age in cases of pregnancy or when couple has a living child born out of wedlock.
(m) Unless parties are 18 years of age or over, or woman is pregnant, or applicants are the parents of a living child born out of wedlock.
(n) Generally no, but may be recognized for limited purposes, e.g., legitimacy of children, workers' compensation benefits, etc.
(o) Three days if parties are under 18 years of age.
(p) However, contracting such a marriage is a misdemeanor.
(q) No minimum age.
(r) No provision in the law for parental consent for males.
(s) Permission of judge also required.
(t) Maximum period between blood test and date of intended marriage.
(u) If under 16 years of age, consent of family court judge also required.
(v) However, marriage may not be solemnized within 3 days of date on which specimen for blood test was taken.
(w) Mental competence.
(x) Tuberculosis.
(y) Some marriages prohibited if a party is severely retarded.
(z) License valid 3 days after application signed and valid for 30 days thereafter.
(aa) Court order needed if party is weakminded, insane, or of unsound mind.
(ab) May be waived if certain conditions are met.
(ac) Affidavit of mental competence required. Also, no epilepsy in Puerto Rico.
(ad) Maximum time from blood test to expiration of license.

6. Generally, a marriage contract is entered into in a ceremonial marriage performed by a civil or religious official authorized by the state to perform such a ceremony.

7. More than simple agreement is required before the parties can enter into a contract of marriage. They must obtain medical examinations and licenses, make a ceremonial exchange of vows before witnesses, and have the marriage recorded.

Table 1 shows some of the requirements for marriage in the various states.

AGE

The marriage of a person under the *age of consent* is void where state statute so provides; and otherwise, such a marriage is usually voidable. However, it is universally held that such a marriage may be ratified and made completely valid and binding when the underaged party reaches the age of consent. This ratification may be as simple an act as the parties continuing to live together as husband and wife after the age of consent is attained.

MENTAL CAPACITY

As to mental capacity, the test seems to be whether the person has the capacity to understand the nature of the marriage contract and the duties and responsibilities created. Even if a person is subject to temporary or periodic insanity, the marriage will be valid if performed during a lucid time.

If a person is so intoxicated by drugs or liquor as to be incapable of understanding the nature of the marriage contract, the marriage may be voidable. However, any lesser degree of intoxication will have no effect on the validity of the marriage.

Once again, a marriage that is voidable because of mental incapacity or intoxication can be made valid if the incompetent person freely lives with the other as husband or wife after regaining sanity or during lucid intervals or after the period of intoxication.

PHYSICAL HEALTH

There are very few requirements as to the physical health of the parties, except that most states require a physician's certificate that the parties do not have any venereal disease before a marriage license can be issued. In some states, if a woman is pregnant by anyone other than her husband-to-be and this fact is unknown to the husband when they enter the marital state, the marriage is voidable.

If one of the parties is impotent (that is, unable to have sexual intercourse) and this impotency is permanent, incurable, unknown to the one not under disability, the marriage is voidable. Sterility, which is the inability to have children, is not a disqualification for marriage if the parties can have sexual intercourse.

CONSENT

Free and voluntary consent, understandingly given, is essential to a valid marriage. Without such consent, a marriage ceremony is a nullity; and where such consent is obtained by fraud or duress, the marriage is voidable.

PARTIES TO A MARRIAGE

Under the Uniform Marriage and Divorce Act §207(a), the following marriages are prohibited:

1. A marriage entered into prior to the dissolution of an earlier marriage of one of the parties.
2. A marriage between an ancestor and a descendant (parent and child or grandparent and grandchild) or between a brother and a sister, whether the relationship is by the half or whole blood or by adoption.
3. A marriage between an uncle and a niece or between an aunt and a nephew, whether the relationship is by the half or the whole blood, except as to marriages permitted by the established customs or aboriginal cultures.

Parties to a marriage prohibited under this section who cohabit after removal of the impediment are lawfully married as of the date of the removal of the impediment. Children born of a prohibited marriage are legitimate. Finally, although certain states may have other or additional prohibitions, all states provide that a marriage must be made between a male and a female to be valid.

Marriage between first cousins was not prohibited at common law, and nearly one-half the states permit such marriages.

COMMON LAW MARRIAGES

Not all states recognize common law marriages. They are recognized in Alabama, California (if entered into before 1895), Colorado, District of

Columbia, Florida, Georgia, Idaho, Indiana, Iowa, Michigan (if entered into prior to January 1957), Minnesota (if entered into prior to April 26, 1941), Mississippi (if entered into prior to 1956), Missouri (if entered into prior to March 31, 1921), Montana, Nebraska (if entered into prior to 1923), New Jersey (if entered into prior to Novembet 30, 1939), New York (if entered into prior to April 29, 1933), Ohio, Oklahoma, Pennsylvania, Rhode Island, South Carolina, South Dakota, and Texas.

For a common law marriage to be valid, the parties must agree either in writing or orally to the marriage, hold themselves out to the public as being husband and wife, and cohabit—that is, openly live together as a married couple. There is no requirement of a ceremonial wedding.

A common law marriage carries with it the same rights and incidents as a ceremonial marriage, such as the rights of inheritance, descent and distribution, dower, and other property rights. Also, in the absence of a statute providing otherwise, there is a general rule that an intent to evade local marriage law by going to another state to contract a marriage that could not lawfully be entered into in the home state has no effect on the validity of the marriage. That is, marriages valid where contracted are valid everywhere.

RIGHTS AND INCIDENTS OF MARRIAGE

Where a valid marriage exists, certain rights and responsibilities go with it. Some of these are given below.

Community Property

In the states of Arizona, California, Nevada, Texas, and Washington, and to a limited extent in states that have adopted the uniform dissolution of marriage, all property acquired by either spouse during marriage is held as *community property.* Upon divorce, this community property is equally divided between the former spouses. At the death of one spouse, one-half of the community property goes to the heirs and representatives of the deceased, not to the surviving spouse.

Property acquired before marriage remains separately owned by each individual and becomes community property only if the spouse owning it transfers it in such a way as to convert it to community property.

Among persons who live together in an illicit relationship under the color of marriage, when such living together is in good faith on the part of one seeking the division of property acquired during this relationship, the courts generally will divide the property between the parties equitably. However, if this living together is done knowing it is illicit, the courts are divided as to whether to apportion the property. Some courts feel they should leave the parties where they found them, while other courts feel that not to divide the property enriches the property holder and refuse to enrich one wrongdoer over another.

Finally, where a man and woman lived together as husband and wife, knowing their relationship is illegal, the law generally will not infer a promise on the part of the man to pay for the services rendered by the woman during the relationship. If there was an express agreement between the parties that the services were to be paid for, some recovery has been allowed. Since the case of *Marvin* v. *Marvin*, involving movie star Lee Marvin, the courts and the public are taking another look at these relationships.

Inheritance, Descent, Distribution, and Power

As a married person, a spouse who survives the death of the other is entitled to inherit certain property of the decedent, depending in what manner the property title is held and the applicable state law. These rights are covered in Chapter 17.

Antenuptial and Property Settlement Agreements

Sometimes, to avoid the division of property as provided by statute in the case of death or by a court in the event of divorce, the parties enter into an agreement before, but in contemplation and consideration of, an impending marriage. In this agreement, the property rights and interests of the prospective husband and wife in property presently owned and property to be acquired in the future are determined in advance of marriage.

These agreements are best developed when both parties are represented by legal counsel. They usually provide that the property of each spouse is to be separate and independent from that of the other and that neither spouse is to acquire any interest in the estate of the other. They also specify any other arrangements the parties agree upon as to the control and ownership of and contribution toward any property owned or to be acquired.

Breach of Promise

Where one qualified person offers to marry another and subsequently refuses to marry that person, the person to whom the offer was made sometimes has a right to bring suit for damages for *breach of promise of marriage*. In some states, the damages sought are actual: that is, amounts of money paid out or lost because the party relied on the promise. The party does not sue for punitive damages, which would compensate for the wrong the party felt was done to him or her. Because of the abuse of this cause by unscrupulous women for blackmail or unjust enrichment, some states have completely abolished any action for breach of promise.

Because this remedy, although provided by statute, is not looked upon with favor by the courts, the statutory provisions must be followed exactly. It is therefore suggested that legal counsel be used to proceed in such a cause of action. A promise to marry need not be made in writing. There does not even have to be a formal engagement. A promise to marry may be inferred from the conduct of the parties.

DUTIES OF HUSBAND AND WIFE

Marriage not only gives the parties certain rights but also places upon them certain responsibilities and duties. Among these is the duty of a wife to follow her husband when he leaves a community, even though this departure will break ties with her friends and relatives and cause an emotional hardship on her. However, a husband has the duty not to make his choice of where to live unreasonable or arbitrary. A husband is under a duty not to beat his wife, and a wife is under a duty not to refuse her husband sexual intercourse so long as such intercourse does not affect her health or well being and is considered normal by community standards.

Commonly, it is the husband's duty to provide his wife and children with food, shelter, clothing, education, medical and dental care, and other essentials of life. However, in this time of equal rights for women, some courts have taken the position that where a wife is as able as or better able than the husband to provide these necessaries, it is her duty to provide them for the family.

Finally, although the law can list the rights and duties of a husband and wife, a marriage that has to rely on the law rather than the good faith give and take of reasonable people is probably headed for rough water, if not in fact for an actual breakup.

16

ANNULMENT, SEPARATE MAINTENANCE, AND DIVORCE

Despite their best efforts, many couples reach the conclusion that the marriage they entered into so blissfully is over and that they do not love each other any more. The solution seems to be to sever the marriage; and while the law does not favor divorce, it does provide a way to accomplish this severance if circumstances warrant it.

ANNULMENT

The first way to dissolve a marriage is by *annulment*. In theory, an annulment is different from a divorce. A divorce is a means of severing a legal marriage; an annulment is a judicial decision that the marriage never took place.

The basis for an annulment is demonstration that the marriage was entered into by one of the parties because of fraud or duress, that there was a violation of a statute, or that there was incapacity of a party—and therefore that the contract is void or voidable.

When there is an annulment, the court decides that a marriage never took place. For this reason, neither spouse is entitled to alimony or separate maintenance, and it is also possible that child support may be denied to the custodial parent. Of course, where there are religious restrictions (or in states where there are legal restrictions) regarding the right of divorced persons to remarry, they do not apply if a marriage is annulled.

Fraud As a Basis for Annulment

Where it can be shown that one person entered into a marriage only because of the fraud of the other, the marriage can be annulled. The elements of fraud to be proven must be essential to the marriage relationship and its duties and obligations. Promises of future conduct or misrepresentations about birth, social position, fortune, character, or health are not enough for annulment.

The kinds of fraud that are grounds for annulment include the following.

1. Concealing the fact that one is impotent at the time of marriage.

2. Concealing the fact that one is lesbian or homosexual.

3. Concealment by a woman that she is pregnant by another or that an existing child is illegitimate. In some states, a man can annul a marriage he entered into only because his wife fraudulently represented to him that she was pregnant by him when she was not pregnant at all. In other states, this is not a ground for annulment.

4. Refusal to bear children. While promises of future conduct are not grounds for annulment, if one refuses to have children after there was a premarital understanding that the couple would have children, or if one repudiates a written agreement entered into before marriage to raise the children in a certain religion, the marriage can be annulled.

Duress As a Basis for Annulment

The amount of duress or force sufficient to provide grounds for annulment is difficult to determine. However, such duress must have been unlawful, have influenced the party into entering the marriage contract, and have been brought about by the other party directly or indirectly or by his or her connivance. For example, a woman can legitimately threaten to charge a man with being the father of her child unless he marries her only if this is true. If she threatens such suit although he is not the father, a marriage entered into because of such threat can be annulled.

Violation of a Statute As a Basis for Annulment

Marriage between first cousins in a state where such marriages are illegal is the kind of violation of a statute that can be used to annual a marriage.

Lack of Capacity As a Basis for Annulment

If a person becomes insane after marriage, it is not a ground for annulment; but if he or she is insame at the time the marriage ceremony takes place, the marriage can be annulled. If a person is so drunk that he or she did not know the nature, meaning, or consequence of the marriage contract, the marriage can be annulled if legal proceedings to do so are started within a few weeks after the ceremony.

State statutes require that the parties be of a minimum age before they can enter into a valid marriage contract. Therefore, if either party is under the age of parental consent, the underaged party or that party's parents can annul the marriage, unless the parties cohabit or continue the marriage relationship after reaching the age of consent.

SEPARATE MAINTENANCE

An agreement for separate maintenance is a contract entered into between a husband and a wife who are living apart or will soon be living apart. In this contract, the rights each spouse can exercise over the property brought to or acquired during marriage is settled, the rights and obligations regarding separate maintenance are provided, and each spouse releases his claims against the other party's estate.

In most states, these agreements can be entered into independently; and if they are fair and fairly obtained, they will be enforced. In Louisiana, such an agreement is binding only if it is incorporated into a divorce decree or entered into after the marriage is dissolved. In Massachusetts, New Hampshire, and Vermont, a trustee, as in the early days of common law, must be appointed before the agreement will be recognized. In the trustee situation, the husband's promise to support the wife runs to the trustee, who uses the funds for the wife's use and benefit and protects the husband from any debts incurred by the wife. In Nebraska, a separation agreement will be upheld only where legal grounds exist for separation or divorce.

Reasons for Separate Maintenance

If a married couple can no longer live together as husband and wife and do not desire to enter into the delay, expense, inevitable bitterness and possible publicity of divorce, they can enter into a contractual agreement for separate maintenance. In this agreement, the rights and duties of the spouses to each other, their property, and their children are set out. The agreement is then approved by a court; and if either party violates the terms of this legal separation, the violator may be jailed for contempt of court. While there are oral separation agreements and separation agreements not presented to a court for approval, such agreements can be enforced only as in any other breach of contract action.

Essentials of a Separation Agreement

For there to be an enforceable separation agreement, certain things are required.

1. There must be a valid existing marriage.
2. The husband and wife must already be living separate and apart or be about to live separate and apart. An agreement to live separate and apart at some future time will void a separation agreement.
3. The parties must make full disclosure to each other of their assets and income, and the agreement based on these disclosures must be fair and arrived at fairly.
4. The agreement should specify the division of the property of the parties, the custody and visitation rights in regard to their children, the amounts of support to be paid by and to a spouse and for the childrens' support, and waivers of claims against each other's estate. Of course, the agreement should also assert that irreconcilable defferences have arisen between the parties and that they are now living or intend immediately to live separate and apart.
5. The agreement can be oral or written. Aside from the obvious problem of proving the terms (or even the existence) of an oral agreement, only a written agreement can be presented to a court for approval. In this way, violations can be punished by incarceration of the violator. In addition, to ensure that support payments are deductible for United States income tax purposes, the agreement must be in writing.

EFFECT OF SEPARATE MAINTENANCE AGREEMENTS

A separation agreement cannot relieve a spouse of an obligation imposed by law to support the other spouse, since such an unsupported spouse could then become a public charge and a burden on the public to support. A separation agreement cannot relieve a parent of his duty to support his children.

While under the terms of a separation agreement, each party lives separate and apart, free from harrassment or control of the other party, they are still legally married. Therefore any nongroup dating or extramarital relationship may present the other spouse with a claim of adultery which puts *fault* on the dating spouse and is a ground for divorce.

Should the parties resume living together or engage in sexual activity together with the intention that the reconciliation be permanent, the agreement is terminated. However, it is the intention, and not the act, which controls.

DIVORCE OR DISSOLUTION OF MARRIAGE

The final judicial way to end a valid marriage is divorce, in some states now called *dissolution of marriage*. Just as a marriage itself must conform to certain legal requirements in order to be valid, a divorce or dissolution of marriage must also follow certain prescribed legal formulas.

Divorce can be granted only when grounds for seeking dissolution of the marriage exist. Such grounds are not just any reasons for dissolving the marriage; they are specific acts that each state legislature has set forth in its state statutes as grounds for the courts to grant a divorce. Because each state has its own grounds and laws are subject to change, divorce proceedings should be placed in the hands of a knowledgable attorney who is acquainted with the divorce laws of the state where he lives.

Grounds for Divorce

As of January 1981, grounds for divorce in each state are as follows:

Alabama

1. Abandonment for more than one year
2. Adultery
3. Crime against nature before or after marriage
4. Cruelty or any cause justifying divorce, if plaintiff desires separation only (also known as a partial divorce)
5. Final decree of partial divorce in effect for more than two years
6. Five successive years in insane asylum after marriage, the person so confined being hopelessly and incurably insane when divorce is filed.
7. Habitual drunkenness or drug addiction contracted after marriage
8. Imprisonment in penetentiary for two years under sentence of seven years or more
9. Incapacity
10. Incompatibility
11. Nonsupport of wife by husband for two years will permit wife to obtain divorce
12. Physical violence
13. Pregnancy of wife at time of marriage without husband's knowledge will permit husband to obtain divorce
14. Irretrievable breakdown of marriage

Residency: Six months
Remarriage: Sixty days

Alaska

1. Adultery
2. Conviction of a felony
3. Cruelty impairing health or endangering life or personal indignities rendering life burdensome
4. Failure to consummate at time of marriage and continuing until commencement of legal action
5. Habitual and gross drunkenness, begun after marriage and continuing for one year.
6. Habitual addiction to drugs after marriage
7. Incompatibility of temperament
8. Incurable mental illness if spouse is confined to an institution for at least eighteen months prior to the filing of the divorce
9. Wilful desertion for one year.
10. Wilful neglect by the husband to provide necessaries of life for the wife for twelve months, when failure is because of his idleness, profligacy, or dissipation

Residency: None
Remarriage: No restriction

Arizona

Court will enter decree of dissolution of marriage if residency requirement is met, conciliation provisions either do not apply or have been met, marriage is irretrievably broken, and, to extent it has jurisdiction, court has considered and provided for child custody and support, spousal maintenance, and property disposition.
Residency: Ninety days
Remarriage: No restriction

Arkansas

1. Adultery
2. Conviction of felony or infamous crime
3. Cruel and barbarous treatment endangering life of innocent party
4. Desertion for one year without reasonable cause
5. Habitual drunkenness for one year
6. Indignities to person of innocent party
7. Insanity—continuous confinement to institution for three years or adjudicated insane more than three years before filing of suit

8. Impotency at time of marriage continuing to time of bringing action for divorce
9. Parties having lived apart for three consecutive years without cohabitation
10. Spouse by former undissolved marriage living at time of marriage
11. Wilful nonsupport

Residency: Sixty days preceding commencement of action

Remarriage: No restriction

California

1. Incurable insanity, requiring proof on competent medical or psychiatric testimony
2. Irreconcilable differences which have caused irremediable breakdown of marriage

Residency: Six months

Remarriage: No restriction

Colorado

Irretrievable breakdown of marriage relationship must be proven as essential element of action

Residency: Ninety days

Remarriage: No restriction

Connecticut

1. Adultery
2. Fraudulent contract
3. Habitual intemperance
4. Incompatibility causing parties to live apart for continuous period of at least eighteen months with no reasonable prospect of reconciliation
5. Infamous crime involving a violation of conjugal duty and punishable by imprisonment for more than a year
6. Intolerable cruelty
7. Irretrievable breakdown of marriage
8. Mental illness causing legal confinement for an accumulated period of at least five years within the six year period next preceding complaint
9. Sentence to imprisonment for life
10. Seven years' absence, unheard from
11. Wilful desertion for a year

Residency: One year
Remarriage: No restriction

Delaware

1. Separation caused by incompatibility
2. Separation caused by respondent's mental illness
3. Separation caused by respondent's misconduct, including adultery, bigamy, conviction of a serious crime, physical or oral abuse, desertion, homosexuality, refusal to perform marriage obligations, contracting venereal disease, habitual alcoholism or drug abuse

Residency: Six months
Remarriage: No restriction

District of Columbia

1. Parties living separately for one year
2. Parties living separately voluntarily for six months

Residency: Six months
Remarriage: No restriction

Florida

1. Marriage irretrievably broken
2. Mental incompetence of a party for three years

Residency: Six months
Remarriage: No restriction

Georgia

1. Adultery
2. Conviction of offense involving moral turpitude with penalty of two years or more in penitentiary
3. Cruel treatment, consisting of wilful infliction of pain, bodily or mental, upon complaining party such as reasonably justifies apprehension of danger to life, limb, or health
4. Force, menaces, duress, or fraud in obtaining marriage
5. Habitual addiction to drugs
6. Habitual intoxication
7. Impotency at time of marriage
8. Incurable mental illness for two years

9. Irretrievably broken marriage
10. Mental incapacity at time of marriage
11. Pregnancy at time of marriage, unknown by husband
12. Relationship between parties such that marriage prohibited
13. Wilful and continued desertion for one year

Residency: Six months

Remarriage: Judge or jury determines rights and disabilities of parties

Hawaii

1. Expiration of term in decree of separate bed and board without reconciliation
2. Living separate and apart for two years or more
3. Marriage irretrievably broken
4. Satisfaction of court that divorce would not be harsh, oppressive, or contrary to public interest

Residency: Six months

Remarriage: No restriction (if wife remarries, alimony must be modified)

Idaho

1. Adultery
2. Conviction of a felony
3. Extreme cruelty
4. Habitual intemperance
5. Irreconcilable differences determined by court to be substantial reasons to dissolve marriage
6. Living separate and apart five years
7. Wilful desertion
8. Wilful neglect

Residency: Six weeks

Remarriage: No restriction

Illinois

1. Adultery
2. Another husband or wife at time of marriage
3. Attempt on life of spouse by poisoning or other means showing malice
4. Conviction of a felony or infamous crime
5. Desertion for one year
6. Excessive use of addictive drugs for two years

7. Extreme and repeated mental or physical cruelty
8. Habitual drunkenness for two years
9. Impotency
10. Infection of spouse with veneral disease

Residency: Ninety days
Remarriage: No restriction

Indiana

1. Conviction of infamous crime
2. Impotency at time of marriage
3. Incurable insanity for two years
4. Irretrievable breakdown of marriage

Residency: Six months, and in county filed three months
Remarriage: Verified application. No license issued to male with dependent children from prior marriages reasonably dependent on him for support, unless person provides proof with his application that he is supporting or contributing to support of his children by prior marriages and complying with court support orders

Iowa

Breakdown of marriage in that legitimate objects of matrimony have been destroyed and no reasonable likelihood that relationship can be preserved
Residency: One year
Remarriage: No restriction

Kansas

1. Abandonment for one year
2. Adultery
3. Confinement in an institution for mental illness or adjudication of mental illness by court without restoration therefrom and without confinement for more than three years; and in either case, a finding by two of three court appointed physicians that defendant has poor prognosis for recovery from such illness
4. Conviction of a felony and imprisonment therefor subsequent to the marriage
5. Extreme cruelty
6. Gross neglect of duty
7. Habitual drunkenness

8. Incompatibility

Residency: Sixty days actual resident

Remarriage: Thirty days after final decree

Kentucky

Irretrievable breakdown of marriage is sole basis for dissolution

Residency: One of the parties must have been maintained in the state for 180 days before the filing of the petition. Must be proved by testimony of one or more witnesses.

Remarriage: Decree of dissolution of marriage

Louisiana

Separation from bed and board may be claimed for

1. Abandonment
2. Adultery
3. Attempt on the life of the other
4. Conviction of a felony and sentence to death or to imprisonment at hard labor
5. Habitual intemperance, excesses, cruel treatment, or outrages if such conduct is of such a nature as to render living together insupportable
6. Having been charged with a felony and having fled from justice
7. Intentional nonsupport
8. Public defamation
9. Voluntary living separate and apart for one year without reconciliation

Separation may be allowed when spouses have lived six months separate and apart voluntarily and they execute affidavit to that effect, including statement of existence of irreconcilable differences to such degree and nature as to render their living together insupportable and impossible.

Divorce may be granted immediately for one of the following causes:

1. Adultery
2. Conviction of a felony and sentence of death or imprisonment at hard labor.

Divorce on any of the other grounds may not be granted unless separation from bed and board has been decreed and one year has elapsed thereafter without reconciliation. When married persons have been living separate and apart for two or more years, either party may sue for absolute divorce.

Residency: None, except as stated above

Remarriage: Where divorce is granted on ground of adultery, guilty party is now permitted to marry his or her accomplice

Maine

1. Adultery
2. Cruel and abusive treatment
3. Extreme cruelty
4. Gross and confirmed habits of intoxication from use of intoxicating liquors or drugs
5. Impotence
6. Irreconcilable differences
7. Nonsupport
8. Utter desertion continued for three consecutive years

Residency: Parties must have been married here or cohabited here after marriage, or plaintiff must have resided here when cause of action occurred, or plaintiff must reside here in good faith for six months before action is begun, or defendant must be resident of the state.
Remarriage: No restriction

Maryland

1. Abandonment for twelve months without reasonable expectation of reconciliation
2. Adultery
3. Any cause rendering marriage null and void from the beginning under Maryland law
4. Conviction of a felony or misdemeanor and sentence of at least three years or indeterminate sentence in penal institution, twelve months of which have been served
5. Cruelty
6. Excessively vicious conduct
7. Impotency
8. Permanent and incurable insanity
9. Uninterrupted separation without cohabitation for three years
10. Voluntary separation without cohabitation for twelve consecutive months without reasonable expectation of reconciliation

Residency: One year. Insanity, two years.
Remarriage: No restriction

Massachusetts

1. Adultery
2. Cruel and abusive treatment
3. Gross and confirmed habits of intoxication caused by voluntary, excessive use of liquor or drugs

4. Gross and cruel failure to support
5. Impotency
6. Irretrievable breakdown of marriage
7. Sentence to confinement for life or five years in penal or reformatory institution
8. Utter desertion for one year

Residency: Plaintiff must live in commonwealth for one year, and cause must have occurred within commonwealth

Remarriage: Allowed after divorce; if spouse remarries after seven years of mate's absence, not guilty of polygamy

Michigan

Breakdown of marriage relationship to extent that objects of matrimony have been destroyed and there remains no reasonable likelihood that marriage can be preserved

Residency: Plaintiff must have lived in state 180 days unless marriage was solemnized in state and plaintiff lived in state from marriage to bringing suit.

One spouse must have resided in county ten days before bringing suit.

If not voluntary appearance, defendant must live in state when divorce filed or when cause arose, unless brought in by publication or personally served with process within state or personally served with order for appearance and publication anywhere.

When cause happened outside Michigan, one party must live in state for one year

Remarriage: No restriction

Minnesota

Irretrievable breakdown of marriage—defenses abolished

Residency: One party must live in state 180 days

Remarriage: Immediate

Mississippi

1. Adultery, unless collusion or condonation
2. Consanguinity within prohibited degrees
3. Habitual cruel and inhuman treatment
4. Habitual excessive use of drugs
5. Incurable insanity, if insane party has been under treatment and confined to institution for three years

6. Insanity or idiocy at time of marriage, unknown to complaining party
7. Irreconcilable differences if not contested and if provisions are made for custody after sixty days
8. Pregnancy by other than husband
9. Prior marriage undissolved
10. Natural impotency
11. Sentence to penitentiary, unless pardoned

Residency: One party must live in state for six months unless residence acquired to secure divorce

Remarriage: No restriction, but in case of adultery court may prohibit remarriage.

Missouri

Irreconcilably broken marriage with no reasonable likelihood it can be preserved

Residency: Ninety days

Remarriage: No restriction

Montana

Irretrievable breakdown of marriage supported by

1. Not having lived together for 180 days
2. Serious marital discord adversely affecting one of the parties

Residency: Ninety days

Remarriage: No restriction except during appeal challenging finding that marriage was irretrievably broken

Nebraska

Marriage irretrievably broken

Residency: One party for one year with bona-fide intent of making state his home, or married in state and one party has stayed there since marriage

Remarriage: No restriction

Nevada

1. Incompatibility
2. Insanity for two years
3. No cohabitation for one year

Residency: Six weeks unless action happened in county while both lived in state. Mere intention to make state residence is not adequate
Remarriage: No restriction

New Hampshire

1. Abandonment and refusal to cohabit for two years
2. Adultery
3. Disappearance for two years
4. Desertion for two years
5. Extreme cruelty
6. Habitual drunkenness for two years
7. Impotency
8. Imprisonment for more than one year
9. Irreconcilable differences leading to irretrievable breakdown of marriage
10. Joining any religious sect or society forbidding cohabitation of husband and wife and six months refusal to cohabit
11. Treatment such as to seriously injure health or seriously endanger reason

Residency: Both parties lived in state when action commenced. Plaintiff lived in state and defendant served in state. Plaintiff lived in state for one year
Remarriage: No restriction

New Jersey

1. Adultery
2. Deviate sexual conduct voluntarily performed by defendant without consent of plaintiff
3. Desertion for one year or more
4. Extreme cruelty for three months before filing
5. Imprisonment for eighteen months, provided that if imprisonment ended before filing couple did not resume cohabitation
6. Institutionalization for mental illness for two years or more after marriage
7. Separation for eighteen consecutive months, if no reasonable prospect of reconciliation
8. Voluntarily induced addiction or habituation to narcotic drug or habitual drunkenness for twelve months after marriage

Residency: Either party bona-fide resident of state and has stayed such, except that no divorce can be commenced on grounds other than adultery unless one of the parties has lived in state for one year
Remarriage: No restriction

New Mexico

1. Abandonment
2. Adultery
3. Cruel or inhuman treatment
4. Incompatibility

Residency: Six months
Remarriage: No restriction

New York

1. Abandonment for one year
2. Adultery
3. Cruel or inhuman treatment
4. Imprisonment of defendant for three years after marriage
5. Living apart for one year

Residency: Parties married in state and lived there for one year.

Parties lived in state as husband and wife for one year. Cause occurred in state and either party lived there for one year.

Cause occurred in state and both parties lived there when action commenced.

Either party lived in state two years before action commenced
Remarriage: No restriction

North Carolina

1. Adultery
2. Bestiality
3. Crime against nature
4. Impotency at time of marriage and continuing
5. Incurable insanity causing separation for three years
6. Pregnancy of wife by another at time of marriage without knowledge of husband
7. Separation for one year

Residency: Six months by plaintiff or defendant
Remarriage: No restriction

North Dakota

1. Adultery
2. Conviction of a felony

3. Extreme cruelty
4. Habitual intemperance for one year
5. Insanity with five years confinement in an institution
6. Irreconcilable differences
7. Wilful desertion for one year
8. Wilful neglect for one year

Residency: Twelve months for plaintiff if a citizen of the United States or has declared intent to become one.

For insanity, complainant must have lived in state five years

Remarriage: Cannot remarry, except as permitted by court. Court must specify if can remarry and when

Ohio

1. Adultery
2. Extreme cruelty
3. Fraudulent contract
4. Gross neglect of duty
5. Habitual drunkenness
6. Imprisonment in penitentiary
7. Impotency
8. Lived apart for two years
9. Lived apart for four years if one party in mental institution
10. Other spouse living at time of marriage to this one
11. Procurement of divorce outside of state by spouse
12. Wilful absence for one year

Residency: Six months for plaintiff

Remarriage: No restriction

Oklahoma

1. Abandonment for one year
2. Adultery
3. Extreme cruelty
4. Fraudulent contract
5. Gross neglect of duty
6. Habitual drunkenness
7. Impotency
8. Imprisonment for felony at time action was filed
9. Insanity for five years
10. Pregnancy of wife at time of marriage by one other than husband

11. Procurement of divorce by spouse in other state
12. Incompatibility

Residency: Six months in good faith, thirty days in county of residence. Five years for grounds of insanity

Remarriage: Six months after divorce decree or thirty days after disposition of appeal.

Cohabitation within said time with spouse married outside state constitutes adultery.

Oregon

1. Either party lacked legal age or sufficient understanding and has not been sufficiently notified
2. Irreconcilable differences
3. Marriage procured by force or fraud

Residency: None if married in state; otherwise six months

Remarriage: Sixty days after appeal

Pennsylvania

1. Adultery
2. Conviction of certain crimes resulting in two or more years sentence
3. Consanguinity or affinity
4. Cruel and barbarous treatment
5. Desertion for two years
6. Endangering life
7. Existing prior marriage
8. Incompatability
9. Indignities suffered rendering condition intolerable and life burdensome
10. Insanity or serious mental disorder
11. Uncondoned fraud, force, or coercion

Residency: If respondent lived in county one year or more, residence of libellant in state not required; otherwise libellant must live in state one year

Remarriage: Either may remarry, but defendant guilty of adultery may not marry other party to adultery during life of plaintiff.

Puerto Rico

1. Abandonment for over one year
2. Absolute incurable impotency occuring after marriage

3. Adultery
4. Attempt to corrupt son or prostitute daughter and commerce in such corruption or prostitution
5. Conviction of a felony which may involve loss of civil rights
6. Cruel treatment or grave injury
7. Habitual drunkenness or excessive use of drugs
8. Incurable insanity if it seriously prevents spouses living together spiritually
9. Proposal of husband to prostitute wife
10. Separation for two years

Residency: One year, unless ground arose in Puerto Rico or while one spouse lived there

Remarriage: Not prohibited, but woman must show if pregnant if remarriage within 301 days of divorce.

Rhode Island

1. Adultery
2. Any other gross misbehavior or wickedness repugnant to and in violation of marriage covenant
3. Continued drunkenness
4. Extreme cruelty
5. Habitual, excessive intemperate use of narcotics
6. Impotency
7. Irreconcilable differences
8. Marriage originally void or voidable by law
9. Neglect or refusal for one year of husband to provide for subsistence of wife if he is of sufficient ability
10. Party deemed to be or is treated as if civilly dead, for crime committed
11. Separation for three years
12. Wilful desertion for five years

Residency: One year for either party; or in case of divorce from bed, board, and future cohabitation (not just from bond of marriage) must have resided in state for such time as court deems sufficient.

Remarriage: No restriction

South Carolina

1. Adultery
2. Continuous separation for one year
3. Desertion for one year

4. Habitual drunkenness caused by alcohol or narcotics
5. Physical cruelty

Residency: One year if both parties are residents when action commenced, must have been residents three months prior to action

Remarriage: No restriction

South Dakota

1. Adultery
2. Extreme cruelty
3. Wilful desertion
4. Wilful negligence
5. Habitual intemperance
6. Conviction of a felony
7. Incurable chronic mania or dementia of either spouse five years or more while under confinement by order of court or of an insanity agency.

Residency: Resident of state

Remarriage: No restriction

Tennessee

1. Adultery
2. Attempts on the life of the other by means showing malice
3. Bigamy
4. Conviction of an infamous crime
5. Conviction of a felony
6. Desertion for one year without reasonable cause
7. Habitual drunkenness or drug abuse
8. Impotence
9. Irreconcilable differences
10. Refusal of wife to move to Tennessee and absence from husband for two years
11. Wife pregnant at time of marriage with another man's child without knowledge of husband

Residency: No requirements if plaintiff lived in state when acts were committed.

If one or other lived in state six months before filing, complaint can be filed on acts committed elsewhere

Remarriage: No restriction

Texas

1. Abandonment for one year
2. Adultery
3. Cruel treatment which makes living together insupportable
4. Discord or conflict of personalities that destroys legitimate ends of marriage and prevents reasonable expectation of reconciliation
5. Felony conviction and imprisonment if twelve months after final judgment (and not if pardoned or convicted on spouse's testimony)
6. Living apart for three years
7. Mental illness with three-year hospitalization without hope for permanent recovery

Residency: Six months in state, ninety days in county

Remarriage: No restriction after thirty days

Utah

1. Adultery
2. Desertion for one year
3. Felony conviction
4. Habitual drunkenness
5. Impotency at time of marriage
6. Permanent insanity
7. Physical or mental cruelty
8. Separation for three years
9. Wilful neglect to provide common necessities of life

Residency: Three months in state and county

Remarriage: Prohibited during appeal or period allowed for appeal

Vermont

1. Adultery
2. Failure to provide suitable maintenance if able to do so
3. Insanity commitment for five years
4. Intolerable severity
5. Prison confinement for hard labor for three years
6. Separation for six months with resumption of marital relations not reasonably probable
7. Wilful desertion or absence for seven years

Residency: Six months.

Two years for insanity

Remarriage: No restriction

Virginia

1. Adultery
2. Cruelty, after one-year separation for it
3. Desertion for one year
4. Felony conviction for one year
5. Separation for one year without cohabitation
6. Sodomy or buggery outside marriage

Nos. 1 and 6 not valid if parties voluntarily cohabited after knowledge of such act, if it happened five years earlier, or if it was committed by procurement or connivance of party alleging it.

Residency: Six months

Remarriage: Allowed after appeals

Virgin Islands

Breakdown of marriage relationship without likelihood that marriage can be preserved

Residency: Six weeks

Remarriage: No restriction

Washington

1. Marriage irretrievably broken
2. Marriage invalid—grounds for invalidity:
    - A. Consanguinity
    - B. Insufficient age
    - C Lack of capacity to consent or consent obtained by force, duress, or fraud
    - D. Lack of parental or court approval
    - E. No voluntary cohabitation after attaining age of consent after cessation of force or duress or discovery of fraud
    - F. Prior undissolved marriage

Residency: No specific duration

Remarriage: No restriction, except during appeal of finding that marriage is irretrievably broken

West Virginia

1. Abandonment for six months
2. Adultery

3. Child abuse or neglect
4. Cruel and unreasonable treatment or fear of bodily hurt
5. Drug addiction
6. Felony conviction
7. Habitual drunkenness
8. Insanity
9. Irreconcilable differences (sixty-day waiting period required)
10. Separation for one year

Residency: One year

Remarriage: No restriction

Wisconsin

Irretrievably broken marriage, marriage being irretrievably broken if

1. Both parties so state
2. One party so states and one year separation
3. One party so states and judge finds no possibility of reconciliation
4. One party so states and, after judge finds marriage not irretrievably broken, either party states under oath that it is irretrievably broken

Residency: Six months in state, thirty days in county

Remarriage: Six month waiting period

Wyoming

1. Insanity confinement for two years
2. Irreconcilable differences

Residency: Plaintiff must reside in state for sixty days, unless marriage was solemnized in state and petitioner has lived there since

Remarriage: No restriction

Definitions

Some of the grounds may need definition or elaboration.

Habitual Drunkenness

A fixed habit of drinking to excess or such frequent use to a condition of drunkenness as to show an inability to control the appetite for drink constitutes habitual drunkenness.

The fact that a spouse cannot attend to business during regular hours because of drunkenness may be considered in an action for divorce, but that fact in and of itself is not a ground for divorce. Neither is it necessary that a person be continually in an intoxicated condition in order to come within the definition of habitual drunkard and entitle the other spouse to divorce on statuatory ground of habitual drunkenness. The same reasoning is applied to define addiction to drugs.

Impotency

This means one must be incurably impotent, whether the impotency results from a defect caused by nature or from accident or from the acts of the parties.

Impotence in the male is the inability to achieve an erection of the penis for normal intercourse with the wife. Oral sex is not considered normal in the eyes of the law, and the insistence on such acts against the will of the other spouse may constitute a ground for divorce in those states in which cruelty is a ground.

Premature ejaculation that occurs before the penis enters the vagina is also considered a form of impotence to constitute a ground for divorce.

Adultery

The voluntary sexual intercourse of a married person with a person other than the offender's wife or husband, whether the other is married or single, is adultery.

Even though adultery may be proven by circumstantial evidence, the proof offered must be of the clearest and most convincing character. To prove adultery, it is not necessary to present the direct evidence of photographs of the parties performing the act or direct testimony of witnesses who observed the act itself. It is sufficient to prove that the parties were disposed to commit the offense and that they had the opportunity and access to each other.

Cruelty

Physical cruelty refers to physical acts of violence, bodily harm, or suffering as to endanger life or limb or raise an apprehension of great bodily harm. Slight acts of cruelty or bad temper, petulance, rude language, want of attention, or angry or abusive words do not constitute physical cruelty as a ground for divorce.

A husband who compels his wife to submit to excessive sexual intercourse will not be subject to causing physical cruelty as a ground for divorce, unless such compulsion is persisted in by the husband against his wife's will and he knows that the act will be injurious to her bodily health.

Mental cruelty as a ground for divorce is conduct that causes embarrassment, humiliation, and anguish so as to render life miserable and unendurable or to cause a spouse's life, person, or health to become endangered. Some of the acts considered by some courts to be mental cruelty are

1. A husband spending three or four nights per week out of the house and returning in an intoxicated state.
2. Public belittlement of a spouse.
3 A wife swearing at her husband, throwing things at him, and threatening to kill him.
4. Verbal abuse.
5. Telling one's spouse one does not love him or her and wishing one were not married.

Abandonment or Desertion

The absence of a spouse, to constitute abandonment or desertion as a ground for divorce, must be against the will of the abandoned spouse. That is, if the separation is by the mutual agreement of the parties, it cannot be a ground for divorce.

Where a husband lives, so must his wife. Therefore, if a husband must move to a different location because of employment or some other necessary reason, his wife must accompany him, or her refusal can constitute desertion as a ground for divorce.

Contrary to the requirement for an action of separate maintenance that the parties must live in separate houses or apartments, divorce has a concept called *constructive desertion*. If one spouse refuses to cohabit with the other, moves out of their joint bedroom, and refuses to fulfill his or her marital duties, these acts may constitute *desertion by constructive desertion* as a ground for divorce, even though the parties live under the same roof.

Loathsome Disease

The courts usually have interpreted the loathsome diseases with which a spouse must be infected to constitute a ground for divorce as venereal diseases like syphilis or gonorrhea.

Vagrancy

This is usually interpreted as idle wandering from place to place without a visible means of support.

Defenses to a Divorce Action

First of all, if a defendant does not want to contest a divorce and there are no children and no question of support or property to be divided, it is not necessary to file a defense. In fact, it is not even necessary for the defendant to hire a lawyer. The defendant need do nothing, and the plaintiff will obtain a divorce by way of a default action. In a default action, the plaintiff, and if required a witness or witnesses, testify for the plaintiff. No one appears to testify for the defendant; and if the plaintiff sets out all of the residency requirements and a basis on which the court can find a ground for divorce, the plaintiff will be awarded a judgment of divorce. In states that have adopted a dissolution of marriage act, the marriage is dissolved by the court's decree. This is preferable to judgment of divorce, since it is not entered in favor of or against either party. It merely recites that the marriage of the parties is dissolved.

If a defendant decides to contest the cause of action, several defenses are available. First, all the motions and defenses available to a defendant in any civil suit are available in a divorce action. In addition, a defendant may raise certain defenses unique to a divorce action.

Condonation

Condonation is the forgiveness of a marriage offense on condition that it not be repeated. If the offense is repeated, however, the original offense is revived. For example, if a husband beats a wife, and if the wife forgives him and continues to live with him, she has condoned his acts. If he beats her again, the condonation is revoked; and the wife may obtain her divorce.

In some states, the only ground for divorce that cannot be condoned is adultery, because the idea is so abhorrent.

Recrimination

Divorce is a remedy provided only for an innocent party; so when each party has cause for divorce against the other, neither should be granted a divorce. Therefore, if a husband charges a wife with desertion and she defends against the action by charging her husband with physical cruelty, if both sides prove their allegations, neither side will be given a divorce. Thus, recrimination (or countercharge) is a defense to a ground for divorce.

In some states, if adultery is proven, recrimination of some other offense cannot be a defense to a ground for divorce. However, a proven defense of adultery to a charge of adultery can be a bar to a judgment of divorce.

In states that have adopted the uniform dissolution of marriage act, the concept of recrimination is not used, and so long as an offense is proven against the defendant, it does not matter that the plaintiff was also guilty of some offense. The marriage will be dissolved.

Collusion

Since the public also has an interest in the marriage relationship and in its proper maintenance, if the parties agree that one of the parties will commit an offense or that an offense will be pretended or that evidence will be made up or suppressed, a divorce will not be granted, if the court discovers such a collusive agreement.

Other Defenses

In addition, other defenses may be raised, such as fraud or invalidity of the marriage (which are discussed earlier in the section on annulment) or want of capacity to commit the offense alleged (for example, one who is impotent cannot commit adultery).

Since the plaintiff must be without fault, proof by the defendant that the acts alleged were provoked by the plaintiff constitutes a defense. For example, if a wife charges a husband with physical cruelty but the husband can prove that he hit her only after a series of episodes when she became drunk and abused him verbally in public and screamed at and beat him with some object in private, he could prove he was provoked by his wife into his actions, and the divorce would not be granted.

Finally, there is the defense that the court is without jurisdiction to rule in the case. This would be raised early in the case by a motion to dismiss the plaintiff's cause of action.

In states that have adopted the principle of no-fault divorces, defenses have been abolished.

Residency Requirements

Besides demanding that a plaintiff have grounds for divorce, each state also requires that a plaintiff reside in that state for a minimum period of time before filing a complaint for divorce. Residence requirements range from a minimum time of six weeks in Idaho and Nevada to two years in Massachusetts, New York (in certain circumstances), Rhode Island, and Wisconsin.

Therefore, when considering divorce, one should consider whether a state provides for no-fault divorce, what grounds for divorce (which can be as liberal as incompatibility or irreconcilable differences) are required, and what the minimum residency requirements may be.

Divorcing couples sometimes shop for a state with liberal grounds and minimum residency requirements. The plaintiff then moves to that state for the minimum required time, grounds such as incompatibility are alleged, both parties obtain legal representation within the state, the plaintiff (and if required, a witness or two) testifies, and within a few minutes a divorce is granted.

The law requires that the establishment of residency be genuine. In contested divorces, therefore, if a plaintiff moves to another state only to avoid the longer residency requirement of the home state, the defendant may allege that the testimony as to residency was perjured and the divorce was therefore fraudulently obtained. The divorce decree, even though it has already been granted, may be set aside.

Alimony

Alimony is an amount a court may order one spouse to pay the other so that that spouse may be supported while the suit is pending and after a decree for divorce is issued. Usually the husband must pay the wife this alimony; but in this time of women's liberation, wives have been ordered to pay support to their husbands if they are better able to pay. For example, if the wife is a corporate executive earning a large salary and the husband an unemployed invalid, the wife will probably be ordered to support the husband.

Whether or not alimony will be granted is discretionary with the court. Many times, if a wife is at fault, the court will not award her alimony. It is therefore sometimes better for a wife to file for divorce. She can thus allege that her husband was at fault and that she is entitled to alimony as the innocent party.

There is another reason why a wife might want to file first. In states that require that a court find one party at fault in order to grant a judgment of divorce, court files, with the complaint and judgment, are public records available for anyone to examine. The wife may be embarrassed to have a public record reflect that she was charged with adultery, drunkenness, desertion, or infection with a loathsome disease.

Just as the court awards (or denies) alimony, it also determines the amount of alimony. The purpose of alimony is not to punish the one committing the marital offense (assume the husband) but to permit the wife to live in the style in which the parties lived while they were married, consistent with the ability of the husband to pay. It was once a rule of thumb that the husband would pay one-third of his net income as alimony. Today, however, courts consider a wife's earnings, other sources of income, and estimated expenses, as well as the husband's net income and expenses, when they order alimony payments.

It should be noted that the wife's actual income, not her potential income is considered. That is, a wife, no matter how skilled or talented, is under no obligation to work to reduce her former husband's alimony payments. Of course, the same observations apply equally if the wife is ordered to pay alimony to the husband.

Temporary alimony, called *alimony pendente lite* is awarded while the suit is pending. Permanent alimony is awarded when the divorce is granted. This amount is usually paid until the death of the husband or wife or until her remarriage. In some states, courts award alimony for a limited period only, considering the duration of the marriage and the wife's ability to earn her own support.

A court retains jurisdiction over the parties and the divorce action, even after a decree of divorce is granted. Therefore, if there is a substantial change in the circumstances of the parties after the divorce, the court, upon petition by one of the spouses, can either increase or decrease the amount of alimony, depending on the change in circumstances. However, the change must be substantial. For example, if the husband becomes unemployed on a long-term basis or is hospitalized, the payments may be decreased. On the other hand, if the wife loses her job or the husband receives a promotion or changes jobs for a large increase in pay, alimony payments may be increased.

What if the alimony payments are not made as ordered? A person failing to make such payments could be in contempt of court. Upon petition by a wife alleging that she was not paid alimony, the court will order the husband to appear to explain why the payments were not made. Unless he can show extenuating circumstances, he can be jailed for contempt of court until he complies with the alimony payment order.

Many problems and additional court appearances can occur if alimony extends over a period of time. Parties often want to end contact with each other after a divorce. They therefore work out some arrangement whereby alimony is paid in one lump sum. Once this sum is paid, there are no adjustments for changes in circumstances and no problems of arrearage or failure to pay. The wife is then completely independent and on her own; and if she decides to remarry, there is no reduction or cessation of the alimony. Since this procedure has advantages and disadvantages to both parties, an attorney should be consulted before any agreement to such a settlement is reached.

Child Support

When one of the parties is awarded custody of the minor children born to or adopted by the parties, the court may order the noncustodial parent to help pay for the support of the children. Again, such payment is not to be used as a punishment of the paying parent but to be determined by the amount necessary to support the minor children. Therefore, the court considers the style in which the family lives, the income and expenses of the paying parent, and the income requirements for the support of the children.

While the purpose of support is to sustain the children during their minority, the court may order that payments continue through undergraduate college or its equivalent if a child elects that kind of education. Child support, unlike alimony, cannot be waived. For example, many times a wife is so anxious to be divorced from her husband that she agrees to support herself and waives any alimony she may be entitled to. If she voluntarily and knowingly waives this alimony, she cannot later request a court to award it to her. In the case of child support, however, even if there is a written agreement between the parties, the judge can inquire into the child-support provisions and change them where he feels it is necessary. The welfare of the child or children is the judge's concern, both when he awards custody to one of the parties and when he approves or sets the amount of child support.

Even after a divorce is final, some parties continue to irritate, aggravate, or harrass each other. A favorite weapon one parent uses against the other is their child. The scenario is often as follows.

The noncustodial father decides that his former wife is using child-support payments to support herself or her new boyfriend, so he stops paying the court-ordered child support. In retaliation, the mother refuses to permit the children to visit with their father, even though the court has ordered such visitation. Each party feels justified in his or her acts, and each party is wrong.

Child support and child visitation rights are mutually independent. Therefore, a father who fails to make his child-support payments as ordered can be summoned to court; and if he cannot show good financial reasons why he has not made the payments, he can be held in contempt of court and jailed until he makes the delinquent payments and agrees to keep his payments current. If the mother refuses to permit the children to visit with their father, she can be ordered into court; and unless she agrees to permit the children to visit their father as the court ordered, she too can be held in contempt of court and jailed until she complies.

The only reason for denying the noncustodial parent visitation with his or her children is that such visitation would be dangerous to their physical or mental health. For example, if the noncustodial parent beats or otherwise abuses his or her child during visitation, the judge can order the visitation to take place in the presence of the other parent or terminate it altogether.

THE EFFECT OF LEGAL SEPARATION OR DIVORCE ON INCOME TAX REQUIREMENTS

Although income tax is usually not a consideration when people are considering divorce, legal separation and divorce play an important role in determining how much tax each party pays after the marriage ties have been broken.

First, the marital status of the parties is determined as of the end of the year. Suppose a man and woman are divorced on December 31. When they file their tax returns, they must file as single people for the entire year—even though they were divorced for less than a day—without any pro-ration for the time they were married. Therefore, people sometimes speed up or defer divorce to take advantage, or escape the consequences, of the tax laws.

One exception to this rule occurs in the case of legal separation. The tax code says "an individual legally separated from his spouse under a decree of divorce or of separate maintenance shall not be considered as married." This means that if a decree of separate maintenance is issued, the parties must file as unmarried persons, even though they are not divorced. The tax code later liberalized even this rule to provide that if a person lives separate and apart from his spouse for an entire year, maintains a home for himself and a dependent child for whom he may claim an exemption, and pays over half the cost of maintaining the household, that person may file a separate return as if not married, even without a legal decree of separate maintenance.

If a party is ordered to pay alimony or support under a decree of divorce or of separate maintenance, this alimony or support may or may not be an allowable tax deduction by the person paying or become part of the taxable income of the one receiving, depending on the way the payments are made. Such payments have tax consequences if they are considered *periodic payments.* If they continue for more than ten years or if they are of a fixed amount for a period that could be less than ten years, but if they will terminate with the death, remarriage, or change in the economic status of either spouse, they are periodic payments. When payments are made under a separation agreement, this agreement must be in writing for them to qualify as periodic payments. Payments for child support are not periodic, and therefore they are not tax deductible by the individual paying them nor includible as income by the custodial spouse or minor children.

If a payment is ordered for alimony or maintenance *and* child support but the decree does not allocate an amount to each, the whole payment may be considered periodic if it meets the other requirements as to period of payment or termination.

Finally, there is one tax trap in divorce that often rubs salt into a wound. The Internal Revenue Tax Code says that someone who pays an obligation with property is taxed on any gain in value of that property from the time he acquired it. In 1962, the United States Supreme Court held that if a spouse transfers property to the other spouse in exchange for any marital rights (such as dower, alimony, right of renunciation of a will, or the right to contest a divorce), this is a taxable event; and the contributing spouse must pay a capital gains tax on any increase in the fair market value of the property. The receiving spouse's basis in the property then becomes its fair market value at the time it is transferred.

For example, a husband and wife agree to divorce. The wife gives up her right to alimony in exchange for the husband's General Motors stock, which has a value of $100,000. Because the husband paid only $20,000 for the stock, he will have to include a taxable capital gain of $80,000 in his income for that year. The wife will now consider the stock's basis to her to be $100,000 if she disposes of it at any time in the future.

When a husband leaves his lawyer's offiice after losing his wife and children and giving all his stock to his wife, he often feels completely whipped when the lawyer says, "Oh, by the way, you will have to pay tax on the amount of increase in that stock you gave your wife." With apologies to Gilbert and Sullivan, sometimes a lawyer's lot is not a happy one.

17

WILLS

Mrs. Brown meets Mrs. Jones on the street and the following conversation takes place:

"Gee, Mrs. Jones, did you hear about that nice Mr. Smith? He died last month."

"Yes, I heard about his dying, but I don't think he was so nice."

"Really? Why not? After all, he put one of his sons through medical school and paid for the education of another who is now a successful engineer, and he's been taking care of his sick wife and infant son for these last three years."

"Sure, but when he died, his poor old sick wife received only half of his estate. His infant son and his rich sons, the doctor and the engineer—who, by the way, have not spoken to Mr. and Mrs. Smith since their graduations—shared the other half. Obviously, Mrs. Smith needs the money more than their ungrateful sons, but she'll never see it."

"In addition, while Mrs. Smith is the guardian of her infant son, she had to be appointed by the court, and I understand she had to pay for and provide a bond as protection for her own son from her wrongdoing, and she has to file a report every year with the court to show how, on what, and why she spent the money on her own son. Imagine!"

"That's terrible, but of course when her son reaches eighteen, he can take his money, and she won't have to pay for any more bonds or file any more reports. I'm not sure that's such a good idea either, giving an eighteen-year-old boy unsupervised control over all that money."

"I understand also, that if Mrs. Smith dies before her son is eighteen, the court can select a guardian for him. Wouldn't it be terrible if some stranger or money-grabbing relative was appointed?"

"I'm not sure how much will be left anyway. I understand the death taxes will be at least 32 percent of Mr. Smith's taxable estate, probably more, so there won't be much left for anyone."

And so the conversation goes on. These women are only talking about some of the problems one can cause a family if one dies without leaving a will.

Many people are superstitious about wills. They are afraid making one will make them die sooner, or they insist that wills are only for rich people and their estates are too small to need one. However, many problems that have nothing to do with the dollar amount of the estate can be settled by making a will.

A will directs how your estate will be disposed of after your death. Your estate consists of more than merely the money you have. It also includes real estate and personal property, including heirlooms and items of sentimental value. Stocks, bonds, notes, accounts receivable, and your interest in any businesses are also part of your estate.

In your will, you name some person or some institution, like a bank qualified to act, as the executor of your estate. This executor is responsible for gathering all your assets (all the things you own); investing, disposing of, or preserving them; and seeing that they are distributed as you directed. Your executor is also responsible for the preparation and filing of any federal estate tax return, state inheritance tax returns, fiduciary tax returns and income tax returns required as a result of your death and for paying any taxes due from your estate—within the legal time limit and before final distribution of your estate. All of these actions are done under the supervision of the probate court and are part of what is called *probating a will.*

To probate a will, the executor must go into court and by oral testimony (in some states an affidavit will do) prove that while you were of sound mind and memory and in the presence of the required number of witnesses, as determined by each state statute, you signed a document you knew to be your last will and testament. The executor then asks the probate court to accept this document and officially grant him as your named executor the power to act on behalf of your estate. In making a will, you should always name a successor executor, someone to serve as executor if the first executor named refuses or is unable to act. If no successor executor is named, the court will appoint one.

FAILURE TO LEAVE A WILL

If you die without leaving a will, you are said to have died *intestate*. In such a case, the court will appoint someone to take on the duties of the executor; but this person, to distinguish him from an executor, is called an *administrator*. If you die without a will, no one can know with certainty how you wanted to distribute your estate; and the courts will not permit someone to make the decision for you. However, since the estate must be settled, the statutes of each states specify how the estate of an intestate decedent will be distributed. These statutes differ from state to state.

The administrator appointed is usually a member of the family, but he or she may not be the person you would have picked to gather and distribute your estate. And you would most probably have wanted your estate distributed in a way different from the one state law directs. In the illustration in the beginning of this chapter, either the decedent's aged wife or one of the selfish sons could have been appointed administrator. The wife might not be capable of gathering all the required information, filing the reports, and keeping the records even if she sought outside help; but the ungrateful sons are surely not the ones the decedent would have selected to administer his estate. In addition, he probably would have wanted his entire estate to go first to his wife and then to his infant son, with only a small token, if that, to his prosperous older sons. However, in some states, upon one's death the surviving spouse gets only one-half the estate, while the children share the other half equally. In some states, a widow or widower gets less than one-half, sometimes only one-third, of the decedent's estate. State statutes also provide for distribution if there is no surviving spouse and/or children.

It is therefore beneficial if not necessary to have a will, and the selection of an executor should be carefully considered.

REQUIREMENTS OF A WILL

A will has no binding effect during the testator's life. It is intended to become effective only upon his death. Since the use of a will to dispose of property is not a natural right but a privilege of statute, certain formalities must be observed to try to assure that the testator's intent is carried out.

Capacity of Testator

If there is no statute to the contrary, a male of fourteen years or older and a female of twelve years or older can make a valid will. Generally the statutes require that a person who disposes of property by will be eighteen years old or older.

A testator must also be of *sound mind and memory*. This is not the same mental capacity necessary to transact business or enter into a contract or manage an estate. All that is necessary for someone to be of the sound mind and memory to dispose of his property by will is that he

1. Understand that he is arranging to dispose of his property after his death by use of a will.
2. Know what property he owns.
3. Know who he wants to receive his estate upon his death.
4. Be able to give away his property according to a plan formed in his own mind.

The fact that a person has failing memory, suffers from forgetfulness or absent-mindedness, or has peculiar or unsound prejudices or beliefs does not affect his testamentary capacity (ability to dispose of property by will).

FORMALITIES OF A WILL

Now that we have seen what is required of a testator before he can make a will, let us examine what is required of a will before it will be accepted by a court for probate.

Writing

Since a will is intended to take effect after the death of the testator, and since a will can be changed or revoked as often as the testator desires in his lifetime, it is required in many states that a will be in writing. The will does not have to be in any particular form or use any particular words, so long as the intention of the testator is clear. The court will not guess or substitute its judgment for that of the decedent.

When a will is to be amended, it must be changed by a separate document, called a codicil, which must conform to all of the formalities of the will itself. A will cannot be amended by altering the will itself, and any such changes usually are of no effect whatsoever.

In certain circumstances (among military people in fear of death or mariners at sea) and in certain states, an oral will made during the last illness of the deceased in the presence of witnesses, is valid. Oral wills are called *nuncupative wills*, but each state's statutes should be examined to determine the limitations and formalities that must be observed to make such wills acceptable.

As an example, a soldier wounded during maneuvers fears that he is dying. He tells the chaplain that he wants his sister to have his car. This is a legally recognized will, even though it is not written.

Signature

A will must be signed by the testator or by someone in his presence and at his direction. Even if the will is in the testator's own handwriting and he mentions himself by name throughout the will, it is not valid unless it is signed by him or for him at his direction and in his presence. The location of the signature is not important, so long as it shows the decedent's intention to sign the writing as his will.

The testator's signature can be made by a sign he uses for his signature (such as an X) or it can be incomplete, if it was intended to be his signature and he was prevented from completing it only because of his weak physical condition. If someone at the request of the testator guides or assists him in signing his will, or even signs for him in his presence and at his direction, this signature will satisfy the requirements of the statute.

What is required is some evidence that he knew the document was his will and knew its contents and intended to sign to indicate this knowledge.

Holographic Wills

A holographic will is one written entirely in the handwriting of the decedent. It can be as informal as a note or a letter, and it can be written in pencil or ink. The letter or note should be dated, and the statutes of the state where the will is to be admitted to probate should be consulted to determine if such wills are acceptable and if the will in question meets all legal requirements.

A woman writes a letter to her daughter telling her that when she dies she wants her to have all of the family silverware, china, and furniture, as well as her fur coat. If the mother is killed in an automobile accident, this could be a valid will in a state that recognizes holographic wills.

Witnesses

Unless state law requires it, witnesses do not have to see a testator sign the will; but many statutes require that the testator sign the will in the presence of a specified minimum number of witnesses and that the witnesses sign in the presence of the testator and at his request.

The contents of a will need not be told to the witnesses. They have to know only that the document is the last will or codicil of the testator. They must believe him to be of sound mind and memory at the time of signing, and where required by statute, they must see him sign in their presence. They will then sign a paragraph attached to the will, called an *attestation clause*, in which it is recited that they saw the testator, whom they believed to be of sound mind and memory, sign the will in their presence and that at his request they signed as witnesses in his presence and in the presence of each other.

Although the statutes usually require that the testator and the witnesses sign in the presence of each other, this stipulation does not necessarily mean that they must all be in the same room. For example, if the testator is confined to a hospital bed and all of the witnesses cannot simultaneously be in the room with him, so long as the witnesses see each other sign the will and so long as the testator also sees the witnesses sign the attestation clause, this is a valid will.

If a testator is blind or illiterate, the contents of the will must be read or explained to him so he knows what it contains. However, it is not necessary that this reading or explanation be made in the presence of the witnesses.

Unless statute requires it, it is not necessary that the testator sign the will in the presence of the witnesses if by some act or word he acknowledges his signature before them. For example, if in the presence of the testator the document is referred to as the testator's will and it is said that it bears the testator's signature and the witnesses are asked to sign as witnesses, the testator may by some gesture, or even by mere silence, if he is then of sound mind and memory, acknowledge that these are his will and his signature. The witnesses, however, must know that this is the testator's will, and they must be able to see his signature.

Because a witness may be called upon to testify in court, he must be competent. This means that the witness cannot be legally disqualified from giving testimony. If someone is both a beneficiary under the will and a witness, the statutes generally provide that the gift to him by the will is void but the will is otherwise valid. The attorney who prepares a will and others from his office are not disqualified from acting as witnesses.

Because of the difficulty of locating the witnesses several years after a will has been signed, many states now allow an attestation clause to the will instead of personal testimony of the witnesses in court. In this clause, the witnesses further swear by affidavit under oath before a notary public that each of them was present and saw the testator sign the will, that the will was attested by each of them in the presence of the testator and each other, and that they believed that the testator was of sound mind and memory when he signed the will and they signed as witnesses. This affidavit can then be substituted in court for the testimony of the witnesses when the will is probated.

Revocation of a Will

A testator may revoke his will at any time. This revocation must be accomplished by mutilating or destroying the original will or by writing a new will. In some states, a divorce automatically revokes the bequests to the former spouse in a will drawn during marriage. In some states, the marriage of the testator automatically revokes a will signed before the marriage.

The destruction of a will must be intended by the testator to revoke the will, and any accidental destruction or mutilation of the will does not revoke it. A will can be mutilated by burning, tearing, cancelling, or obliterating it. This destruction can be done by the testator himself or by someone else, but only in the presence of the testator and by his direction and consent.

If a will is made in duplicate and the testator keeps one copy while his bank or lawyer keeps the other, should the testator destroy his copy, the will is revoked, since the revocation of the copy in the testator's possession revokes all copies.

Drawing lines through parts of a will or making changes in parts of the will and initialling them has no effect in revoking the will. For example, Mr. Stone executed a proper will with proper attestation. In his will, he left his entire estate to his friends Mary and Verne Snow. Later he changed this will in his own handwriting and initialed the changes (without witnesses) to make George and Jenny Winter the beneficiaries of his estate rather than the Snows. Mr. Stone then died. The amended will was contested when it was presented for probate, and the court held that the original will should be effective because the will was not revoked by the proper method of destruction or rewriting.

An insane person cannot revoke his will, because it takes as much mental capacity to revoke a will as it does to execute one.

A will cannot be revoked orally.

Terms of a will can be changed only by a properly executed and witnessed codicil.

Of course if a testator leaves someone a specific property and that property no longer exists at the time of the testator's death, for all practical purposes that provision of the will has been revoked. For example, Mr. Brown bequeaths his Rolls Royce to his son John. Before he dies, however, he either sells the car or gives it to his daughter Mary. Through the sale or gift by Mr. Brown, John's bequest is revoked.

Renunciation of a Will

Sometimes a testator leaves an heir a ridiculously small amount as a token of his displeasure. The will clause may read "and to my son Harry I leave one dollar." Harry may have the last laugh, however. He may renounce his portion under the will (that is, he may declare to the probate court that he does not want the share given to him by will). In that case, he can elect to receive the amount he would have been entitled to under state statute if the decedent had died intestate. This could be one-third or even one-half of the estate, or it could be zero. It depends upon the statute of the state involved.

Renunciation is also sometimes used when a beneficiary already in a high tax bracket is bequeathed some high-income property by a will. In this case, the benficiary may even elect to forego his statutory share and let it pass on to the beneficiaries who would be entitled to the balance of the estate.

Undue Influence

There are two grounds for contesting the mental capacity of a testator. One is to allege that the testator was insane when the will was executed; the other is to allege that someone exercised undue influence over him so as to deprive him of his own freedom of choice in the disposition of his property after death. Advice, suggestion, persuasion, or honest argument do not constitute undue influence. There must be a confidential and trusting relationship between the testator and the alleged influencer, and the influence must be such as to deprive the testator of his own freedom of choice. The burden of proving undue influence lies on the person alleging it as an objection to the admission of the will to probate.

Joint and Mutual Wills

A *joint will* is a single will that acts as the will of two or more people and is signed by them at the same time.

Mutual wills are separate wills by two or more people in which the terms of the wills are reciprocal to each other.

In each of these types of wills, there is a presumption of a contract between the parties to make these wills based on mutual promises to enforce the wills mutually.

Such wills can be revoked by one or more of the parties while all of the parties are alive. Upon the death of one mutual or joint testator, his will is probated, however; and if the other joint or mutual party then tries to revoke his portion of the will, he can be sued as in a breach of contract action. Berle and Hattie Coffee were married in 1960. Berle had two children from a previous marriage, and Hattie had one child from a previous marriage. They executed mutual wills leaving their estates first to each other and then to the three children equally upon the survivor's death. In 1970, Berle died and Hattie inherited his entire estate under Berle's mutual will. Hattie then executed a new will leaving everything to her son. When she died in 1971, Berle's children filed a breach of contract action against the estate to prevent Hattie's second will from being probated instead of the mutual one she executed in 1960. The court said that once a party to a joint or mutual will dies, the reciprocal will is legally enforceable and will be enforced in equity. Hattie's estate was divided equally among the three children.

Joint Tenancy

To avoid making a will or to avoid probate or to avoid paying attorney's fees, some people leave all their property in joint tenancy with one or more other people. If John Smith buys a vacation cottage in joint tenancy with his wife Mary, each joint tenant owns an undivided interest in the property. Upon the death of one, the title to the property is automatically transferred to the surviving joint tenant or joint tenants immediately and without anything further needing to be done. This automatic succession of title continues so long as the property remains in joint tenancy until there is just one survivor, who then takes title to it all.

Since only the assets a decedent owned in his name at his death are probated, and since the title to any property held in joint tenancy was immediately transferred out of his name at death, property is not subject to probate.

Under certain limited circumstances, joint tenancy may be the best way to hold title to certain property. Owning title to property in joint tenancy does not save inheritance and estate taxes, however; and in some cases, it may greatly increase these taxes, leaving less for the testator's heirs. In addition, owning title to a property in joint tenancy may cause that property to go to beneficiaries not intended. For example, Mr. Jones, who has two children from a previous marriage, marries Mrs. Light, who also has two children from a previous marriage. Mr. Jones and Mrs. Light do not adopt each other's children. Mr. Jones owns and maintains some commercial property from which he collects substantial rents with the help of his two sons. Mrs. Light seldom sees her children, who live with her former husband. Even though Mr. Jones bought his commercial property solely with his money and it is successful only because his efforts and those of his sons, he puts its title in joint tenancy with his wife so that she will have the income during her life. Mrs. Light promises that if Mr. Jones dies first, she will bequeath the title to the property to Mrs. Jones's sons, but she makes no will. At this point, Mr. Jones and his wife are involved in an automobile accident and Mr. Jones dies immediately. Although Mrs. Light survives Mr. Jones for two days, she remains in a coma until she dies. Upon Mr. Jones' death, the title to the commercial property immediately went to Mrs. Light. Upon her death, since she is intestate, the title to the property by statute goes to her sons (whom Mr. Jones had never even seen). They can throw out Mr. Jones' sons and have the commercial property all to themselves.

Other advantages and disadvantages of joint tenancy are discussed in Chapter 13.

Because of the potential problems and complications in disposing of an estate, it is always better to discuss your situation with a competent lawyer in whom you have faith and rely on him to advise you as to your need for a will and the type that best suits your circumstances.

GLOSSARY

The following glossary provides brief definitions of the legal terms used in this chapter.

Acknowledgement. Words or actions by the testator to the witnesses to indicate that the instrument they are about to sign is his will and that the signature on it is his.

Administrator. A person appointed by a court to administer the estate of a deceased if there is no will.

Alteration. Change in terms of a will accomplished by use of a codicil.

Attestation clause. A paragraph attached to and made a part of a will. This paragraph is signed by the witnesses to a will who state in the clause that they signed the will as witnesses at the request of the testator.

Beneficiary. One named to receive a benefit or gift under a will.

Bequest. Personal property, such as jewelry, silverware, books, and the like passing under a will.

Codicil. An instrument used to alter, amend, or revise a will. This instrument is in writing and executed with the same legal formality as to signatures and witnesses as the will it amends.

Decedent. One who died.
Devise. Real property, such as a house, passing under a will.
Execution. Signing and dating of an instrument in writing.
Executor. A person named in a will by the testator to carry out its provisions.
Heir. A person entitled to inheritance of one who died intestate.
Holographic will. A will entirely written in the testator's own handwriting. It must be entirely written, signed, and dated by the testator, and it may not require witnesses.
Intestate. An estate where the decedent died without leaving a will.
Legacy. Usually money passing under a will.
Nuncupative will. An oral will. Usually valid as to personal property and often only up to a certain amount, made in testator's last sickness or fear of dying, as by one in the military.
Renounce. A disclaimer by a beneficiary of his benefits under a will.
Residuary beneficiary. One entitled to the balance of a testator's estate after satisfaction of all debts and specific bequests, legacies, and devises.
Revocation. The act of recalling, cancelling, or setting aside a will, equivalent to its destruction.
Testate. An estate where decedent died leaving a valid will to dispose of his estate.
Testator. A person who executes a will.
Will. Usually an instrument in writing executed by a testator disposing of his property and usually witnessed by people who have no interest in or benefit under the will.

18

CRIMINAL LAW

"You have the right to remain silent. If you give up that right, anything you say can and will be held against you. You have the right to have an attorney present. If you can't afford an attorney, one will be appointed for you without charge." For those accused of criminal acts, many criminal cases begin with these words, sometimes called the "Miranda warning" because of the 1966 case from which it was popularized.

This so called warning is really a reminder to the accused that he has certain rights guaranteed to all citizens under the Constitution of the United States of America. The accused is reminded that although he may voluntarily give evidence against himself, no one can be forced to testify against himself in a criminal matter. He is also advised that to protect this right, he may have a lawyer present while he is being questioned to advise him and to protect his interests. Finally, he is implicitly told that this right is fundamental, so that if he can't afford to hire a lawyer to protect him but wants one, the court will appoint a lawyer for him; and all police questioning must stop until this lawyer is present. This protection is intended to prevent police from using any heavy-handed methods to force confessions from either the innocent or the guilty.

Why are the courts so zealous in protecting the rights of an accused? In a civil case, a defendant who loses may have to part with some money or property; but in a criminal case, a defendant who loses can lose his liberty for a long time, or even his life. Therefore the Constitution of the United States, as well as the constitutions of the several states, set up strict guidelines that police, states attorneys, district attorneys and United States attorneys must exactly and completely follow when prosecuting someone for a crime.

A *crime* is an antisocial act that embodies a wrong against the entire public, even if it involves only two people—a criminal and a victim. A *tort* is a private wrong against an individual or a group of individuals that does not offend the entire society.

For example, a murder may involve only a murderer and a victim. Because murder is such a repulsive act, however, and because it would be dangerous to others to let a murderer roam the streets, all of society is affected, and the public's lawyer—the states attorney or district attorney—will prosecute the murderer for his crime.

If a person drives his car negligently and strikes a person crossing the street, he has committed a tort. It is a private wrong; and the injured person may sue the driver of the car for medical bills, damage to his property, loss of wages, pain and suffering, and any other damages he may have suffered. The injuries may be gruesome and permanent (and these factors will be considered by the jury in awarding damages to the injured person) but the act is still a private wrong and not a crime.

Of course there are some acts, like assault and battery, that may be both crimes and torts; and a person can be tried in both a criminal case and a civil case for the same act.

Crimes are classified according to one of three levels of seriousness.

The most serious crimes are *capital crimes* and *felonies*. Capital crimes comprise treason, murder, and kidnapping, for which the death penalty may be inflicted. Felonies include rape, manslaughter, robbery, embezzlement, and other offenses for which the perpetrator can be sentenced to a penitentiary.

Crimes of moderate seriousness are *misdemeanors*. A misdemeanor is punishable by a fine or imprisonment in a facility other than a penitentiary or both a fine and imprisonment. Such crimes include theft under $150, possession of a small amount of some narcotic, or driving while under the influence of intoxicating liquor or narcotics.

The least serious crimes are *ordinance violations*. These include driving violations, permitting barking dogs, growing noxious weeds, or the like. Violation of these ordinances is punished by fine only without any imprisonment.

WHO CAN COMMIT CRIMES?

Although it might seem obvious that all people can commit crimes, under some circumstances, defenses may be raised if certain people are charged with committing crimes. Most crimes, particularly capital crimes or felonies, require an intent to commit the crime or knowledge that the act performed is illegal. Therefore, if a person charged with a crime does not have the mental capacity required by law to commit the crime, he cannot be guilty, even if all the other acts making it a crime were performed.

For example, if a three-year-old child finds his father's gun, sights down the barrel at his mother, pulls the trigger, and kills her, he cannot be found guilty of murder. All state statutes require that a person be above a certain age (older than three) before he can form the necessary intent to murder.

Lack of Capacity Because of Age

Children below a certain age, usually seven years, are conclusively determined to be incapable of committing crimes. This means that there is no way a child under this age can be tried for a crime. In most states, for children above the minimum age but younger than a certain older age, there is a presumption of the incapability of committing a crime. Such presumption of incapacity can be overcome if a prosecutor for the state can present strong and convincing proof that the child actually did have the ability to understand what he was doing and knew that what he did was wrong.

Lack of Capacity Because of Insanity

If a person charged with a crime was insane at the time the crime was committed, he did not have the mental capacity to commit the crime, so he cannot be punished for the act. The question of when one is legally insane has caused the legal community no end of trouble. While psychiatrists can diagnose persons as abnormal or neurotic or even psychotic, it is very difficult for them to define the term *legal insanity*. To complicate the matter even further, there are two common legal definitions of insanity that conflict with each other.

The oldest rule regarding insanity in criminal matters holds that only if the accused was unable to tell the difference between right and wrong can he be legally insane. That is, no matter what devils he has running around in his head, if he knew his act was wrong, he could not have been legally insane.

The other rule, called *McNaughton's rule* is based on a case in England in 1843, entitled "M'Naghten's Case" (10 Clark and Fin. 200). In this case, the House of Lords said in effect, that if a person acts because of an "irresistable impulse" to do something even if he knows it is wrong he cannot be convicted of a crime because he is "legally insane."

Some states have adopted the "right from wrong" rule; others the "McNaughton rule." Some states started with one rule then switched to the other; and some have switched back and forth so many times it is difficult to tell where their courts stand on the question of legal insanity.

If we add to this the conflicting opinions of the psychiatrists who testify for each side in a criminal case, we can see what a gigantic job it is for any jury to decide if an accused was legally sane or insane at the time the crime was committed. Nevertheless, this is the question a jury is always asked to decide where the defense of insanity is raised.

One other matter must be understood when we discuss insanity. The issue is not whether the accused was insane before the crime was committed or insane at the time of his trial. The issue is always whether the accused was insane at the time he is supposed to have committed the crime. If he was insane before the crime was committed, it is irrelevant. If he is insane at the time of the trial, he cannot assist or cooperate with his lawyer during the trial and must be institutionalized until he is sane before he may be brought to trial. But if he was legally insane *at the time the crime was committed,* he will ultimately be released, since he cannot be tried for a crime he did not have the mental capacity to commit.

Sometimes an accused is found to be in need of mental treatment and confined to a mental hospital until he returns to normal. The point at which he recovers is determined by the opinion of the treating doctors at the mental hospital. Therefore, an accused found insane may be confined to a mental hospital for a longer period than he would have had to serve in prison if he had been found guilty.

Drunkenness As a Defense

Again, because most serious crimes require a certain mental condition, if a person is so drunk that he does not know what he is doing, he cannot be guilty of a crime. However, most states have modified this rule to say that if an accused caused himself to be in a drunken condition, he cannot use drunkenness as a defense. That is, you cannot bring a condition upon yourself and then use it as a defense.

A corporation can also be convicted of a crime. Of course, a convicted corporation cannot go to jail, but it can be fined, and its property can be taken and sold to repay for damages. And since a corporation acts through its officers, directors, and agents, those who participated in the crime can be sent to jail for their acts.

CAPITAL CRIMES AND FELONIES

Although each state has its own definitions of crimes, the examples here identify and generally define some crimes as they are defined in the United States Code and the statutes of the state of Illinois. Three terms that run throughout all of the code or statutes should be given serious consideration. These terms are (Illinois Revised Statutes, Chapter 38—Section 4)

Intent or Intentionally

A person intends, or acts intentionally or with intent, to accomplish a result or engage in conduct described by the statutes defining the offense when his conscious objective or purpose is to accomplish that result or engage in that conduct.

Knowledge

A person knows, or acts knowingly or with knowledge of the nature or attendant circumstances of his conduct, described by the statute defining the offense, when he is consciously aware that his conduct is of such nature or that such circumstances exist. Knowledge of a material fact includes awareness of the substantial probability that such fact exists.

A person also knows the result of his conduct, described by the statute defining the offense, when he is consciously aware that such result is practically certain to be caused by his conduct. Conduct performed knowingly or with knowledge is performed wilfully.

Wilfully

(California Jury Instruction, 1946). The word *wilfully,* when applied to the intent with which an act is done or omitted . . . implies simply a purpose or willingness to commit the act or to make the omission in question. The word does not require in its meaning any intent to violate law, or to injure another, or to acquire any advantage.

Destruction of an Aircraft or Aircraft Facility—A Federal Crime

Whoever wilfully sets fire to, damages, destroys, disables, or wrecks any aircraft engine, propeller, appliance, or spare part with intent to damage, destroy, disable, or wreck any such aircraft; or places any destructive substance in, upon, or in proximity to any such aircraft, . . . or material . . . intended to be used in connection with the operation of the aircraft . . . or cargo . . . intended to be carried on any such aircraft or . . . causes . . . such aircraft . . . or other material to be unworkable or unusable or hazardous; or wilfully sets fire to, damages, destroys, disables, or wrecks or places any destructive substance in, upon, or in proximity to any shop, supply, structure, station, depot, terminal, hangar, ramp, landing area, air-navigation facility, . . . or wilfully incapacitates any member of the crew, shall be fined $10,000 or imprisoned not more than twenty years or both.

The same prohibitions apply to motor vehicles used in interstate travel, with the same penalty.

If the acts result in death, the death penalty or life imprisonment can be invoked as the penalty.

If any person knowingly gives false information as to an attempt or alleged attempt to commit any of these crimes, he shall be subject to a civil penalty of not more than $1,000. If the false information is wilfully and maliciously conveyed, the crime is subject to a fine of not more than $5,000 or five years imprisonment or both.

Abortion—State Statute

No abortion shall be performed except by a physician after he determines that, in his best clinical judgment, the abortion is necessary. Any person who knowingly performs an abortion contrary to the requirements of this paragraph commits a Class 2 felony.

Arson—State Statute

A person commits arson when, by means of fire or explosive, he knowingly

1. Damages any real property, or any personal property having a value of $150 or more, of another without his consent.
2. With intent to defraud an insurer, damages any property or any personal property having a value of $150 or more.

This felony is punishable by fine or imprisonment or both. The federal act also punishes arson within special maritime jurisdiction as a felony.

Armed Violence—State Statute

A person commits armed violence when, while armed with a dangerous weapon, he commits any felony defined by Illinois law.

This felony is punishable by fine or imprisonment or both.

A dangerous weapon is a pistol, revolver, rifle, shotgun, spring gun, sawed-off shutgun, stun gun, taser or knife with a blade at least three inches in length, dagger, dirk, switchblade knife, stiletto, bludgeon, black-jack, slingshot, sandbag, sandclub, metal knuckles, billy, or other dangerous weapon of like character.

Assault—Federal Crime

It is a felony to assault, resist, oppose, impede, intimidate or interfere with any United States judge, attorney, marshall or deputy marshall, FBI employee, Post Office employee, Secret Service or Bureau of Narcotics employee, penal or correctional institution employee, Customs, Immigration, or Internal Revenue employee, Department of Agriculture, Interior, National Park Service, Land Management, Indian Field Service, National Aeronautics and Space Administration, or Department of Health, Education or Welfare employee, or any Coast Guard officer or enlisted man, or security officer of the Department of State or Foreign Service, while in the performance of his official duty.

It is also a felony to assault, strike, wound, imprison, or offer violence to the head of a foreign state or government, foreign minister, ambassador, or other public minister, in violation of the law of nations.

Attempt—State Statute

A person commits an attempt when, with intent to commit a specific offense, he does any act which is a substantial step toward commission of that offense.

It is not a defense to a charge of attempt that it is impossible to commit the crime because of a factual impossibility (for example, attempting to pick an empty pocket) or a legal impossibility (for example, attempting to receive stolen goods when the goods were not stolen).

This is a felony punishable as above.

Bankruptcy Fraud—Federal Crime

It is a felony to conceal assets or make a false oath or false claim or fraudulently receive or transfer assets in a bankruptcy proceeding.

Assault, Battery, and Aggravated Battery—State Statute

Under the statutes of the State of Illinois, when without lawful authority a person engages in conduct that places another in reasonable apprehension of receiving a battery, he has committed an *assault.* This is a misdemeanor.

If a person intentionally or knowingly without legal justification and by *any means* causes bodily harm to an individual or makes physical contact of an insulting or provoking nature with an individual, he has committed a *battery.* This battery is also a misdemeanor, *unless* in committing the battery he causes great bodily harm or permanent disability or disfigurement in which case he has committed an *aggravated battery,* which is a felony.

He may also commit an aggravated battery if, in committing the battery, he uses a deadly weapon or is hooded, robed, or masked or knows the individual to be harmed is a school teacher or other school employee on school grounds or park employee on park grounds or employee of a state or county department of public aid and the battery occurs on the department's grounds or upon the grounds of a public aid applicant or recipient or the person harmed is a peace officer or fireman in the execution of his official duties or the person battered is in a public place or a driver or passenger in a facility for transportation of the public for hire.

A person may also commit aggravated battery if he causes another without his consent and for other than medical purposes to take any intoxicating, poisonous, stupefying, narcotic, or anesthetic substance.

Bribery—State Statute

Any person who, with intent to influence any person participating in, officiating at or connected with any professional or amateur athletic contest, sporting event, or exhibition, gives, offers, or promises any money, bribe, or anything of value or advantage to induce such participant, official, or other person not to use his best efforts in connection with such contest, event. or exhibition commits a felony.

There is also a federal act making bribery of sporting events carried on in interstate or foreign commerce a felony.

The state statute also makes the failure to report a bribe a misdemeanor and a bribe in a commercial affair a crime punishable by fine only.

Bribery

Anyone who offers or promises anything of value to a public official with intent to influence any official act; or any public official who solicits or accepts anything of value for himself or some other person or entity in return for being influenced in his performance of any official act; or anyone who offers or solicits or accepts anything of value in exchange for influencing testimony as a witness before a court or hearing shall be guilty of a felony.

Civil Rights

If two or more persons conspire to injure, oppress, threaten, or intimidate any citizen in the free exercise or enjoyment of any right or privilege secured to him by the Constitution or laws of the United States, they shall be fined $10,000 or imprisoned not more than ten years or both, and if death results, they shall be subject to imprisonment for any term of years or for life.

Counterfeiting

Whoever with the intent to defraud makes, forges, passes or attempts to pass, or alters any obligation or other security of the United States shall be fined not more than $5,000 or imprisoned for not more than fifteen years or both.

If one buys, sells, exchanges, delivers, or receives these counterfeited items with the intent to pass them as true and genuine, he shall be fined not more than $5,000 or imprisoned for not more than ten years or both.

Criminal Usury

Any person commits usury when he charges interest on a loan or discounts it at a rate greater than 20 percent a year.

Customs

One who effects any entry of goods by falsely classifying them as to weight, measure, quality, or value or by paying less duty than legally due shall be fined not more than $5,000 and imprisoned not more than two years or both.

Damage to Property

Where by fire or stink bomb one damages the property of another or injures a domestic animal of another without his consent and the damage to the property exceeds $150, he has committed a felony.

Shooting at a railroad train is also a felony.

Deadly Weapon

A person commits the offense of unlawful use of a deadly weapon as a felony when he (*1*) Sells, manufactures, purchases, possesses, or carries any weapon from which eight or more shots or bullets may be discharged at a single firing, any shotgun having one or more barrels less than 18 inches in length, or a bomb, bomb-shell, grenade, or molotov cocktail; or (*2*) Carries or possesses in a vehicle or on or about his person any pistol, revolver, stun gun or taser, or firearm when he is hooded, robed or masked.

There are other acts involving use of a deadly weapon, but these are misdemeanors and are not listed here.

Espionage

Whoever gathers information respecting the national defense with intent or reason to believe that the information is to be used to the injury of the United States shall be fined not more than $10,000 or imprisoned not more than ten years or both.

Whoever, with intent or reason to believe that it is to be used to the injury of the United States, communicates that information to a foreign government shall be punished by death or for any term of years or for life.

Anyone who levies war against the state or gives aid and comfort to its enemies is guilty of a felony under the state statutes. The person cannot be convicted except on the testimony of two witnesses to the same overt act or on his confession in open court.

Anyone who withholds his knowledge that another has committed treason against the state or advocated the violent overthrow of the existing form of government is also guilty of a felony under the state statutes.

Extortion

Whoever threatens by mail the life of or bodily harm to the president or vice president of the United States, or who under the threat of informing against any violation of any law of the United States demands or receives money (blackmail), or who by force, intimidation, or threat of procuring dismissal from employment obtains money from a public works employee, is guilty of a felony under the federal criminal code.

Foreign Governments—Agents

Section 951 of Chapter 45 of Title 18 of the United States Code says "Whoever, other than a diplomatic or consular officer or attache, acts in the United States as an agent of a foreign government without prior notification to the Secretary of State, shall be fined not more than $5,000 or imprisoned not more than ten years or both."

Gambling

Gambling in Illinois is a misdemeanor. However, a second conviction for gambling converts it to a felony.

Under the federal law, anyone who owns a ship used principally for gambling has committed a felony.

Habitual Criminals

In Illinois, if a person is convicted of any of the following crimes three times (not necessarily for the same crime), he is considered an habitual criminal and shall be imprisoned in the penitentiary for life and never be eligible for release, or receive the death penalty: treason, murder, rape, deviate sexual assault, armed robbery, aggravated arson, or aggravated kidnapping for ransom.

Juice Racketeering

Juice racketeering occurs when one lends money with the corrupt intent of receiving more in repayment than authorized by law and resorts to intimidation, threats, or any violent or criminal act against the borrower or his family or business to enforce collection.

Kidnapping

Kidnapping occurs when a person knowingly and secretly confines another against his will, or by force or threat of imminent force carries another from one place to another with intent to secretly confine him against his will, or by deceit or enticement induces another to go from one place to another with intent secretly to confine him against his will.

In Illinois, confinement of a child under the age of thirteen years is against his will if the confinement is without consent of his parent or legal guardian.

If one with intent to violate a court order removes a child under the age of fourteen years from Illinois without the consent of the person lawfully having custody or conceals the child within Illinois, he has committed a felony called *child abduction.*

If anyone transports a person unlawfully seized or held across state lines or to a foreign country, he has committed the federal crime of *kidnapping,* for which the punishment can be death or life imprisonment.

Manslaughter

Manslaughter is the unlawful killing of a human being without malice. It is of two kinds:

1. Voluntary manslaughter occurs upon a sudden quarrel or in the heat of passion.
2. Involuntary manslaughter takes place in the commission of an unlawful act not amounting to a felony or in the commission in an unlawful manner or without due caution or thought of a lawful act that might produce death.

Murder

Murder is the unlawful killing of a human being with malice aforethought. In Illinois, there is a further provision that if in performing the acts which cause the death one is attempting or committing a forcible felony other than voluntary manslaughter, he can be tried for murder even if the killing was not intentional or was done by a confederate. This is known as the *felony-murder rule.* In nearly three-quarters of the states, there are various degrees of murder. Most states recognize two degrees of murder, describing the first degree as killing with malice aforethought, and the second degree as killing during the commission of a felony. It is to this latter definition that Illinois has addressed its additional provision without giving a lesser penalty, as most states do, for felony murder. In brief, the Illinois statute provides that if in the commission of a forcible felony, such as robbery, rape, or kidnapping, a person is killed without lawful justification, the person committing the felony can be tried for murder, even if the killing was not intentional or if the killing was done by a confederate without the connivance of the defendant.

Notice that in both murder and manslaughter the killing must be unlawful. Therefore, if one kills another during war or if a policeman must kill another person in the performance of his duty, he is not guilty of murder or manslaughter, since such killing is not unlawful.

Obscenity

It is a violation of the federal criminal code to send obscene material through the mail. However, the United States Supreme Court has been unable clearly to define an obscenity standard, so enforcing this provision is difficult.

Robbery and Burglary

A person commits *robbery* when he takes property from another by use of force or by threatening the use of force. If a person enters a building with intent to commit a felony or theft, he commits *burglary*.

Theft

A person commits theft when he knowingly

1. Obtains or exerts unauthorized control over property of the owner.
2. Obtains by deception control over property of the owner.
3. Obtains by threat control over property of the owner.
4. Obtains control over stolen property knowing the property to have been stolen by another.

If the value of the property is more than $150, its theft is a felony. If the value is $150 or less, it is a misdemeanor. Theft of a firearm is a felony regardless of its value.

Rape

A male person of the age of fourteen years or older who has sexual intercourse with a female, not his wife, by force and against her will, commits *rape*. So long as there is any penetration of the female sex organ by the male sex organ, however slight, this amounts to sexual intercourse.

Deviate Sexual Assault

Any person fourteen years old or older who, by force or threat of force, compels any other person, male or female, to engage in an act of sexual gratification involving the sex organs of one person and the mouth or anus of another commits *deviate sexual assault.*

Indecent Liberties with a Child

A person seventeen years old or older commits indecent liberties with a child when he or she performs or submits to any of the following acts with a child under the age of sixteen:

1. sexual intercourse.
2. deviate sexual conduct.
3. any lewd fondling or touching of either the child or the person, done or submitted to with the intent to arouse or to satisfy the sexual desires of the child or the person or both.

Any person regardless of age commits indecent liberties with a child when he or she photographs, videotapes, films, or make reproductions by similar means of any of the above acts between a person less than sixteen years of age and another person or a person less than sixteen years of age and an animal or of a person less than sixteen years of age excreting or urinating or being bound in a sexual context or engaging in masturbation.

It is also a crime of indecent liberties to solicit a child to perform these acts, or as a parent or guardian to knowingly permit them to take place.

However, anyone accused of indecent liberties who reasonably believed the child was sixteen years old or older or knew the child had previously been married, may use these conditions as defenses to these charges.

Incest

Any male or female person who shall perform an act of sexual intercourse or deviate sexual conduct with a person he or she knows is his or her daughter or son commits *aggravated incest.* Such acts between brother and sister, of either whole or half blood, are *incest.* Both are felonies.

Bigamy

If a person marries, then marries another, he or she commits bigamy, unless

1. The prior marriage was dissolved by divorce or annulment.
2. The accused reasonably believed the prior spouse to be dead. There is no waiting period involved for this defense to take effect. For example, if the

husband is dead, she can remarry. If her first husband later turns up alive, she has a defense to any charge of bigamy.

3. The prior spouse had been continually absent for a period of five years, during which time the accused did not know the prior spouse to be alive.

4. The accused reasonably believed that he or she was legally eligible to remarry.

Prostitution and Pandering

In Illinois, prostitution is a misdemeanor, but one who compels a person to become a prostitute, called a *panderer,* commits a felony.

MISDEMEANORS

Misdemeanors are lesser crimes than felonies, and they are usually punished by fines, although a jail term may sometimes be imposed. In some cases, if a misdemeanor is repeated, the second offense raises the crime to a felony. Here are some examples of misdemeanors.

Criminal Defamation

A person commits criminal defamation when with intent to defame another, living or dead, he communicates by any means to any person matter that tends to provoke a breach of the peace. In other words, if one libels or slanders another, it could be criminal defamation if it tends to provoke a breach of the peace, such as yelling, fighting, or some other disorder.

Libel is an untruth in writing that depreciates another's reputation.

Slander is an untruth by word of mouth that defames another's reputation.

In criminal defamation, the communication may even be made to the person defamed, and it is a crime. The communication needs only "tend" to provoke a breach of the peace; it need not actually cause such a disorder.

Disorderly Conduct

A person commits disorderly conduct when he knowingly does an act in such unreasonable manner as to alarm or disturb another and to provoke a breach of the peace; or sends a false fire or bomb alarm; or acts as a Peeping

Tom; or as a collection agency or employee of a collection agency attempting to collect a debt makes a telephone call to the debtor and harasses, annoys, or tries to intimidate the alleged debtor.

There are many other misdemeanors, such as deception, picketing of a residence, interference with a school, and violations of civil rights by refusing one the use of public facilities because of race, religion, color, national ancestry, or physical or mental handicap.

19

CRIMINAL PROCEDURE

From Chapter 18 we know some of the acts considered by the law to be crimes. A long road must be traveled between the crime and the sentencing of someone tried and convicted of committing that crime.

The heaviest burden along this road lies on the police and the prosecutor, whether they be local, state, or federal officials. A person accused of a crime does not have to do anything, but the arresting and prosecuting authorities must take the initiative and force the action. If they misstep along the way and violate any of the accused's rights (for example, by an improper arrest or search), he may be set free.

Setting strict rules and constitutional restrictions on prosecution is altogether fit and proper. After all, the state and federal governments have all of the power and authority. They also have money, people, and all the newest sophisticated investigative equipment and techniques at their disposal. Therefore, these restrictions are set up to protect us, the people, from an abuse of this power and authority.

Lawyers are often asked, "How can you represent a man if you know he's guilty of committing a crime?" The answer is, "It is not for us to find him guilty or not guilty; that is for a judge or jury. Our job is to see that his rights have been and are protected, and it is only by protecting his rights that we help to protect your rights from abuse."

ARREST

Let us now walk through the criminal procedure. When a crime has been committed, the police conduct an investigation; and if they have reason to suspect someone, they arrest him.

An *arrest* is the first stage in a criminal proceeding. It is the taking of a person into custody either by actual restraint or by his submission to custody. Merely stopping a person or talking to him or calling him over to a squad car is not an arrest. These acts may be part of a police officer's investigation, but they are not arrests.

In any arrest, certain questions must be considered.

1. Was the arrest made with or without an *arrest warrant*?
2. Was any incriminating evidence seized by the officer?
3. Was this evidence obtained with or without a *search warrant*?

These questions illustrate some of the constitutional protections mentioned above. If evidence was illegally obtained, it may be suppressed (that is, denied admission at the trial of the accused). Without the use of this evidence, the state may not be able to prove its case; and the accused may be set free. Therefore, police officers, prosecutors, and defense lawyers examine the search and arrest procedure used by the police with great care.

Privilege against Arrest

The constitutional privilege of senators and representatives from arrest during their attendance at a session and in going to and returning from a session of the Congress or a state legislature applies only in civil cases. Legislators are not priviledged from arrest for the commission or threatened commission of public offences.

A member of the armed forces of the United States while under orders in active service is not subject to arrest upon an order of a state court. However, a federal officer or employee, including a mailman whose arrest would delay mail delivery, is not exempt from arrest for violation of the criminal laws of the state.

An ambassador or minister representing a foreign country is exempt from all local jurisdiction, as are members of his household and official staff.

Where a statute so provides, judges and lawyers are privileged from arrest during the term of court and while going to or returning from the court.

Arrest with a Warrant

Requiring a warrant to make an arrest places a neutral official between the government and the citizen and protects citizens from unlimited and unreasonable arrest.

An arrest warrant is issued by a magistrate after a complaining witness or police officer appears before him in person or by affidavit and under oath gives information that causes the magistrate to believe that an offense has been committed and that the named accused, if known, committed the crime. This is called *probable cause*. If the name of the accused is not known, the warrant must adequately describe him so he can be identified. In other words, a warrant must be specific and certain as to the person to be arrested.

A police officer generally serves a warrant, and a private person cannot serve a warrant unless he has first been properly deputized. However, a peace officer may call upon a private citizen to assist in an arrest. In such a case, the private citizen is protected from any charge of false arrest.

Only the person named in the warrant can be arrested under the warrant.

Arrest without a Warrant

The state statutes specify when an arrest may be made without a warrant. Where the facts justify it, a person may, and has the duty to, arrest without a warrant. However, when a person arrests without a warrant, he does so at his peril and he must prove that the arrest was lawful.

Arrest by a Peace Officer

A peace officer may arrest a person without a warrant when he has reasonable grounds to believe that a warrant for the person's arrest has been issued or has reasonable grounds to believe that the person is committing or has committed an offense.

Arrest by a Private Person

Any person may arrest another when he has reasonable grounds to believe that an offense other than an ordinance violation is being committed.

SEARCH

When a lawful arrest is made, a peace officer may reasonably, without a warrant, search the person arrested and the area he can reach for the purpose of

1. Protecting the officer from attack.
2. Preventing the person from escaping.
3. Discovering the fruits of the crime.
4. Discovering anything that may have been used in the commission of or may be evidence of an offense.

However, if it is not a transitory or emergency situation, a search warrant should be obtained before a search is made. The standards for issuing search warrants are the same as those for issuing arrest warrants.

1. There must be a written complaint under oath which states facts sufficient to show probable cause that the place or person to be searched, which must be particularly described, contains things that may constitute evidence of the offense in connection with which the warrant is issued.
2. The things to be seized by use of this warrant must also be particularly described.

It should be noted that all necessary and reasonable force may be used to effect an entry into any building or property to execute a search warrant. This means that in making a search with a warrant the peace officers are authorized to break down doors and use whatever other force is necessary if the situation requires it.

The things seized in a search must be inventoried and delivered to the judge issuing the warrant. The judge then issues an order providing for the custody of these items until trial.

PRELIMINARY HEARING

A person arrested is taken to jail where he is photographed, fingerprinted, and may be held until a judge is available. When a judge is available, a person arrested without a warrant is taken before the nearest and most accessible judge and charged with his crime. A person arrested on a warrant is taken without unnecessary delay before the judge who issued the warrant, or if he is absent or unable to act, before the nearest or most accessible judge in the same county.

The judge

1. Informs the defendant of the charge against him and provides him with a copy of the charge.
2. At that time, advises the defendant of his right to a lawyer; and if the defendant cannot afford a lawyer, the judge must appoint a public defender or licensed attorney at law of the state to represent him.

3. Should hold a preliminary hearing to determine whether the defendant should be held in custody any longer.
4. Should set bail so the defendant can be released from custody.

Bail is neither a punishment nor a fine. It is money deposited with the court to insure that the defendant will appear for the next step in the proceeding.

Unless a defendant pleads guilty, the question of his guilt or innocence is determined only by a trial. Until trial, the court only wants to assure itself that the defendant will appear as required for the various steps in the proceeding. Therefore, if the defendant is charged with a lesser felony or misdemeanor, if he is a stable individual with a job and family, or if he attends school or owns property or otherwise appears reliable, the bail may be very low. In some cases, a judge may be so convinced that the defendant will appear that he releases him on his *own recognizance,* that is, on the strength of his word and without cash bond. However, if the defendant has a history of not appearing or of running from previous hearings, the judge may set a very high bail to insure that he will appear. If the defendant is unable or unwilling to post bond, he is returned to jail to await trial.

In most states, all crimes are bailable offenses except murder or other crimes punishable by death.

At the preliminary hearing, the guilt of the defendant need not be established beyond a reasonable doubt. The judge need only determine that there is probable cause that the defendant committed the crime.

CHARGING THE DEFENDANT WITH THE CRIME

After the preliminary hearing, if the judge or magistrate determines that a crime has been committed and that there is probable cause to believe that the defendant committed it, the defendant must be *formally* charged with the crime.

He is formally charged with the crime in one of three ways: by a complaint, by an information, or by an indictment.

A *complaint* is generally used to charge someone with an ordinance violation or a misdemeanor, and it is usually used in actions before a magistrate, associate judge, or justice of the peace.

An *information* is the formal presentation of a criminal charge against a person by the state's attorney or district attorney. This method is generally used when the crime is a misdemeanor. If, however, prosecution of a felony by indictment is waived, such prosecution may be by information or complaint.

The most common way of formally charging a defendant with a crime is by an *indictment.* An indictment is returned by a grand jury. The majority of states, by constitution or statute, and the Constitution in federal criminal cases require the prosecution of some or all serious crimes by indictment.

A grand jury is composed of a number of citizens, usually twelve to twentythree, who are selected from voting lists, tax rolls, or by some other statutorily prescribed method. They sit in private without any judicial officer present. Generally, only the prosecutor, a stenographer, and the testifying witness are present during testimony to a grand jury. In some states, a testifying witness is permitted to have his lawyer accompany him. The lawyer cannot in any way participate in the hearing, but he can advise his client.

The witnesses testify under oath, and the jury may call any witnesses it pleases. Generally, the prosecutor presents the case against the defendant or defendants and suggests the witnesses the jury should hear.

When the prosecutor completes his presentation, the grand jury considers whether or not to indict the defendant. Everyone but the members of the jury are excluded during these deliberations. If a majority of the jury votes to indict the defendant, it returns a *true bill.* If the jury decides that not enough evidence was presented, it returns *no bill.* If the latter occurs, all further proceedings generally end, and the defendant is set free.

ARRAIGNMENT

The purpose of an *arraignment* is to inform the defendant of the charge against him in open court. He at that time pleads to the charge. He may plead *guilty, not guilty, not guilty by reason of insanity,* or *no contest to the charge,* (Nolo contendere). This last plea is the same as a guilty plea, but the defendant's admission of guilt cannot be used elsewhere. During the arraignment, many defense attorneys raise their objections to what took place before, asserting that

1. The defendant was arrested illegally.
2. The evidence was seized or the search was conducted improperly.
3. Any confessions the defendant made were made illegally or improperly obtained.
4. The warrant, either arrest or search warrant, was defective.
5. The grand jury was selected improperly or prejudiced by publicity or unauthorized persons were present during jury deliberations.
6. The charging paper (indictment, information, or complaint) fails to charge an offense.

7. The charging paper does not give the court venue to hear the case.

8. The defendant is protected against being charged for this crime because he has already been tried for it. This is called *double jeopardy,* which is unconstitutional.

At the arraignment, the defense lawyer also makes his motions to discover as much of the prosecutor's evidence as is permitted. These motions are in writing and request the court to order the prosecutor to provide whatever material he has, up to the limits set by the law, to the defense attorney. If the prosecutor refuses or fails to provide this material, the case can be dismissed and the defendant freed.

TRIAL

If the defendant understandingly pleads guilty at the arraignment, the judge may order a presentence investigation, have a sentence hearing after the investigation, and sentence the defendant. Prior to the arraignment, the prosecutor, the defendant, and his lawyer may often discuss the merits of proceeding with the case. If the prosecutor feels his evidence and/or witnesses will not support a more serious charge, he may agree to accept a guilty plea to a lesser charge rather than run the risk of losing altogether. The defendant, on the other hand, may be concerned with his past record or the type of crime or the quality of the evidence against him and therefore agree to plead guilty to a lesser crime or to the crime as charged with a recommendation by the prosecutor for a reduced sentence. To reduce the backlog of his overworked office or because of his knowledge of the community or the reputation or unmarred record of the defendant, the prosecutor may agree to the terms of the negotiated plea. This course of action also saves the court time and the community the expenses of a trial.

If the defendant pleads not guilty to the charge, the case is set for trial. In a criminal trial, a defendant is entitled to a jury unless he knowingly waives this right. If he waives this right to a jury trial, he is tried only by a judge in what is called a *bench trial.*

Once the jury has been selected or the judge is ready to hear the case if a jury has been waived, *opening statements* are made. The purpose of the opening statements is to advise the jury of what each side is going to present and to identify and explain the significance of the evidence and witnesses that will be presented during the trial.

Since the burden in a criminal case is on the prosecutor, who must prove the guilt of the defendant, the prosecutor has the right to address the jury or judge first.

When the prosecutor has finished his opening statement, the defendant's attorney may make his opening statement. Since the defendant need not prove his innocence and need not even testify or present witnesses, relying on the failure of the prosecutor to carry the burden of proof of guilt, a defense attorney frequently waives the right to make an opening statement.

After the opening statements, the prosecution begins to present its case. The prosecutor does this by calling his first witness to testify to the facts as he knows them, under oath. After the witness has testified in full for the prosecution, the defendant's attorney may cross-examine the witness.

The purpose of cross-examination is to disclose to the judge or jury any ulterior motive the witness may have in testifying against the accused. For example, is he biased or prejudiced against the defendant? Does he have an interest in testifying, such as a reward or revenge? Another reason for cross-examining a witness is to identify any reasons why the witness should not be believed. For example, he may have participated in the crime and be pointing his finger at the accused to save himself; or he may have something in his history and background that would cause the jury to question his truthfulness. For example, he may have been convicted of perjury. His recollection of the facts may be weak or may not square with other known facts. He may have testified under oath or given a statement elsewhere directly contrary to his testimony in this trial. If the witness testifies as an expert witness and the defense attorney can show that his expertise is flawed, this goes a long way toward destroying the prosecution's case.

At any rate, the prosecutor presents his witnesses one by one; and after each one testifies, the defense attorney has the right to cross-examine him.

After the prosecutor has called all his witnesses and presented all his evidence, he rests his case. This means he has presented all the direct evidence he has linking the defendant with the crime.

At this point, the defense attorney routinely asks the judge to direct the jury to return a verdict of not guilty. This is called a *motion for directed verdict* or *motion for acquittal* or a *demur to the evidence*. What it says is that the judge should tell the jury that a reasonable juror, crediting the prosecution witnesses' testimony and giving it the benefit of all rational inferences in its favor, still could not find the defendant guilty of the crime under the facts or under the law. If the judge grants the defense motion and so instructs the jury, the trial is over and the defendant is set free. If the judge denies the defendant's motion, the defendant presents his side of the case. The defendant's attorney presents his evidence and calls his witnesses to testify one by one. After each witness testifies, the prosecutor can cross-examine that witness.

After the defense has presented its evidence and witnesses and rests its case, the prosecutor can call additional witnesses to rebut any evidence or testimony presented by the defense.

After all the testimony is concluded, each side makes a *closing argument*, each pointing out the weakness in the opponent's case and emphasizing why his own side should prevail. Since the prosecution must prove the defendant guilty, he gives the first closing argument. The defense attorney then gives his closing argument. After the defense attorney finishes his argument, the prosecutor has one more opportunity to address the jury. This is called *rebuttal argument*, and its purpose is to rebut those points raised by the defense attorney in his argument.

After the attorneys finish their arguments, the judge instructs the jury as to what the law is and how they should apply it to the facts. The jury then retires to the jury room to decide, on the basis of those facts and the law, whether the prosecution has proved the defendant guilty of the crime as charged beyond a reasonable doubt.

To find the defendant either guilty or not guilty, the jury must be unanimous in its decision. If the jury cannot agree on a verdict, it is called a *hung jury*. If, after a period of time discretionary with the judge, the jury remains hung, the jurors are dismissed. In that situation, the prosecutor can decide to retry the defendant before a different jury or to take no further action.

If the defendant is found not guilty, he is set free and that is the end of the matter.

The defendant's lawyer will probably make a motion for a new trial. As grounds for a new trial, he will allege one or more of the following:

1. The evidence was insufficient to support the verdict.
2. Most of the evidence was in favor of the defendant and so the verdict was wrong.
3. A new trial should be granted in the interests of justice.
4. There were errors in the pretrial stages of the proceeding.
5. There were errors by the judge in his rulings during the trial.
6. There is newly discovered evidence that was not available at the time of trial.

If the motion for a new trial is denied the judge will order some agency of the court, like the probation department, to make a presentence investigation of the history, family, and environment of the defendant in order to determine if there are any unusual circumstances that will act to cause the judge to reduce or increase the length of the sentence. After the judge receives the written presentence report, he sets a date for sentencing. At the sentencing hearing, the prosecutor may or may not take a position on the sentence to be imposed. Defense counsel is always given an opportunity to argue some reasons why the defendant should get a reduced sentence, medical care, probation, or some sort of work release instead of prison. The defendant usually is also given an opportunity to address the judge, if he so desires, to tell the judge how he feels about his crime and add anything he wants. These final arguments are informal and are not subject to the strict rules of evidence under which the trial took place. The judge then sentences the defendant.

Once the sentence has been handed down, the defendant can appeal the verdict or the sentence or both. The defendant may or may not be released on bail during appeal. This release is discretionary with the judge and is in large part influenced by the seriousness or viciousness of the crime and the attitude and history of the defendant. The points raised for appellate review should all be properly raised claims of error in the pretrial and trial rulings of the judges, the sufficiency of the evidence to support the verdict, or plain or fundamental errors which occurred, even if they were not raised before or during the trial.

If the appeals are denied, the defendant serves his sentence, making application periodically for release from prison on parole. If the appeal is granted, the defendant may be set free or returned to the trial court system for a new trial.

20

YOUR INCOME TAX RETURN

THE INDIVIDUAL TAX RETURN

To understand income tax, one must understand what is taxed. Not all increases in assets are income. Any gain in an asset must be realized to be income. In other words, if you buy stock for $100 and it increases in value to $150, there is no income to be taxed unless you sell the stock. Not all receipts are income either. For example, if you lend your brother $500, when he pays it back to you you receive only your own money.

Gross Income

Gross income is defined as all items of income from whatever source, unless specifically excluded. By this definition, it is easier to list what is excluded and call whatever is left gross income. While the following list is not exhaustive, it does state the majority of items excluded from gross income.

1. Unrealized gains.
2. Repayment of loans.
3. Return of capital.
4. Gifts.
5. Inherited property.
6. Insurance proceeds received by reason of death.

7. Social Security benefits.
8. Welfare payments.
9. Certain amounts of unemployment compensation.
10. Interest on municipal bonds.
11. Personal injury awards.
12. Gains from the sale of a personal residence where the proceeds of the sale are reinvested in another residence or the taxpayer or spouse is fifty-five years of age or older.

Trade, Business, and Investment Deductions

From the gross income, certain deductions are allowed. Some of these include

1. Expenses incurred in a trade or business.
2. Sixty percent of the gain on capital assets (which are defined later) held more than one year.
3. $200 of interest, as well as $200 of dividends received during the year ($400 if a joint return is filed).

The balance we may refer to as gross taxable income. From this figure other items can be deducted:

1. Travel expenses away from home as an employee.
2. Transportation expenses as an employee. However, the cost of commuting from home to the first business stop at the beginning of the business day and from the last business stop to home at the end of the day is not deductible.
3. Certain business expense like secretarial help, telephone, entertainment and meals for customers incurred by a salesman while working away from his employer's place of business.
4. Contributions to self-employment (Keogh) or IRA pension plans.
5. Interest forfeited because of premature withdrawals from savings accounts.
6. Alimony.

The resulting balance is called *adjusted gross income*. Before going on, it should be remembered that no deductions may be taken by a taxpayer unless they are expressly permitted by the tax laws.

Itemized Personal Deductions

From the adjusted gross income, the taxpayer is permitted additional deductions for certain personal expenses. These include five areas: medical expenses, taxes, interest, charitable contributions, and casualty losses.

Medical expenses in excess of 3 percent of adjusted gross income plus one-half of medical insurance premium up to $150 are deductible. Deductible insurance premiums must cover medical and hospital insurance, not insurance to reimburse lost wages.

If any medical expenses paid during the year are reimbursed to the taxpayer by insurance or otherwise, these expenses must be reduced by this reimbursement before they are deducted.

Transportation to and from a hospital is deductible as are meals and lodging furnished to an in-patient incident to treatment.

Certain improvements to a house may in some cases be deductible. These improvements are in the nature of air cleaners or filters or conditioners. However, their cost may be depreciated only over the life of the improvement and only if the improvement is added principally for a good medical reason and after being prescribed by a doctor for care and use of the patient.

Not all taxes are deductible, and some taxes—like employment taxes, auto licenses, and gasoline taxes—are deductible only as expenses of a trade or business and not as personal expenses. Deductible personal taxes are

1. Real estate taxes. On a real estate sale, the tax must be apportioned between the buyer and the seller according to the number of days in the real property year each holds title to the property.
2. Personal property taxes.
3. State and city income taxes.
4. City and state retail sales taxes.

The penalty charge for prepaying a mortgage is deductible as interest. Finance charges on a retail installment contract, revolving credit charge account, bank credit card, or gasoline credit card are interest.

Charitable contributions cannot be more than 50 percent of adjusted gross income. Services rendered to a charitable institution are not deductible. However, the cost of using an auto, traveling, using a telephone, and making other out of pocket unreimbursed expenses are deductible as contributions. If a ticket to a charitable event, such as a ball, bazaar, show, or athletic contest is purchased, it is presumed that its cost represents the value of the item purchased. The burden is on the taxpayer to show that the payment exceeds the fair market value of the admission. The purchase price of a raffle ticket is not deductible.

If the taxpayer has cancelled checks or receipts to verify his cash contributions, he needs only to list the total of these contributions. If he does not have supporting documentation for his other cash contributions, he must list the recipients and the amounts contributed. For noncash contributions, the taxpayer must attach a schedule giving the details of these contributions, describing the items and their value.

Contributions of appreciated property may also be made and can result in greater tax benefits than the cost of the property contributed. This kind of contribution should be planned by the taxpayer and his accountant and attorney before the year end. It is complex, and the timing of the contribution can be important.

When one loses property from fire, storm, or shipwreck and if that loss is due to some "sudden and unexpected" cause, some of the loss may be deductible. This does not refer to sales of stocks or bonds or other capital assets, but it does refer to the loss of personal items, such as jewelry, one's home or some part of it, trees or shrubs, or other possessions. It should be noted, however, that for the loss to be deductible it must be from a "sudden and unexpected" cause. If one's porch collapses because of termite damage, the loss is not deductible. Although the damage may have been unexpected, the termites had been at work for a long time, so it was not sudden. The same rationale is applied in disallowing the loss of trees or shrubs from disease or insects.

The amount of loss deductible is the amount of the loss in excess of $100 from each casualty or theft. For example, if a man is transporting his expensive television set in his car when his car is stolen, only one $100 amount is applied even though two items were lost. Contrary to this, if this man's car is stolen one week, his television set the next, each loss would be reduced by $100, since they did not result from the same casualty.

If a husband and wife file a joint return, their combined loss from a casualty is subject to only one $100 amount. However, if each files a separate return, each is subject to the $100 amount applied to his or her individual loss.

The amount of loss deduction to which the $100 limit is applied is the most difficult part of the claim. The burden of proof as to a deduction of any item is on the taxpayer; and with respect to a casualty loss, the regulations state that the amount of casualty loss deductible is limited to the difference between the value of the property immediately preceding the casualty and its value immediately thereafter, less insurance. The value of the property after the loss is not difficult to prove. However, determining the value (not necessarily the cost) of the property before the casualty is often difficult. Therefore, it is important for taxpayers to keep pictures, records of costs, and anything else that might prove useful to an appraiser and to the Internal Revenue Service to determine value before the casualty.

Finally, an individual is allowed to deduct certain other items from adjusted gross income.

1. Investor expenses, such as counseling fees, investment loose-leaf services, or transfer taxes.
2. Union dues and certain employee business expenses.
3. Job hunting costs.
4. Education-related expenses.
5. Moving expenses.
6. Uniforms and special clothing that do not replace items of ordinary clothing.

Zero Bracket Amount

Some taxpayers do not have any of these personal itemized deductions or do not have much in the way of such deductions. To be equitable to these taxpayers, the government has built a deduction into the tax schedules and tables, called *zero bracket amount.* This amount varies, depending on the taxpayer's filing status. At the present time, the amount is $2,300 for unmarried individuals and heads of households, $3,400 for married individuals filing jointly, and $1,700 each for married individuals filing separately.

If the taxpayer's itemized deductions are less than the zero bracket amount, he merely uses the tax table or tax rate schedule as determined by his filing status, taxable income, and exemptions to determine his tax. If the itemized deductions are more than the zero bracket amount, the deductions are reduced by that amount, and the excess deductions are used to reduce the adjusted gross income. The resulting balance is called *tax table income.*

If the tax table income is not in excess of a ceiling amount as provided by the Internal Revenue Code and the personal exemptions do not exceed the maximum number permissible, the taxpayer refers to government-provided tax tables to determine the tax.

If the tax table cannot be used at this point because of the Tax Table Income amount or the number of exemptions, this figure must be reduced by the taxpayer's allowable exemptions.

Exemptions

Taxpayers who cannot use the tax tables but must use the rate schedules are permitted to further reduce their taxable income for their personal exemptions.

Each person is entitled to a $1,000 exemption. Thus, a husband and wife are entitled to at least $2,000 of exemptions. In addition, if a taxpayer or spouse is blind or 65 years of age or over, he is entitled to another $1,000 exemption. For example, if a husband and wife file a joint return and each is blind and each is 65, they are entitled to $6,000 of exemptions.

In addition to their personal exemptions, taxpayers are entitled to $1,000 of exemption for each dependent they support. Five tests must be met before an exemption is allowed for a dependent:

1. The claimed dependent must have less than $1,000 of gross income for the calendar year, except if the dependent is a child of the taxpayer and is either under age nineteen at the close of the calendar year or is a full-time student.

2. Over half of the dependent's support for the calendar year must have been furnished by the taxpayer.

3. The dependent must fall within the specified class of dependents:

   a. Child, grandchild, or stepchild
   b. Brother, sister, stepbrother, or stepsister
   c. Parent or grandparent
   d. Stepparent
   e. Niece or nephew
   f. Aunt or uncle
   g. In-laws
   h. A person (other than the taxpayer's spouse) who during the taxpayer's entire year lives in the taxpayer's home and is a member of the taxpayer's household (but not if the relationship is in violation of local law)

4. The dependent must not have filed a joint return with a spouse.

5. The dependent must be a citizen of the United States, Canada, or Mexico at some time during the year or an alien child adopted by and living with a United States citizen in a foreign country as a member of his household for the entire year.

Tax Due or Refund

After the income has been reduced by the exemptions, the balance is the *taxable income.* By locating the amount of the taxable income on the appropriate schedule X, Y, or Z (depending on the status under which the taxpayer is filing; i.e., single, married filing jointly, married filing separately, or head of household) the tax liability can be computed.

This liability may be further reduced by certain tax credits which the government allows. These credits are a direct reduction of the tax, while deductions and exemptions only reduce the income to which the tax rate is applied. Some of these credits are

1. *Investment tax credit,* which is a credit for investment in business machinery and equipment and energy saving devices used in business.
2. Credit for the elderly.
3. Credit for federal tax on gasoline, special fuels, and lubricating oils.
4. Credit for political contributions.
5. *Earned income credit,* which is available for a low-income worker who maintains a household which is the principal abode of the worker and a child or children.
6. *Child and dependent care credit,* which is a credit for qualifying-child or dependent-care expenses paid for the purpose of being employed.
7. *Residential energy credits* for amounts spent in buying and installing qualifying insulation and other energy saving components in an individual's principal residence located in the United States.

After the tax liability has been reduced by the credits, this balance is compared with the income tax withheld from wages plus any estimated tax paid during the year. If there is still tax due, it should be paid with the return. If there is an overpayment of tax during the year, this overpayment may be refunded to the taxpayer or carried forward to next year's estimate, as the taxpayer chooses.

SUPPORTING SCHEDULES

In addition to the basic income tax return, which for an individual is either a Form 1040 or short version of the return called a 1040A, there are several supporting schedules or documents that must accompany the return.

For example, the W-2 form, which lists earnings from employment and the taxes withheld from those earnings, should be stapled to the return along with the taxpayer's check for any tax due. If the taxpayer received income of more than $400 in either interest or dividends, Schedule B should be prepared. If the taxpayer owns his own business as a sole proprietor, he prepares Schedule C, which lists business income and expenses, and Schedule SE, which computes Social Security tax due on business income. Schedule D is used for reporting capital gains and/or losses and Schedule E for reporting income from pensions, annuities, rents, royalties, partnerships, estates, trusts, and tax option corporations. A farmer reports his farm income and expenses on Schedule F. Schedule G is used for income averaging, and Schedule R or RP is used for claiming credit for the elderly. Schedule TC is for computing the income tax of taxpayers who cannot use the tax tables.

In addition, there are several other numerical forms, like Form 3468, which is used to compute investment credit; Form 4136, which is used to compute federal tax on gasoline, special fuels, and lubricating oil; Form 5696, which is used to compute residential energy credit; Form 2441, which is used to figure child and dependent care credit; and Form 2106, for employee business expenses. This is not a complete list of all the forms available or needed in filing a tax return. However, such a list usually can be obtained, along with copies of any forms one may need, from a local Internal Revenue Service office.

Other Returns

Just as an individual must file a Form 1040, businesses must also file returns. A corporation files a tax return on Form 1120; and just like an individual, it may owe tax or be entitled to a refund. If the corporation is a tax-option corporation in which the income is taxed to the shareholders, an information return is filed on Form 1120S.

A partnership does not pay a tax. Its income is destributed to the partners who include this income on their individual returns. However, a partnership information return is filed on Form 1065.

Although a trust or estate may or may not owe a tax, a Form 1041 is filed for it. This return may require a payment or a refund, or it may be only an information return. Generally, this depends upon whether the trust or estate income is accumulated or distributed to the beneficiaries.

TAX PLANNING

The federal government wants every individual to pay every cent he owes in taxes, and federal agents will go as far as legally possible to collect these taxes. However, the government does not want anyone to pay more taxes than he owes. Therefore, there is nothing illegal or immoral about planning to make it possible to pay the minimum amount of tax. Such tax planning usually involves some of the following techniques:

1. Selecting a recognized method of reporting income and expenses that will result in the minimum amount of tax.
2. Selecting a form of business operation that will do the same; that is, determining whether to operate as a sole proprietor, partnership, or corporation, whichever will result in the smallest amount of tax.
3. Deferring or bunching receipts or expenses in one year where it is legally possible to do so.

4. Selling or holding capital assets.

Whatever tax planning you do, it is strongly suggested that you:

1. Do it well in advance of the year end.
2. Do it with the assistance of a competent lawyer and a competent accountant.
3. Keep records.

CAPITAL ASSETS

Throughout this chapter, the term *capital assets* has occurred repeatedly. Transactions involving capital assets can materially effect one's taxes. A *capital asset* is any property, whether or not used in a trade or business, except the following:

1. An item of inventory.
2. Property held primarily for sale to customers in the ordinary course of the taxpayer's trade or business.
3. A note or account receivable acquired in the ordinary course of trade or business for services rendered or from the sale of stock in trade or property held for sale in the ordinary course of business.
4. Depreciable business property .
5. Real property used in the taxpayer's trade or business.
6. A copyright, a literary, musical or artistic composition, a letter or memorandum, or similar property (but not a patent or invention) held by the taxpayer who created it, or by one whose basis in the property is determined by reference to the basis of the one who created it, or in the case of a letter, memorandum or similar property, a taxpayer for whom such property was prepared or produced.
7. A non-interest-bearing federal or state obligation issued on or after March 1, 1941 on a discount basis and due one year or less from the date of issue.
8. A U.S. Government publication (including the Congressional Record) held by a taxpayer who received it other than by purchase at the price that the publication is offered to the public.

Thus stocks, bonds, and goodwill are capital assets. So are household furnishings, personal residences, automobiles, personal jewelry, and other personal items for the purpose of computing capital gains. However, losses from the disposal of personal assets are not recognized for income tax purposes, except for casualty losses as discussed previously.

It is important to determine if an item is a capital asset. If it is, it must be determined how long it was held by the taxpayer. If the asset is held for one year or less (called a short term), the gain or loss from its sale is treated as any other gain or loss. If, however, the holding period is more than one year (called a long term), the gain is given special favored treatment. In addition, if long-term losses exceed any short-term gains, these losses are also applied to reduce income in a different manner than usual deductions.

The favored treatment afforded long-term gains operates as follows. If there is a short-term gain, all of the recognized gain is added to the taxpayer's other income, and the tax is calculated as previously described. However, if there is a long-term gain, only a portion of the gain is included in income. At the present time, only 40 percent is included. Therefore, if a taxpayer has a recognized short-term capital gain of $1,000, all $1,000 is included in his taxable income. But if it is a long-term gain, only $400 is included in his taxable income.

If an item sold at a loss is of a personal nature, the loss is not deductible and there is no effect on the taxpayer's income. However, if the loss is of a capital asset, the capital gains are offset by this loss. If the losses are greater than the gains, not only are all of the gains eliminated, but some of the excess loss can also be used to reduce other income. Under current tax laws, up to $3,000 of other income can be reduced by excess long-term losses. If the loss is not used up on one year, any unused loss can be carried forward to future years and applied to reduce capital gains and income.

A long-term capital loss must be reduced by 50 percent before it can be used to reduce other income. In other words, if a taxpayer has excess long-term capital losses of $1,600, all $1,600 are needed to eliminate $800 of other income.

EXAMINATION OF TAX RETURNS

Almost all tax returns filed are verified for mathematical accuracy. This examination is not used to determine the correctness of the items of income or expense. It is used only to determine if the taxpayer's addition and subtraction are correct and if he used the right tables and schedules and reported his exemptions and withheld and estimated tax prepayments correctly. Corrections are made by the Internal Revenue Service, and any adjustments are automatically applied to any refunds requested or bills for tax due without any further action from the taxpayer.

After returns are checked for mathematical accuracy, they are examined again. The purpose of this review is to select some returns for audit. Some of the reasons that cause an audit are

1. The amount of reported income of the taxpayer.

2. The business or profession of the taxpayer.

3. The reporting of certain expenses in an amount greater than the IRS profile shows proper.

4. Certain areas of reporting income or expenses in which the IRS has decided to emphasize review.

The audit review can be performed in one or more of the following ways:

1. The IRS may request the taxpayer to mail certain documentation to a given address to support an item on a tax return. This method is usually used when the IRS wants the taxpayer to prove payroll tax or estimated tax deposits or contributions of property or other items that can be proven by submitting just a few documents.

2. The taxpayer may be requested to come into the local IRS office with all his supporting documentation. This is called an *office audit,* and it usually is used for a nonbusiness taxpayer where several items on the tax return are being audited and/or the documentation required may be voluminous.

3. An audit that involves a review of business records usually takes place at the taxpayer's place of business. This is called a *field audit.*

No matter where or how the audit is performed, there are some things that should be kept in mind. First, the burden of proving the correctness of the income and expenses and the amounts is on the taxpayer. If the taxpayer is unable to prove those items questioned by the agent, they will be resolved against the taxpayer. Therefore, it is essential to obtain, keep, and organize as much written documentation as you can to support the income and expense items on your tax return.

If an agent wants to disallow certain deductions or include certain income during an audit, he will write a report including the change in taxes that results from his determinations. The agent will discuss this report with the taxpayer. If the taxpayer agrees with the agent's finding, he can sign a Form 870, by which he consents to the assessment of the deficiency; and this generally closes the case.

If the taxpayer disagrees with the agent's finding, he can request a district conference or an appellate division hearing within thirty days after receipt of a letter from the IRS advising him of this right.

If the taxpayer does nothing after receiving such a letter, he will receive a formal notice of the deficiency. This notice will advise him that if he still disagrees with the agent's finding, he can file a petition with the tax court for redetermining the deficiency. This petition must be filed with the tax court within ninety days of the date of the notice. Upon receipt of the petition, the matter is set for trial.

If he disagrees but still does not want to go to the tax court, the taxpayer may pay the tax deficiency as assessed and then file a suit for refund in the United States district court. The choice of court usually is based on the previous decisions of the tax court and the district court in the matters the taxpayer is contesting.

The taxpayer can represent himself in any of these hearings. However, if the taxpayer wants other representation, he may be represented by a certified public accountant, by an attorney, or by a person other than a certified public accountant or attorney who has passed a test administered by the Internal Revenue Service that permits him to act as an enrolled agent.

In any case, any representative must receive and display to the Internal Revenue Service agent a signed power of attorney from the taxpayer authorizing that representation.

Most tax audits are intended to determine any additional tax that may be due. However, if the Internal Revenue Service makes an examination that involves criminal penalties, the examination will be conducted by a *special agent*. Therefore, if a taxpayer asks an agent for identification, which he has every right to do, and the agent's identification card shows that he is a special agent, the taxpayer is well advised to break off all further conversation with the agent and immediately contact his lawyer.

Finally—it is worth repeating—in any tax matter, plan early, get good advice, and keep records.

INDEX

Index